North to Alaska

North to Alaska

KEN COATES

M&S

Canadian Cataloguing in Publication Data

Coates, Kenneth, 1956–
   North to Alaska

ISBN 0-7710-2164-X

1. Alaska Highway – History. I. Title.
FC4023.9.A4C6 1991   388.1'09711'8   C91-094448-2
F1060.92.C6 1991

Map: James Loates
Design: ArtPlus Limited/Brant Cowie
Electronic Assembly: ArtPlus Limited/Valerie Phillips

Printed and bound in Canada. The paper used in this book is acid-free.

McClelland & Stewart Inc.
The Canadian Publishers
481 University Avenue
Toronto, Ontario
M5G 2E9

Contents

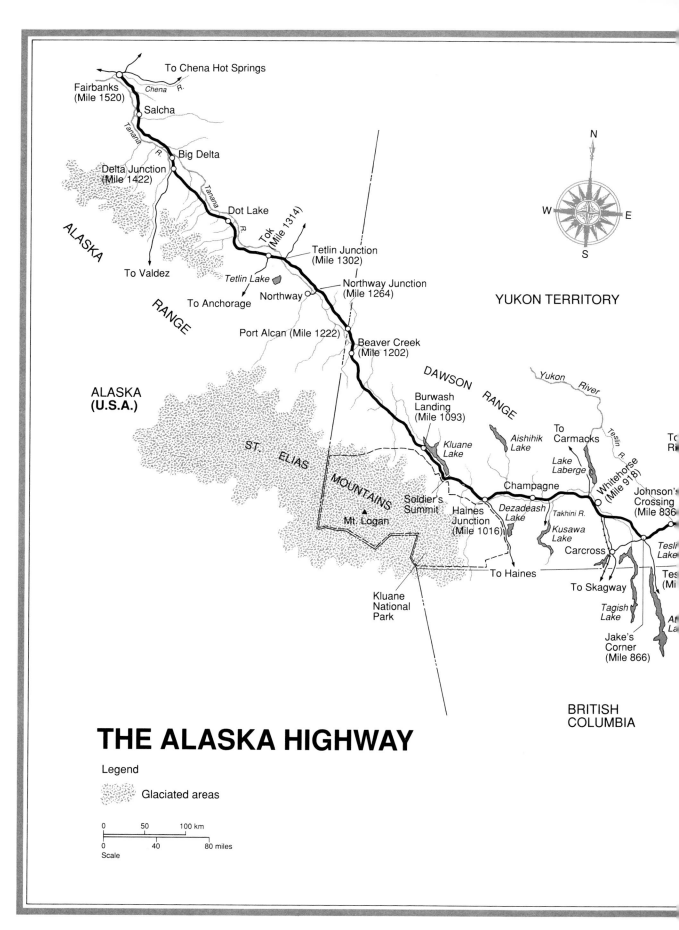

THE ALASKA HIGHWAY

To Chena Hot Springs

Chena R.

Fairbanks
(Mile 1520)

Salcha

Tanana R.

Big Delta

Delta Junction
(Mile 1422)

ALASKA

Dot Lake

Tok
(Mile 1314)

Tetlin Junction
(Mile 1302)

To Valdez

RANGE

Tetlin Lake

Northway

Northway Junction
(Mile 1264)

To Anchorage

Port Alcan (Mile 1222)

Beaver Creek
(Mile 1202)

**ALASKA
(U.S.A.)**

YUKON TERRITORY

Yukon River

DAWSON RANGE

Burwash
Landing
(Mile 1093)

*Kluane
Lake*

*Aishihik
Lake*

To
Carmacks

Teslin R.

*Lake
Laberge*

To
R

ST. ELIAS

MOUNTAINS

▲ Mt. Logan

Soldier's
Summit

Haines
Junction
(Mile 1016)

*Dezadeash
Lake*

Takhini R.

Champagne

Whitehorse
(Mile 918)

Johnson's
Crossing
(Mile 836

*Kusawa
Lake*

Carcross

*Tesli
Lake*

Kluane
National
Park

To Haines

To Skagway

Tes
(Mi

*Tagish
Lake*

*At
La*

Jake's
Corner
(Mile 866)

**BRITISH
COLUMBIA**

Legend

Glaciated areas

```
0        50      100 km
|————————|————————|

0        40       80 miles
|————————|————————|
Scale
```

N
W   E
S

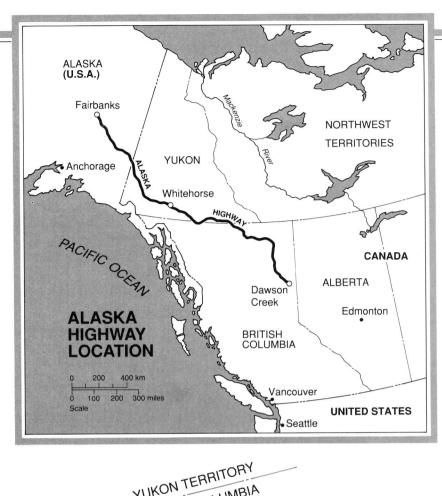

ALASKA
(U.S.A.)

Fairbanks

Anchorage

YUKON

Whitehorse

ALASKA

HIGHWAY

NORTHWEST
TERRITORIES

Mackenzie River

CANADA

ALBERTA

Edmonton

Dawson
Creek

PACIFIC OCEAN

**ALASKA
HIGHWAY
LOCATION**

BRITISH
COLUMBIA

Vancouver

0   200   400 km

0   100   200   300 miles

Scale

UNITED STATES

Seattle

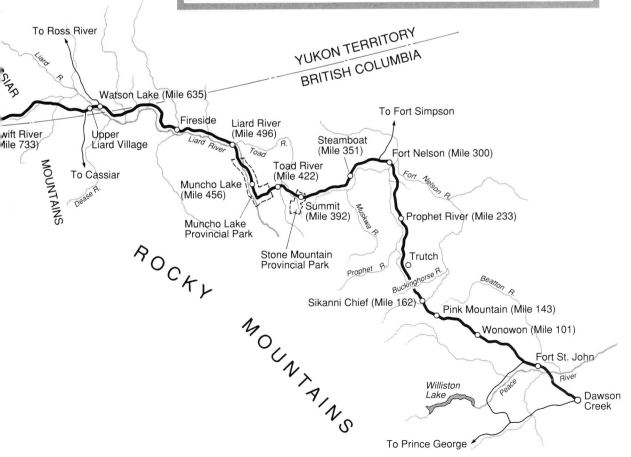

To Ross River

Liard R.

CASSIAR

Swift River
(Mile 733)

Watson Lake (Mile 635)

Upper
Liard Village

To Cassiar

MOUNTAINS

Dease R.

Fireside

Liard River

Liard River
(Mile 496)

Toad R.

Muncho Lake
(Mile 456)

Muncho Lake
Provincial Park

Toad River
(Mile 422)

Summit
(Mile 392)

Stone Mountain
Provincial Park

YUKON TERRITORY

BRITISH COLUMBIA

To Fort Simpson

Steamboat
(Mile 351)

Fort Nelson (Mile 300)

Fort Nelson R.

Muskwa R.

Prophet River (Mile 233)

Prophet R.

Trutch

Buckinghorse R.

Beatton R.

Sikanni Chief (Mile 162)

Pink Mountain (Mile 143)

Wonowon (Mile 101)

Fort St. John

Williston
Lake

Peace River

Dawson
Creek

R O C K Y

M O U N T A I N S

To Prince George

Introduction

YOU CANNOT describe the Alaska Highway as a road. The Queen Elizabeth Way in southern Ontario is a road; the I-5 freeway linking Seattle, Washington, and San Diego, California, is a road; even the Trans-Canada highway, for all its political significance, is really just a road, ranging widely in quality and significance, linking eastern Canada and the West Coast. One can make something of a case for the Blue Ridge Parkway in Virginia, but this beautiful and well-travelled route lacks the mystique and aura that surround the 1,523 miles of mostly paved road stretching from Dawson Creek, British Columbia, to Fairbanks, Alaska.

The Alaska Highway is more than a road, carrying vehicles from one point to another; it is a holiday excursion all by itself. Each summer, thousands of American and Canadian travellers strap a second spare tire onto their vehicle, purchase headlight shields and even wire screens for the front of their cars, and head to the Far Northwest. While some come to visit Dawson City, home of the Klondike Gold Rush, or Mount McKinley in Alaska's Denali National Park, many more travel just for the adventure of the highway itself. It is every person's outing, affording thousands of North Americans an opportunity to explore the continent's last frontier and to go where few have gone before.

The Alaska Highway stands alone among the many famous routes, trails, and early wagon roads that played such a historic role in the expansion of settlement and development across the continent. These old trails – the Santa Fe, the Cariboo Road, the Oregon Trail, California's Spanish Mission Trail – retain a treasured place in North American history, celebrated by non-Natives as the embodiment of the pioneering spirit and the urge to peel back the frontier of the Far West, but bitterly remembered by Natives as the avenues by which farmers, ranchers, miners, and other developers ventured west to take possession of Indian lands. Most of these old trails are gone, replaced by paved multi-lane expressways. A few, their usefulness long past, lie abandoned, clogged by trees and underbrush and ignored by all but history buffs. There is very little in the modern experience of these roads that harkens back to their origins. A few historic sites and monuments or brightly coloured bumper stickers do little to recreate the time and place of the early explorers, road builders, and travellers.

The Alaska Highway is different. Built during World War II, the road remains an enduring symbol of the determination to protect this continent from Japanese invasion. The road also stands as a symbol of Canadian-American cooperation and friendship. Developed by the United States government, the Alaska Highway is largely located in Canada and was completed with very little interference from Dominion authorities.

But the mystique of the Alaska Highway cannot be explained simply by its mute testament to American resolve and Canadian cooperation during the last World War. There is also the allure of its route. Starting in the agricultural lands around Dawson Creek, British Columbia, the highway stretches 1,523 miles (2,446 kilometres) toward the Northwest. It lies across hundreds of miles of North America's most beautiful, rugged, and pristine landscape. The highway crosses mighty rivers – the Peace, Muskwa, Liard, Teslin, Yukon, White – and scores of smaller streams and creeks; it curls around dozens of mountains and is bordered at one point by the magisterial St. Elias Mountains, the highest range in North America. Frigid, crystal clear lakes – Muncho, Teslin, Kluane – appear alongside the highway as it winds its way north to Alaska. Few roads in the world traverse such beauty and variety, much of it still unbruised by development.

Still, beauty alone does not account for the attraction, although it certainly explains why many travellers fall in love with the northland. The Alaska Highway is also a road into history. The

Far Northwest is one of the continent's most famed lands, home to the Klondike Gold Rush, one of the best-known events of North American history. This is the domain of Robert Service and the "men who moil for gold," of Jack London and *White Fang*, and of Charlie Chaplin's film, *The Gold Rush*. At its end is Alaska, once contemptuously dismissed by a few misguided cynics as "Seward's folly," but today treasured as a resource-rich land of scenic wonders.

The Northwest is one of the coldest places in North America, noted across Canada and the United States as the source of the Arctic fronts that routinely drive freezing air deep to the south. Southerners follow with fascination the vagaries of northern thermometers, wondering how people survive when the mercury falls to minus sixty-five Fahrenheit and snow driven by powerful northerly winds obscures all vision. They watch with awe as the mushers push their dog teams through the gruelling ordeals of the Iditarod and Yukon Quest races. (One of the best T-shirts ever made reads simply, The North: Where the Men are Men and Women Win the Iditarod.) The Far Northwest is one of the most romantic and magical places on the continent, mythologized as a land where humans can test the limits of their endurance and determination and yet experience nature as it was and ought still to be. It is, put simply, North America's last frontier.

The Alaska Highway is the link, the access, between North and South, between overdeveloped regions and unspoiled wilderness, between past and the present. Enfolded in a mystique of its own that goes back to its wartime origins, when, driven by wartime urgency, Americans and Canadians, soldiers and civilians, pushed through a rough pioneer road in less than eight months, the highway affords North Americans an unparalleled opportunity to experience the northern frontier. Travelling in the comfort of cars, campers, and mobile homes, tourists by the tens of thousands annually recreate their own Klondike quest, or relive vicariously the experience of the wartime construction crews. The road is infinitely better now than it was at the end of World War II, but the land it crosses is as unsullied, primeval, and magnetic as it ever was.

The Alaska Highway is far more than a road, for it does far more than simply allow people to travel from the lower forty-eight states and southern Canada to the Yukon and Alaska. As the travellers venture north, putting hundreds of miles between themselves and the congestion and development of more settled areas, they enter a land of history, mystery, majesty, and beauty. But they also enter a homeland, for the Far Northwest is the longest continually inhabited area of North America. First Nations in this area trace their ancestry back between 12,000 and 15,000 years, and some archaeologists push the time of initial occupation back even further. These people are still here, their cultures changed by contact with immigrants and travellers, but they are still very much a part of the land and retain their special knowledge of the sub-Arctic environment.

For the Native people, and the non-Natives who have chosen the North, the Alaska Highway is not a road to adventure, a tourist trail, or an opportunity to discover a lost past. For those who live along the highway in the widely spaced towns, tourist camps, and Native villages, the highway is a lifeline, a connection to the larger world. Supplies that once came by pack train or riverboat now arrive by truck. The highway also provides safe, reliable access to the larger centres – Fort St. John, Whitehorse, or Fairbanks – where hospitals, schools, government offices, and other facilities are available. In the South, such things are taken for granted; in the Far Northwest, the Alaska Highway is the assurance of contact with the "outside" and with the services of the modern world. For northerners, the Alaska Highway has become a linear community, much as the main rivers were earlier, linking families, friends, and businesses throughout the Northwest.

Many travellers look askance at the tiny settlements along the Alaska Highway, places such as Muncho Lake, Johnson's Crossing, Jake's Corner, Destruction Bay, Northway, and Delta Junction. They wonder about the attractions of life in these isolated outposts, noting that many have satellite dishes, electricity, and other accoutrements of modern life, but also remarking on the absence of stores, recreational facilities, and the many other things city-dwellers take for granted. They often overlook the intense attachment of Native people to their homeland and the powerful attraction of the Northwest for some newcomers. Victims of the corridor perception that afflicts North American life, they also fail to look much beyond the highway and do not contemplate the many rivers, lakes, hills, and mountains that sit only a few miles away from the highway itself.

Travellers invariably cling to the road and find that the high-way journey is more than enough of an adventure. In doing so, they miss the true sense of isolation that accompanies life in the Northwest. Pretend for a second that you are standing in Tok Junction, a small highway community in eastern Alaska. Start walking toward the Canada–United States boundary that lies to the east. If you keep to the same latitude, you will cross only one major road, the Klondike Highway, before you reach Hudson Bay, several thousand miles away. There are more isolated and sparsely settled places on earth, but not many, and very few that are accessible to the average North American traveller. The Alaska Highway traverses this wilderness and this homeland, providing access to one of the most unusual human and natural environments to be found anywhere.

The Alaska Highway has loomed large in my own life. My father, Richard K. Coates, was a civil engineer with the Department of Public Works (now called Public Works Canada), assigned first to Banff, Alberta, and later to Revelstoke, British Columbia, where he worked on the Rogers Pass section of the Trans-Canada Highway. In 1964 he applied for a post in Whitehorse. The federal government had transferred responsibility for the Alaska Highway from the Department of National Defence to the Department of Public Works. The prospect of working on the reconstruction of the Alaska Highway was something of an engineer's dream, and so my father was delighted when the job was offered to him. At the age of seven, I was less impressed with the issue of professional opportunity than with the realization that we were leaving our trailer, with its newly built family room, and heading off to some tiny spot on a map, in a place I had never heard of before.

Warned about the brutality of the Alaska Highway, my parents bought a new car for the trip, a light blue 1964 Acadian Beaumont station wagon, a vehicle particularly well-suited for northern driving conditions (although not, as I later proved, for the driving habits of a heavy-footed teenager). My parents jammed suitcases and boxes, a handsome hunting dog named Bingo, me, my brother, my sister, my cousin, and themselves into the car, and we headed off in early August for what must have been, for my parents, a great adventure. By the time we had travelled several hundred miles – not yet even close to the start of the Alaska Highway – fights had broken out with my sister (two years older, and bossy) and my brother (four years younger, and a miserable child). Though not at all at fault, or so I remember these squabbles, I nonetheless seemed to attract a disproportionate share of parental ire. By the time we reached the Peace River country, we three children wanted to go back. Occasional breaks at restaurants and hotels with swimming pools – the ultimate luxury – did little to placate us.

To our dismay, we discovered that the real journey was just beginning. The pavement ran out a short distance north of Fort St. John. Alaska Highway indeed! The road was narrow, constantly dusty, incredibly windy, and rough. Driving was slow, noisy, and for us kids unbelievably boring. Mom and Dad constantly pointed out attractive features – rivers, forests, grand vistas, mountains – but we were singularly unimpressed. I was more interested in picking a fight with my sister – and proclaiming my innocence – and complaining about my brother. We had to slow down whenever traffic approached, a remarkably rare event, while our car was bombarded with a hail of gravel and enveloped in fine, breath-choking dust – although the road, rocks, and dust were not as bad as other travellers had warned. A fire-drill routine, in which all car windows were hastily rolled up, greeted the sight of each vehicle. The windshield miraculously survived the barrage of stones intact, and never suffered the crystalline stars that pock-mark most northern automobiles. And on and on it continued, long past any reasonable test of childhood endurance. Even the normal travelling games – counting farm animals or guessing the colours of oncoming cars – were hopeless along the Alaska Highway, for there were no farms and very few cars; we could count telephone poles, but that also became distressingly monotonous after the first four or five hundred.

Much later, my father explained the rationale behind our rather unusual driving schedule – involving early morning starts and mid-afternoon stops: "We had some good advice," he said. "A friend went up a year ahead of us. He said, 'Don't forget when you come up the highway you are travelling mostly west. Travel early in the morning and don't drive late in the afternoon, because in the afternoon you are looking into the sun. The dust and the sun, in combination, make driving very hazardous.' So we would get up at 5:00 a.m. and get started and drive 300 miles and stop at 2:00 p.m." My mother remembered – and so do the rest of us – that the system didn't work quite as smoothly as Dad laid it out. The 5:00 a.m. starts were attended to religiously, but getting Dad to slow down by 2:00 p.m. took some doing – as we were to discover again and again on our many family journeys along the Alaska Highway.

There was one diversion worthy of note. In an attempt to encourage safe driving, the Canadian army had posted markers at the site of every fatal accident along the Alaska Highway. Solitary markers, indicating the date of the accident and the number of people killed, were sobering enough. At other locations, including several of the numerous sharp curves and blind hills along the highway, we would see a number – five or six – of these signs in a row. With childish glee, we shouted at our father to slow down and quickly counted the number of fatalities, comparing the body-count with that encountered on other twists and turns in the road. Signs indicating the deaths of large numbers in a single accident sparked a great deal of morbid speculation on our part as to its cause.

We stopped at many of the gas stations, hotels, and restaurants, but even that generated little enthusiasm. Many miles passed between stops, at least fifty and usually one hundred or more, with few signs of human habitation. The restaurants and gas stations typically were converted World War II surplus buildings; they looked strikingly similar as we made our way northwest past Pink Mountain, Trutch, Steamboat, Coal River, and Liard. Our silence only temporarily purchased by ice cream or hamburgers, we constantly complained to my parents about our increasing boredom. The hotels were unlike the few we had experienced in the South. There were no swimming pools and, even worse, no television sets. The settings may have been beautiful, particularly at Muncho Lake, which, as the half-way point between Dawson Creek and Whitehorse, was one of the main stops on the highway, but we children were unimpressed.

Our family made it to Whitehorse from Dawson Creek in three days without witnessing a single fatal accident, colliding with a moose, being besieged by caribou herds, having a flat tire, puncturing our gas tank, obliterating the windshield, or otherwise experiencing a *true* introduction to travel along the Alaska

Highway. It was hard to be impressed by Whitehorse. There were few signs of modern life – only the Dairy Queen was of much interest – and the entire place appeared to be covered in a thin layer of dust. The greenery of southern British Columbia was noticeably absent; if I had been old enough, I most certainly would have been depressed. We stayed in the Tourist Services Hotel over the weekend and then moved into our army-issue duplex in Camp Takhini. School started within a few weeks, and we were quickly incorporated into the seasonal rhythms of life in the Far Northwest. We had survived the highway phase of our indoctrination into northern life. Only much later did I discover that most fathers moving to the Yukon to work on the highway dispatched wife and children northward by airplane; my father, anxious to have us share his fascination with gravel pits, road clearances, and sight lines, had decided that the entire family should travel together.

My father's career remained intricately linked with the Alaska Highway for ten years. He became district director for the Department of Public Works in 1967, with supervisory responsibility for the entire length of the road in Canada. Five years later, he helped negotiate the transfer of responsibility for highway maintenance from the federal to the Yukon territorial government. In 1974, over his quiet professional protests, he was transferred to the Vancouver office of Public Works Canada, although he retained a strong personal and professional interest in the Alaska Highway until he retired in 1984.

Living in Whitehorse, I quickly discovered that the Alaska Highway was a dominant influence in all of our lives. The highway brought hordes of tourists north every summer, including the damnable caravans of cars and trailers which clogged the road and kicked up mountainous clouds of dust. It also provided the major route out of the North. Our family headed "outside" (the northern word for the South) every three years, pushing from Whitehorse to Muncho Lake on the first day, and from there to the joyous rediscovery of hotels with pools and drive-in restaurants in Dawson Creek on the second. I learned to drive on the highway, as good a training ground as can be found anywhere, and witnessed its gradual improvement from a rough, unpaved, and poorly sited road to an increasingly well-designed and reconstructed highway.

I also worked along the Yukon portions of the highway for three summers following high school. The first year I had a job straight out of the 1970s: counting cars. Working in eight-hour shifts with two co-workers (I was the "boss"), I sat in a car alongside the highway, radio turned variously to stations in Vancouver, San Francisco, Las Vegas, and occasionally a foreign language broadcast from some unknown country. My job involved noting the number of cars, direction of travel, and country of origin – a task befitting my successful completion of high school. I received a promotion the following year to the sign crew and spent most of the summer tearing out the internationally famous mileposts along the highway and replacing them with the uniformly hated kilometre posts. My last summer, 1975, still with the sign crew, I travelled along the highway replacing intersection signs – more than one traveller was sent into a state of panic and fury when he discovered that the established method of displaying distances in miles had been replaced by the new Canadian metric standard.

I left Whitehorse in 1974 to attend the University of British Columbia, travelling the Alaska Highway in a 1973 Datsun 610 sedan. After a two-year sojourn in physical education, broken by the sudden realization of what I would look like at forty, still chasing teenagers around a high-school gymnasium, I transferred into history and rediscovered my fascination with the Canadian North. As I continued my studies, I found a way to link my personal fascination with the Alaska Highway to my professional activities. Having discovered that Canadian and American historians paid very little attention to the highway, I began work on a series of academic projects relating to the history of the Alaska Highway. I come to this book, therefore, from two directions: as someone raised along the Alaska Highway and familiar with its importance and impact on the Northwest and as a university academic intrigued with the broader political, economic, and social significance of this unique episode in Canadian-American relations.

And now there is this book. In it, I have attempted to capture glimpses of life in the Northwest from World War II to the present. While I have drawn on many written records, from government documents to published memoirs, and from private photographs to personal correspondence, I have relied primarily on the reminiscences of the men and women who worked and lived along the Alaska Highway. Collecting these memories has been one of the most rewarding experiences of my time as a writer, for I have met – in person and by letter – dozens of delightful and friendly people. They have in common a fascination with the Alaska Highway and the Far Northwest, and a remarkable willingness to share their stories and memorabilia. Although I have contacted several hundred people, I know that I have only just scratched the surface, for the highway has attracted many workers and travellers over the years. The story I offer here, culled from thousands of pages of archival documentation, hundreds of hours of interview tapes, and piles of written reminiscences of life along the highway, is of necessity selective. I have attempted to recreate a sense of the time and place and have, wherever possible, let the people speak of their experiences in their own words. Others, of course, have their own stories and would offer different descriptions.

My experience tells me that the Alaska Highway is much more than a road, and that history cannot be told solely through an examination of the political and diplomatic debates that have long surrounded the Alaska Highway. The history of this road is really about the people who lived in the area before the highway was built, the promoters who longed for a road linking North and South, the men and women, soldiers and civilians, who built the initial road, the workers who, over the next forty years, upgraded the highway, the people who lived alongside and helped give it its special character, and the travellers who come north to Alaska each year, drawn by the magic of the place and the mystique of one of the world's truly great adventures: the Alaska Highway. This is their story.

1

Setting the Stage

THE CONSTRUCTION of the Alaska Highway began in 1942. Long before then, however, promoters pushed various schemes for the building of roads, trails, or railways between the Far Northwest and the South. They were unsuccessful, leaving the region isolated within North America. But the idea would not die, kept alive by those who dreamt of a day when the Yukon and Alaska would be linked directly to the rest of the continent.

The visions of a connection to the Northwest are almost a century old. In the last three years of the nineteenth century, thousands of *cheechakos* (newcomers) streamed over the mountains from Skagway and Dyea, heading for Dawson City and gold. Access was limited by the impressive coastal mountain range and the vast distances between the headwaters of the Yukon River at Lake Lindeman and the Klondike. For Canadians the problems went deeper, for Skagway was an American port; the construction of the White Pass and Yukon Route railway from Skagway to Whitehorse during the Gold Rush years only heightened the region's dependence on access via Alaska. The entire Yukon basin was, in all practical terms, cut off from southern Canada, and left hostage to American generosity and goodwill. At a time of considerable tension between the two countries – Canada and the United States were engaged in a long and vigorous diplomatic battle over the Alaska-Canada boundary – Canadians' inability to travel freely and directly to the Klondike was a matter of intense national interest.

Clifford Sifton, Canadian Minister of the Interior, had a solution. He authorized the construction of an all-Canadian railway from the interior of British Columbia through to the Yukon. Agreements had been reached with William Mackenzie and Donald Mann, speculators and contractors *extraordinaire*, who had previously built a number of development railways, including the Canadian Northern, in southern Canada. Sifton made one egregious error: he assumed that the Americans would simply accept his plans for northern development. They didn't. Confronted with plans for a competing line and the likely collapse of Skagway as a trans-shipment port, American authorities dug in their heels and prevented construction of the railway. It was a bitter loss for Sifton and a hard-learned lesson for Canadians.

The abandonment of the all-Canadian route stranded the Yukon Territory, and left Alaska without land-based access to the south. In the years that followed, the North's options disappeared almost as quickly as they arose. By the end of the first decade of the new century, the rich bounty of the Klondike fields had begun to run out. The individual prospectors who had given the Klondike much of its character and flavour were pushed aside by large corporations. Soon massive dredges began to scour the creeks, snaking through the river bottoms, leaving only huge gravel castings behind to mark their passing. Alaska had benefitted from a series of echo-booms that had rebounded through the Northwest following the Klondike strike. Discoveries at Nome, Fairbanks, Ruby, Iditarod, and a dozen smaller sites sparked short-lived rushes and kept alive the dream of another sub-Arctic Eldorado. It was all for naught, and the Northwest slipped slowly into an economic coma that threatened the region's life.

Struggling for survival, the remaining non-Native residents of the region scarcely dared to dream big. A few promoters begged Canadian and American authorities for the money necessary to push a wagon road through from the south, but the vast, unopened wilderness that lay between the Yukon and the nearest settlements of British Columbia and Alberta deterred all but the most naive and enthusiastic. A small regional society emerged, straddling the Alaska-Yukon boundary, and tied together by the umbilical cord of the Yukon River. The British Yukon Navigation Company, mother corporation to the White Pass and Yukon Route and commercial *grande dame* of the Far Northwest, controlled most of the riverboats, and ran an efficient and integrated operation that stretched from Skagway on the Alaskan Panhandle, through Whitehorse and Dawson City, to the lower Yukon River. The northland – the Yukon and the interior of Alaska – knew an internal unity and sense of community that all but ignored the existence of a national boundary. The cohesion of the region was dashed in the early 1920s when the American government pushed through the Alaska Railroad from Seward to Fairbanks. The isolated interior of Alaska now had direct access to the ocean and quickly cast off its ties to the upper Yukon River basin.

There were roads in the region. A small, rough network of trails had been built within both the Yukon and Alaska and in the agricultural districts of northern British Columbia. These roads – seldom more than rugged paths suitable only for horse-drawn wagons – permitted summertime travel between the villages and towns; after the snows came and rivers froze, a slightly larger network of winter roads came into use. Only the greatest optimist found much satisfaction in the northern byways, more suitable for horse and dog-team than for automobile traffic. By now, however, northerners had all but given up hope that southern politicians might look favourably on their request for land access to the rest of the continent.

By the 1920s faint rumblings from the south held out the prospect of change. It was not that politicians from Washington State or British Columbia were particularly concerned about the well-being of the territorians in the Yukon and Alaska; rather, a small group of visionaries decided that the future of the Pacific Northwest lay in the opening of northern British Columbia, the Yukon, and Alaska for mining, lumbering, and tourism. The promoters and politicians guessed, not illogically, that the cities and regions that lay at the southern end of a road from Alaska would corner the market on northern development. This was certainly the case during the Gold Rush, when Seattle, Vancouver, and Victoria had duked it out for commercial supremacy over the Klondike stampeders. Seattle's clear victory provided that city

A Native camp in the Far Northwest.
CAMPBELL COLLECTION.

with an important boost going into the twentieth century. Regional politicians decided that when the next boom came – and come it must – their towns, states, and provinces would be properly placed to capitalize on any opportunities.

Simon Fraser Tolmie, the distressingly ineffectual Conservative premier of British Columbia in the late 1920s, was among the first to boost a road to Alaska. The highway, he argued, offered the immediate benefit of construction jobs for hundreds of British Columbians, while opening the Northwest to American tourists.

He found few supporters, particularly among the Ottawa politicians whom he counted on for the money necessary to build the project. Tolmie pushed hard, sponsoring a caravan of officials from Canada and the United States to northern British Columbia, and repeatedly restating his commitment to the highway adventure. As Tolmie's government withered in the painfully difficult Depression years of the early 1930s, plans for a road north faded. When Tolmie and his party were tossed out of office in 1933 the scheme appeared dead, for the new Liberal premier, T. Duff Pattullo, had opposed Tolmie's plan at every turn.

To the surprise of all but those familiar with him, Pattullo quickly showed himself to be an ardent supporter of the Alaska highway plan. Pattullo had joined the rush to the Klondike in 1897, where his father's solid political connections earned him a job with the Commissioner of the Yukon. He later moved to Prince Rupert and, although frustrated by lack of provincial attention to the area, became convinced that the province's future lay in the North. Pattullo also realized that dreams of northern prosperity ultimately rested on the construction of suitable transportation facilities. A road to the south was, in Pattullo's mind, at the absolute top of the list. So, too, as British Columbians and Yukoners discovered in 1937, were his almost successful plans to annex the Yukon Territory to his province.

British Columbia teetered on the verge of bankruptcy, and faced massive economic chaos and social disruptions as a result of the deepening depression. Pattullo believed that major public works, such as the bridge his government constructed across the Fraser River and a highway to Alaska, were necessary to jump-start the regional economy. His efforts were aided by growing American interest in the highway project. Congress in 1935 provided $2 million for such a project and authorized the president to begin talks with Canada on the matter. The highway project, seemingly off to a racing start, soon foundered in the morass of federal-provincial politics and Canadian-American relations. Pattullo pushed the plan with President F. D. Roosevelt, who was favourably disposed to Alaskan development. The British Columbia premier's interference in diplomatic affairs with the United States, however, infuriated the cautious William Lyon Mackenzie King, Canada's prime minister during these troubled years. Federal officials moved quickly to obstruct provincial initiatives.

The United States had its own promoters of a highway to Alaska. Pre-eminent among them was Donald MacDonald, an engineer and long-time advocate of a road from the contiguous states to the Far Northwest. Although at times an almost solitary voice, MacDonald persisted. The idea, oddly, occasionally ran afoul of Alaskan opinion, as historian Harold Griffin describes: "The cry was raised that if the highway were built Alaska would be thrown open to all the itinerant Okies and Arkies who would migrate there in search of new homes. It was contended that the best way to develop Alaska was to let it develop itself."[1] The idea of a *Grapes of Wrath*, northern style, did not long deter Alaskan promoters, who threw their lot behind MacDonald's dream.

The widening public debate illustrated the complexity of any cooperative project of the scale of the proposed highway to Alaska. Newspaper editors and other public commentators wondered aloud if Canadian sovereignty would survive if Canada permitted the Americans to build a road through to Alaska. Alarmists raised the spectre of Yankee military domination of the Far Northwest. While the press debate supported the notion that Canadian concerns over its independence ultimately scuttled Pattullo's plans, it was actually the intricacies of federal-provincial relations that stamped them out. Prime Minister King, parsimonious at the best of times, believed that the small number of federal seats in British Columbia did not justify massive expenditures from a severely limited national treasury.

The Americans, led by Congressman Warren Magnuson from Washington State, attempted to force the Canadians' hand. In an attempt to speed consideration of the highway project and, less directly, to allay Canadian fears of American intentions, in 1938 the United States government established an International Highway Commission, under Magnuson's chairmanship and with Governor Ernest Gruening of Alaska, former Governor Thomas Riggs, and James Carey, a consulting engineer from Seattle, to consider the matter. Pushed by Pattullo, Prime Minister King agreed to establish a similar commission, although he was quick to point out that the federal government was in no way committed to following the directives of the study team. If King's lack of enthusiasm was not already clear, he made it particularly evident by appointing Charles Stewart as the chairman of the Canadian commission.

Stewart was seriously ill at the time and was not able to assume his duties properly for a full six months.

The work of the two commissions proceeded; the American under Magnuson's enthusiastic guidance, the Canadian team reflecting the prime minister's resounding lack of interest. Deliberations were further clouded by the onset of war with Germany in 1939 and, on the West Coast, steadily increasing concern about the threat from Japan. While most observers claimed that a highway to Alaska would aid in the defence of the Northwest, a few argued that the highway, particularly if near the coast, would provide a Japanese invading force with a golden opportunity to strike at the South. The commissions proceeded as best they could, travelling throughout the area, visiting the Yukon and Alaska briefly, and considering several different route proposals.

There was a great deal at stake in the selection of the highway route. Towns along any new road stood to prosper; those by-passed, even if by only a few miles, were almost certainly doomed. After eliminating frivolous and impractical routes, attention focused on two alternatives: Route A, which ran just to the east of the Alaskan Panhandle and passed through the majestic coastal mountain ranges, and Route B, which ran roughly north from Prince George, British Columbia, to Dawson City, and from there on to Alaska. Route A was favoured for its scenery and its attractiveness to tourists; because it was close to the coast and in the mountains, however, it was sure to be costly to build and maintain. Route B, located several hundred miles inland, was not as physically attractive, but traversed gentler and more heavily mineralized territory. The American highway commission, and the governments of Alaska, British Columbia, and Washington favoured Route A, largely because it promised access to isolated coastal towns on the Alaska Panhandle. The more cautious Canadians offered a less declarative opinion, but gave greatest support to the inland route.

It was all for naught. By the time the commissions had reported, Pattullo had resigned the premiership, Canada was fully involved in the European war, and concern was growing about Japanese aggression in the Pacific. As had so often been the case, the government investigations had delayed serious consideration of a contentious issue and, by offering competing conclusions, had left decision-makers with uncertain guidance for the future. But while politicians from Washington State, Alaska, and British Columbia (Yukon officials scarcely participated in the debate, except during commission hearings in Whitehorse) argued over the choice of route, yet another group was quietly staking out its claim to the highway to Alaska.

The competing interest lay in an odd union of Canadian and American politicians and promoters from the Prairie west. Like their counterparts on the West Coast, the Prairie leaders sought ways of expanding their economic base and making their region the focus for further expansion. Edmonton had long asserted its role as the Gateway to the North, a claim that originated with the dangerously absurd promotion of the Alberta town (then part of the Northwest Territories) as the best place to start an expedition to the Klondike. Many of those unfortunate enough to buy Edmonton's self-interested boosterism suffered severely as a consequence. The stampeders' personal misfortune was not enough to stop the city's promoters from realizing the potential for future schemes. (Edmonton persists in its self-promotion as a Klondike centre, as seen in its annual fair, Klondike Days. Many Yukoners are still offended by the specious claims and regularly protest the naming of the event after a territorial phenomenon.)

Not surprisingly Edmonton emerged at the forefront of a Prairie lobby demanding that any road to Alaska pass through the northern plains. While Washington State and British Columbia debated the relative merits of the coastal and inland routes, F. S. Wright, editor of the *Nor'West Miner* and local booster, argued for a road heading northwest from Edmonton to Alaska: "Cheap construction, better climate conditions, productive areas for farming and mining and also scenic beauty all favor this route."[2] Like most urban promoters, including many of those arguing for Routes A and B through British Columbia, Wright actually had few technical details about the Prairie route at his fingertips; those would come later, after the main battle had been joined and won. Beginning in 1938 he recruited other Edmontonians and petitioned federal and provincial politicians to join his cause.

Wright realized that Edmonton had no hope of winning the battle on its own. During personal travels in the northern United States, he discovered a similar interest in expanding road links throughout the region. The Wahpeton-Portal Highway Association of North Dakota quickly threw its support behind Wright and enthusiastically seconded Edmonton's efforts for a highway to Alaska. At the instigation of American promoters a number of interested municipal, state, and provincial officials met to consider the matter in more detail. The Alaska-United States-Canada Prairie Highway Association was formed with the principal goal of ensuring that the road to Alaska linked up with an expanded prairie road network and not, as Washington and British Columbia would have it, be oriented due south.

In the manner of boosters everywhere, the Prairie promoters did not let logic or geography stand in the way of their vision. Supporters produced fascinating maps of North America, showing large highways originating in southern Florida and crossing the United States and Canada diagonally to reach the Yukon and Alaska. In this conception of North America, North Dakota, Saskatchewan, and Alberta became the continental pivot and assumed central importance in any plan to develop a highway route to the Far Northwest. Municipal promoters and regional politicians fantasized about massive highways carrying hundreds of cars and the wealth and resources of two countries.

For a region suffering through the depths of the Depression and heavily dependent on the wheat crop for economic survival, the potential diversification promised through highway construction sounded like the answer to their prayers. Meetings of the Alaska-United States-Canada Prairie Highway Association were enthusiastically attended. A meeting held in Regina, Saskatchewan, in May 1941 attracted supporters from across the region, including Calgary, Edmonton, and Peace River in Alberta, the Saskatchewan towns of Estevan, Moose Jaw, Saskatoon, Battleford, Regina and Weyburn, and Minot, Kenmare, Devil's Lake, Bowbells, Bismarck, Fargo, Wahpeton, Velva, Portal, and Drake in North Dakota. A few Prairie folks, battered by ten years of hardship, dared free up their imagination and dream big once more.[3]

Few observers gave the Prairie advocates much chance of success. So sure of their case were the promoters from the Pacific Northwest that they paid virtually no attention to the Prairie Highway Association. They saw their routes, resource-rich and infinitely more scenic than a dusty route across the northern plains, as the only logical ones. But the Prairie lobbyists were not easily deterred, even by the likelihood of defeat, and they proceeded to lobby aggressively for their cause. Response from Canadian and American public officials was less than supportive. The Canadian Minister of Mines and Resources, T. A. Crerar, said it was "unlikely" that the United States government – the one likely to provide the funding – would look favourably on an interior route.[4]

Other considerations also affected the final decision on the highway route. In the 1930s, Canadian and British officials had commenced work on a Great Circle air route to the Orient, using the curvature of the earth to shorten the lengthy flight from North America to Japan and China. What was initially conceived as a service to civil aviation took on new importance as hostilities flared in the Pacific. Work started in 1939 on a series of airfields linking Edmonton, Alberta, and Fairbanks, Alaska. The Permanent Joint Board on Defence, a Canadian-American planning agency established in 1941, pushed for further development of the air network. Canada agreed and commenced work on the Northwest Staging Route, an expanded version of the earlier civilian air system in the Northwest. This decision would ultimately have a considerable impact on the location of the Alaska Highway.

Until early December 1941, discussions about a highway route held little continental urgency. Local politicians, particularly in Alaska, British Columbia, and Washington State, pushed the idea, but more from a desire to ensure that they were first in line than the belief that the project was urgent. Even northerners, long used to the South ignoring their pleas for attention and help, expected little action from national governments. Competing interests lobbied for position, particularly as the Prairie Highway Association intensified its efforts and bombarded potentially sympathetic officials with petitions, letters of support, and queries. In the broader scheme of things, with Canada joining its allies in the war against Germany and with many in the United States champing at the militaristic bit and anxious to join in the fray, a highway to Alaska was fairly low in national and international priorities.

Everything changed on 7 December 1941. A surprise raid by Japanese bombers and fighter planes devastated much of Pearl

Harbor in Hawaii and provided the United States' leadership with the excuse needed to enter the war against Japan and its allies. Military planners and politicians were not caught totally unawares by the declaration of war. Anti-Japanese sentiment, fuelled by Japanese aggression in the Far East, had grown steadily through the 1930s as Canadian and American officials grew increasingly concerned about Japanese designs on the West Coast. Among a few anti-Japanese agitators worries mounted about the reliability of the thousands of Canadian and American citizens of Japanese descent living in the region. The onset of war unleashed the thinly veiled race hatred that ran through portions of North American society and provided a moral justification for vicious anti-Japanese attitudes. As the Canadian and United States governments cranked up their promotional machinery for a full international war effort they spared little effort in painting the Japanese as the most treacherous of enemies. The inflated rhetoric of the democracies at war soon convinced the continent that the Pacific Northwest was extremely vulnerable to Japanese attack.

Military planners took immediate action. Canadian and American armies shifted ships and soldiers west, erected gun emplacements near major West Coast cities, and stepped up surveillance activities. Within a few months politicians in Canada and the United States surrendered to those racists advocating the removal from coastal areas and dispossession of Japanese nationals and citizens of Japanese descent, opening an unsavoury chapter in the wartime histories of both countries. As concern for continental defence escalated, it became increasingly evident that there was a gaping hole – Alaska – in the planned defence of the West Coast.

As the westerly islands of the ill-defended Aleutian chain lie closer to Japan than the rest of the North American continent, Alaska presented an obvious target for the Japanese. In the South Pacific, Japanese forces had hopped aggressively from island to island, quickly overrunning hastily constructed defences. Alaska had a few widely scattered and poorly provisioned military posts, but Canada did not have a single soldier in the Yukon Territory. It was quite conceivable, particularly to the hysterics who provided much of the public commentary during World War II, that a successful Japanese attack on Alaska would swiftly be followed by a piercing thrust to the heart of the continent.

With the distance and dispassionate perspective provided by the passage of time it is easy to dismiss, even ridicule, Canadian and American concerns about a potential Japanese invasion. It is now clear that the Japanese did not plan a large land-based invasion of North America; logic certainly worked against any such plan. But, for North Americans engulfed in a global conflagration, particularly a struggle that was not going particularly well early in 1942, even the slightest evidence of an Axis invasion was enough to send shivers across Canada and the United States. The Japanese occupations of Kiska and Attu islands in the Aleutians provided proof that North America was not safe from attack. The Allied powers were in trouble elsewhere. Late in 1941, with Nazi forces occupying most of Europe and North Africa and on the march toward Russia, with Japan in the clear ascendancy in the South Pacific, North Americans had legitimate fears that they might soon stand alone against the Axis powers. An invasion seemed imminent, and many Americans and Canadians were swept up in hysteria and fear during the dark first months of 1942.

Concern about the defence and supply of Alaska and the Canadian Northwest rose significantly on the North American agenda. While it was not quite clear what could or should be done to defend the region, Canadians and Americans demanded action. The United States military offered a variety of opinions on the best means of defence, and the navy argued that the defence and supply of Alaska was best conducted by sea, pointing to the fact that most Alaskan settlements were along the coast and would require maritime protection throughout the war. Consideration was even given to building a railroad northwest from Prince George. General B. Sommervell, commander of the U.S. Army Service Forces, commissioned logistical expert Colonel J. H. Graham to examine the options. Graham made a quick study of the alternatives and came down decisively in favour of a highway from Edmonton to Fairbanks, following the line of the string of airfields – the Northwest Staging Route – then being expanded.[5] President Roosevelt listened to this advice and authorized construction of a highway to Alaska. This plan had the added benefit, not openly discussed at the time, of reassuring North Americans that resolute action in defence of the continent had been taken.

Diplomatic protocol and logic dictated that the United States government seek Canadian approval of the plan. The proposed road, to be built by the United States Army Corps of Engineers and American civilian agencies, would pass through more than 1,200 miles of Canadian territory. Canadian permission to build the road and permit the entry of soldiers and civilian workers was essential before work could commence. The appropriate letters and proposals passed between Washington and Ottawa. Federal civil servants and politicians were singularly unimpressed. Hugh Keenleyside, assistant undersecretary for External Affairs, dismissed the strategic arguments as a "dubious egg" and worried that the entire project might well be a "white elephant." Like his superiors, however, Keenleyside could not find the political justification for turning down a seemingly logical Allied request. Canada made it clear from the outset that it would not participate in the financing or construction of the Alaska Highway or the many related defence projects in the Far Northwest. The United States could proceed with its highway to Alaska, but it would do so on its own.[6]

American military officials now had to decide which was the best route to Alaska. British Columbia and Washington, confident in the success of their proposals, reasserted their claim; so, too, did the Prairie Highway Association. There was no shortage of opinion. Vilhjalmur Stefansson, Arctic explorer-promoter, threw his considerable reputation behind a combined pipeline and highway project that would connect Edmonton, Alberta, the Imperial Oil field at Norman Wells on the Mackenzie River, and Fairbanks, Alaska. The United States government eventually commissioned a pipeline-refinery complex in the Northwest, called the CANOL Project, to support the highway and aerial activity in the region; Stefansson's more grandiose scheme received little support. Under wartime conditions, and with stakes so high, there was no time for regional politics and self-interested arguments. The army wanted to move quickly in order to get construction units into the field before the snow melted and the river ice thawed in the spring of 1942. To do so, it had to know the route immediately.

Working behind the scenes, army officials pushed for the Prairie route. They were not buying the commercial and political arguments of the Prairie politicians, but they saw a certain logic in combining work on the Northwest Staging Route and the new highway to Alaska. In their minds the highway was of dubious benefit to the overall war effort, but they saw it could make a vital contribution to the aerial network, which would be used to ferry hundreds of planes to the Soviet Union under the lend-lease program the U.S.A. had adopted to help its allies before it formally declared war. Alaskan Governor Ernest Gruening, angered by rumours that the route might go elsewhere than along the coast, flitted about Washington during the winter of 1941-42 like a frustrated flea, creating so many waves that his superior, Secretary of the Interior H. Ickes, admonished him to keep his opinions to himself. Clearly, the weight of opinion was shifting toward the Prairie route even though, as one American official noted, such a decision was sure to "break the hearts of politicians in the Pacific Northwest."[7]

While the army moved on its decision, the public debate quickly heated up. Alaskan Congressional Delegate A. Dimond presented a bill, HR 3095, to the Committee of Public Roads early in February 1942. Not surprisingly, given the thrust of Alaskan sentiment on this count, his bill called for the highway to be built through British Columbia to Alaska. The Prairie Highway Association had been caught unawares. Alerted by phone, Halvor Halvorson, the association's president, chartered a plane to Washington and then had to wait patiently for two days until he had a chance to present his case. The Alaska-British Columbia-Washington group brought out the heavy guns: Delegate Dimond, Governor Gruening, ex-Governor Thomas Riggs, and engineer Donald MacDonald. Finally, Halvorson was called to speak.

Modest in victory, Halvorson later recounted that it had been "a little embarrassing" to contradict the earlier speakers. But he did not let embarrassment stand in his way as he launched a careful and detailed assault on the British Columbia route. He pointed out that a proper cost accounting had not been done, that the route was vulnerable to ship-launched aerial attack, and that it routinely experienced heavy winter snows and seasonal rains. Having made his case, Halvorson was, somewhat naively, dismayed that his opponents struck back with fury. The combined Seattle-Alaska business interests were particularly infuriated by the Prairie upstarts and spared few adjectives or vitriol in their counterattack. It was not enough. The Committee on Public Roads decided to support the Prairie option.

The boosters from the plains states and provinces were elated, for they had successfully beaten back a well-organized and heavily financed British Columbia lobby. With the decision now unofficially made – formal announcement of the route would not follow for some time – local officials across the Prairies lobbied for highway construction to connect their towns to the new road to Alaska, or petitioned for the main route to Edmonton, now the cornerstone of plans for highway construction in the Northwest, to pass through their communities. For British Columbia and Washington State, more than a decade of planning, organizing, and lobbying had been destroyed in a few short days. To them, the choice had been between the coastal or the inland route, and they had accepted as gospel that the coastal province and state would win the main battle. Now, in the interests of the Allied war effort, they had to stifle their criticism of the government's decision even as they knew in their hearts that the little-known Prairie route was much inferior to either of the others.

A year later, General J. F. O'Connor, commander of the Northwest Service Command, explained the army's decision in frank terms that made it clear the politicians' agenda had been of little concern: "The primary purpose of this road was the airfields. The secondary purpose was to have an additional route to Alaska in case of difficulties in the Pacific. At the time this road was initiated, our fleet, of course, was knocked out and we had grave fears. Our sole aim in our construction here has been to give a road that would serve the military purpose and not have what we call up here a peacetime road."[8]

The decision to follow the airfields to the Northwest destroyed some dreams, answered some, and frustrated others. Yukoners complained quietly that the highway left Dawson City, territorial capital and centre of the Yukon economy, out of the picture. Whitehorse, formerly a seasonal trans-shipment point, was virtually assured of territorial prominence as a consequence of the U.S. Army's decision to route the highway through the town. Boosters from Edmonton to Fort St. John, and from Fort Nelson to Fairbanks were ecstatic over the route, while promoters in southern British Columbia and Washington State were furious, although the fact that the highway was being built as a wartime emergency project muted any public displays of outrage or disappointment.

Much of the debate occurred before negotiations with Canada had been formally concluded. Discussions continued on a number of technical points – whether American workers would be covered by Canadian workman's compensation agreements and American construction material exempt from tariffs – and on 18 March 1942, Canadian and American officials gathered for an official signing of the agreement. The American engineers had not waited for formalities; they already had surveyors and construction units on their way to the Northwest and were quickly organizing the shipment of massive quantities of road-building equipment and other supplies to Edmonton, Whitehorse, and Big Delta, the three main supply centres for the highway project. The decision to build the highway was not widely celebrated. American officials had requested that Canada "soft-pedal news of all developments...which might tend to attract the attention of our enemies."[9] The American government hardly respected its own advice, for in the following months the North American public was kept well-informed of the Army's hell-bent race to Alaska.

The Army's decision to follow the Northwest Staging Route lifted the specific decision of routing out of the hands of the politicians and passed it quickly to Colonel William M. Hoge, commander of the United States Army Corps of Engineers in the region. Hoge was in Fort Belvoir, a few miles south of Washington, D.C., when the Alaska highway project surfaced. He was experienced in frontier highway construction, having built a series of roads across the rugged Bataan Peninsula in the Philippines. Hoge brought impressive credentials: he was a decorated World War I veteran, a highly trained engineer who had advanced training from the Massachusetts Institute of Technology, and had a solid military record. A good soldier, Hoge tackled his new assignment with determination and energy, although he was not particularly enamoured with it. A. C. McEachern, a professional engineer who met Hoge in Whitehorse, remembers the Colonel: "My impression was that he had no great personal belief in the usefulness of the project, but he had been given a job to do and he was going to work hard at it until he could get an assignment to active duty overseas."

American military planners had already decided that the road would run past Fort St. John, Fort Nelson, Watson Lake, Whitehorse, Northway, and Big Delta, where the main airfields

Colonel William Hoge.

of the Northwest Staging Route were. Hoge had to find a way to connect these isolated sites. It was easy to do in Washington; thick pencil lines on poorly drafted maps identified a basic route for the highway. But on the ground there were mountain ranges, massive rivers, lakes, and miles of solid permafrost and muskeg in the way. The actual highway would have to be carefully surveyed through the Northwest wilderness.

Gathering detailed information on the region proved exceptionally difficult. In mid-February, Hoge, Colonel Robert Ingalls, Lieutenant Colonel E. A. Mueller of the Quartermaster Corps, and Public Roads Administration engineer C.F. Capes arrived in Edmonton to examine the prospects for a highway along the Prairie route. Working northwest from Edmonton, Hoge and his companions met with locals, soliciting advice and comments on the best possible route for the highway. Suggestions came fast, but usable data was sparse.

There was something to build on. Rough trails connected Fort St. John and Fort Nelson; wagon roads existed west of Whitehorse, reaching as far as Kluane Lake. The major gap was between Fort Nelson and Whitehorse. Maps of the area were hopelessly inadequate, and no one knew the most suitable construction corridor. In Whitehorse Hoge recruited local bush pilot Les Cook to fly him over the *terra incognita* (although not unknown to local Indians, who were not consulted until later) and help locate a path for the highway.

Les Cook proved to be an inspired choice. After a series of flights, Hoge gradually learned the lay of the land and was able to sketch out a preliminary route. Hoge later said, "Les Cook was the great one. Les took me every place. He went between the mountains. . . . We got lost, but I got to know the country pretty well, and the streams, by this flying back and forth."[10] With Cook's help, Hoge determined that the best route crossed the mountains about eighty miles east of Teslin, in the southern Yukon. One of the major routing problems had been set to rest. Les Cook, having played such a pivotal role in the early stages of the highway planning, did not live to see the road built. In December 1942, Cook's plane exploded in a fiery crash on the streets of Whitehorse, killing him instantly.

Countless other decisions also had to be made: troops had to be assigned by the Corps of Engineers, arrangements made with the U.S. Public Roads Administration for construction work, supplies and equipment located and shipped north, and provision made for the housing and feeding of more than ten thousand soldiers. As a vital first stage, surveyors had to be rushed into the field to lay out the road plan in detail. Much of this work fell to the Corps of Engineers, although a civilian agency, the Public Roads Administration, played a vital role from the very beginning.

Alaska Highway mythology has always held that the road was built by the U.S. Army Corps of Engineers. Highway construction was regarded as a test of Yankee military ability to construct a military highway across 1,523 miles of sub-Arctic wilderness and to complete the task in less than eight months. But the Army did not build the entire highway, nor was it ever instructed to do so. Its task, more limited but still daunting, was to construct a pioneer road, rough and unfinished, "at the earliest possible date to a standard sufficient only for the supply of the troops engaged on the work."[11] It was given eight months. The actual highway – a road usable by the military supply convoys destined for Alaska and for future civilian traffic, to be ready by the end of 1943 – would be completed by civilian contractors working under the direction of the Public Roads Administration. The image of private contractors, directed by civil servants, building a proper, full-service, all-weather road was not as dramatic as that of American soldiers racing against time and the elements to defend North America, and so received little publicity during the war years. But the Alaska Highway is as much their creation as the army's.

The Alaska Highway, initially called the Alcan Highway, was also only the most important of dozens of other projects undertaken in the Far Northwest at the same time. New airfields were constructed to complement the Northwest Staging Route; additional roads were constructed from Carcross to Jake's Corner in the Yukon, and from Haines, Alaska, to the Alaska Highway; work proceeded on the massive CANOL oil pipeline and Whitehorse refinery; a telephone network was built throughout the Northwest; the army erected dozens of barracks and administrative offices; and maintenance facilities were built from Edmonton to Fairbanks, and from Fort St. John to Big Delta. These projects ranged from the essential to the ridiculous. The CANOL project, ill-conceived and poorly executed, later became a major scandal and a matter of acute embarrassment to the American government. The telephone system, in contrast, contributed enormously to the modernization of the "new North."

The Alaska Highway had been a long time coming. Promoters from North and South had urged the construction of a highway to Alaska for years and now, with lightning speed and little discussion, work was ready to proceed. For some, including

Yukoners and British Columbians, the highway went the wrong way and promised few long-term benefits, but with a war on, this was not the right time to complain. Gritting their teeth in frustration, the losers wished the American government well, and wondered why the Canadian government was so conspicuously absent from deliberations about the highway. But these were now matters for armchair engineers; the U.S. Army had decided to push the highway northwest from the railhead at Dawson Creek to Big Delta, Alaska. The simple challenge now was to gather the thousands of soldiers and civilians and dispatch them to the Northwest. For those in the South, it was the start of an adventure of a lifetime; for the few people in the Northwest, it was the beginning of a period of unprecedented change and dislocation.

2

The Invasion of the North

THE BUILDING of the Alaska Highway has often been discussed in relation to military strategy, wartime priorities, Canadian-American relations, and regional economic development. But the larger geopolitical processes did not mean a great deal to the thousands of men and women, soldiers and civilians, hastily dispatched to the sub-Arctic to work on the highway. Nor did these broader issues really register with the small number of people, Native and non-Native, who lived in the highway corridor. For these people, the coming of the surveyors and bulldozers was a rude introduction to the realities of war and industrial development and a sure sign that the northland that they had known was no more.

There were few people in the Northwest in the winter of 1941-1942. The Yukon had a population of only 4,900; Alaska had many more – 74,000 residents in 1940, most of them living along the coast. The Peace River country around Dawson Creek was something of a northern anomaly, a finger of rich farmland poking northward from Alberta and pointing suggestively toward Alaska. Farmers had begun to put plough to sod in the Dawson Creek and Fort St. John area the previous decade, most of them driven north by the Prairie dust storms of the Great Depression. Wheat grew well in the rich soils during the long summer days, but the settlers had difficulty convincing government and business to second their efforts by expanding rail and road networks in the area. The Northern Alberta Railway ran a short distance north from Edmonton and had been extended northwestward to Dawson Creek, making this farming village the cornerstone of development in northeast British Columbia.

Across the region, there was not one society, but two. North Americans knew most about the white society, a remnant of the world-famous Klondike Gold Rush. Prospectors unable to find gold in the Dawson City area had fanned out across the Northwest, sparking rushes to smaller discoveries and ephemeral strikes at such places as Nome, Iditarod, Ruby, Fairbanks, Atlin, and Livingstone Creek. They found more than gold, including extremely rich silver and lead deposits near Mayo, coal near Carmacks, copper at Kennicott and Whitehorse. Short-lived boom towns sprung up around these discoveries, but many, such as Conrad and Silver City, quickly collapsed, leaving behind a few decaying log buildings to symbolize the many dashed dreams of non-Native miners in the area.

In the forty years after the Klondike Gold Rush, non-Natives created an infrastructure to support their mining activities in the area. Railways operated between Skagway and Whitehorse and between Seward and Fairbanks. Sternwheelers plied the main rivers between the mining camps and fur-trading posts, providing a seasonal lifeline for the Northwest. The main towns in the interior – Whitehorse, Dawson City, and Fairbanks – were governed by the uncertainties of unstable resource industries and the inevitability of bitterly cold winters. They were rough-hewn frontier towns, with only a few signs – such as Dawson's impressive government buildings – of a more stable existence. Hundreds of workers and business people spent only the summer in the North, fleeing for warmer climates before the snows came. The governments of Canada and the United States offered only minimal support for their northern territories (Alaska became a state only in 1959), and British Columbia did just as little for the settlers in the isolated northeast corner of the province.

Miners, workers, government officials, teachers, clergy, and other non-Natives moved in and out of the region with distressing frequency; few set down roots or demonstrated much commitment to the Canadian Northwest. Alaska's record in attracting settlers was markedly better, reflecting a greater enthusiasm for

The "old" North. The Hudson's Bay Company post at Fort Nelson.

J. GARBUS

the territory's long-term prospects and the Americans' continuing fascination with the frontier experience. Canadians were too cautious a lot to be fired by whimsical notions of resource bonanzas in the North. Many in the Yukon were already living in the past, resigned to the fact that they might never again experience a boom. Northern British Columbia, beyond the agricultural districts, had attracted little attention apart from the short-lived Cassiar gold rush in the 1870s and seemed destined to remain an economic backwater in a province oriented toward the southern cities of Vancouver and Victoria.

The Northwest's non-Native population was unstable, transient, and there only for the rapid extraction of personal wealth from the region's rich resources. For most the goal was to make a killing, not a living, and few perceived the region as a permanent home. They saw it as a frigid, dangerous place, a land of adventure, a place for hardy young men anxious to test their mettle against a hostile wilderness. Arriving with their heads filled with fanciful notions originating in explorers' descriptions, Klondike legends, and the stories of Robert Service and Jack London, most discovered that the winters were colder, the wages and riches smaller than expected, and the prospect for adventure minimal. Many quickly abandoned their northern fantasies and fled southward. The distressing cycle of short-lived booms, temporary towns, friends made and abandoned, and lives oriented more toward the South than the North survived intact into the middle of the twentieth century.

But this was only the white man's North. There was another North: that of the First Nations. The indigenous people, mostly Athapaskan-speaking tribes (a major exception was the Tlingit people of the southern Yukon), had inhabited the land for countless generations. Although most non-Natives saw them only as backward and primitive, the indigenous people were well adapted to the North. They knew the land intimately and found solace and certainty in the spirits that inhabited every niche of their surroundings. They knew where to locate food in the rivers and lakes, valleys and mountain plateaus, and found enough to sustain them through the long and bitterly cold winters. Unlike the non-Natives who followed so many years later, the indigenous people did not see the region in relation to other places: it was not particularly cold or hot; it simply was as it was. The North was their home, and although they learned of other places from travellers, they knew the land of their birth would be the site of their death.

The Native people had not remained entirely alone. Sailors arrived off the coast of the Alaskan Panhandle in the late eighteenth century, and in 1789 Alexander Mackenzie sailed down his bitterly labelled "River of Disappointment" to the Arctic Ocean. European trade goods – highly valued metal pots, steel knives, blankets – filtered into the Northwest. Hudson's Bay Company explorers John McLeod, Robert Campbell, and John Bell added the Liard, Pelly, Porcupine, and Yukon (then spelled Youcon) rivers to European maps. On the lower Yukon, traders with the Russian-American Company worked slowly up river. The advent of the fur trade drew the Indians into the European economy, which they embraced with considerable enthusiasm and ability. They were far from the guileless savages of the early history books, throwing aside self-respect and culture in a mad scramble for the wonders of Europe. They approached new trade goods and opportunities with caution and selected those particularly well-suited to their nomadic, harvesting lifestyle.

Native society changed noticeably in the years following these initial contacts. Christian missionaries sped north in an interdenominational contest over heathen souls and quickly painted their baptismal marks on hundreds of Indian foreheads. Gold miners followed, a trickle in the 1870s, a stream in the 1880s, and a torrent in the 1890s, pushing Natives off treasured territories and assaulting the land with a rapacious destructiveness that the Indians had never before witnessed. Government agents followed, providing Natives from Alaska to northern British Columbia with relief handouts — unofficial compensation for lands taken and resources destroyed — and encouraging parents to send their children to schools, where they might learn more about the wonders of Canadian or American society and discover the true "debauchery" and "backwardness" of their parents and grandparents.

It is easy, but incorrect, to assume that Native culture simply collapsed in the face of the onslaught of white society and development. Indigenous people, to be sure, suffered seriously, particularly from epidemics that raged through the Northwest and killed hundreds of them. They also changed their hunting habits to suit the needs of the fur trade and re-ordered their lives to take advantage of seasonal work on riverboats, as woodcutters, or as big-game guides. Many became practising Christians — although they did not necessarily abandon their traditional spiritual view. But they largely remained on the land and very much dependent on the products of their hunting and gathering. They also remained, in Virginia Smarch's beautiful phrase, "part of the land, part of the water."

Natives also formed the core of the second sector of Northwestern society. The fur trade brought them to the trading posts, which dotted the region, on a seasonal basis for trade and resupply. The posts became the centre of tiny non-Native settlements; most had one or two traders, a missionary (although often only for the summer), and, notably on the Canadian side, a policeman. The Royal Canadian Mounted Police operated small jack-of-all-trades detachments at many isolated locations in northern Alberta, the Northwest Territories, and the Yukon; in northern British Columbia, the B.C. Provincial Police provided a similar service. Alaskan coverage of the outstations was more spotty, but U.S. marshalls did patrol Native villages in an attempt to ensure at least partial adherence to American law.

The fur traders and the police had much more to do with the Native people than did the whites in the mining camps and major towns. The Natives were, in fact, their *raison d'etre*. A number of the fur traders took Native wives and, although often contemptuously dismissed by non-Native society as "squaw men," became deeply integrated into Indian life. The missionaries and police tended to come and go with regularity, although a few were so drawn by the people and the place that they abandoned their professional careers and remained in the region.

This, then, was the Northwest in the winter of 1941-1942. Largely cut off from the rest of North America, northerners were nonetheless anxious to do their share for the war effort. Many were convinced the war would pass them by and that their only opportunity to participate would be by sending their young men to fight and their money to southern charities. Canadians did both in large numbers. The Indians of Old Crow, one of the most isolated communities in Canada, became famous for their contributions to the support of children displaced by the Nazi aerial attack on London. The Indians' support was a public relations dream. The British High Commissioner to Canada, Malcolm Macdonald, made a substantial detour on his 1942 expedition throughout the Northwest to deliver a plaque and the thanks of his government.

Even the Japanese attack on Pearl Harbor did little to upset the northern equilibrium. Northerners counted, with good reason, on geography as a first line of defence and felt little direct threat. With very few residents of Japanese ancestry in their midst, they also avoided the racist excesses that engulfed British Columbia and the American West Coast in the early years of the war in the Pacific.

Northerners – Native and non-Native, Alaskan and Canadian – were not consulted on the plans for the highway to Alaska, although a few had participated in the Canadian and American commissions studying road proposals in the 1930s. There were none of the community hearings, environmental assessments, and social-impact analyses that would so frustrate developers and placate residents in later years. There was a war on, and military necessity dictated that a road be built immediately to Alaska. Regional concerns and needs had to be subordinated to Allied priorities. When the war was over there would be time to consider the full implications of the decisions taken in the early months of 1942.

The country was awash with rumours. Government secrecy – ostensibly designed to keep news of the highway project from the enemy – only added to the uncertainty. Wild stories abounded. Harold Griffin was in Edmonton early in the construction period: "Edmonton is a city of rumours, many of them so wild that it is hard to see how they gain credence. A stenographer employed by one of the airlines told me in all seriousness she had heard that British Columbia and Alberta had been ceded by secret treaty to the United States as a condition for construction of the various projects."

Thousands of miles to the south, in army camps from the West Coast, the Deep South, and Virginia, troops prepared for the journey to the North. Engineers in Boulder, Colorado, and Washington, D.C., eagerly accepted jobs in the North. Secretaries in Saskatchewan and Oregon signed on for the money and the adventure. Construction workers in Minnesota, Ontario, British Columbia, and Iowa heard of the boom-time wages and offered their services to the private companies looking for help. It was one of the most diverse, broadly based, and chaotic efforts at recruitment, organization, and allocation of labour ever undertaken in North America. The workers knew little of their objective or obligations. They knew that there was a highway to be built, that it had been assigned the highest military priority, and that they were headed north. Beyond that, the expedition was very much a mystery.

Military recruitment was reasonably logical and orderly. Engineering units assigned to the Northwest packed their duffel bags, said their goodbyes to families and friends, and boarded the troop trains headed to the North. While there was sadness at parting, many soldiers and their relatives must have been relieved that their destination was the Northwest rather than Europe or the South Pacific. Better frostbite than Japanese bullets!

The civilian contractors attempted to put their work crews together close to home. R. Melville Smith, an Ontario-based firm, brought many employees from the central Canadian province. Okes Construction from St. Paul, Minnesota, Dowell Construction and E.W. Elliott of Seattle, and Lytle and Green Construction of Sioux City, Iowa, also did most of their recruiting in their home towns. Trainloads of workers and equipment travelled military-style across the U.S.A. and southern Canada toward Edmonton or Seattle and from there to their work stations in the North.

The construction companies had much to offer – a chance to assist the war effort while earning large sums of money – but they also knew that they were taking the workers into a frontier setting with few amenities. One sign succinctly stated the conditions they faced. Initially published by Bechtel-Price-Callahan, contractors on the CANOL pipeline, but widely posted throughout the Northwest, it read:

THIS IS NO PICNIC

Working and living conditions on this job are as difficult as those encountered on any construction job ever done in the United States or foreign territory. Men hired for this job will be required to work and live under the most extreme conditions imaginable. Temperature will range from 90 degrees above zero to 90 degrees below zero. Men will have to fight swamps, rivers, ice and cold; mosquitos, flies and gnats will not only be annoying but will cause bodily harm. If you are not prepared to work under these and similar conditions

DO NOT APPLY

The workers who chose to come north, the hundreds of men and women stricken with a military version of Klondike fever, came for many reasons: a unique chance for a civilian to join the fight against Japan, the adventure of retracing the famed Trail of '98, an unusual engineering and construction challenge. Perhaps the most important was the opportunity to get in on the boom-time wages being offered.

Willis Grafe was employed as a night-shift maintenance man in the Columbia Aircraft Industries' factory outside Portland, Oregon, when he first learned that there was work to be had up north. He marched to the local Public Roads Administration office and offered his services as a surveyor. A few days later, he was hired. Grafe rushed to the laundromat to retrieve his clothes, hurriedly tossed them and a few other possessions into a footlocker, and quickly departed for Seattle. Along with a few other PRA recruits, Grafe was hurried onto the *Eli D. Hoyle*, which left shortly thereafter for Skagway. About a week after entering the Portland office, he was in Whitehorse, assigned to a survey crew responsible for laying out the road in the Kluane Lake area in the western Yukon. Two days later, Grafe and over a dozen companions were ferried by Yukon Southern Air Transport to Burwash Landing, where they were jammed into several crowded one-room cabins and, amid the snow and muck, began their work.

Bud Schnurstein was several thousand miles away from Portland when he learned that he, too, was heading north. An ROTC officer enrolled in college, Schnurstein was drafted into military service in December 1941. His first assignment was the command of a black engineering unit, the 93rd Engineers, based in Camp Clayburn, Louisiana. Early in 1942, the 93rd was sent by train to Fort Laughton, near Seattle. A shavetail, Schnurstein was designated assistance officer for the journey, with responsibility for buying fresh meat and vegetables for the troops at each stop. He did as requested but neglected to collect receipts for the purchases. Once established in the North, he spent many hours writing to the stores along the train route, attempting to assemble the chits necessary to placate the army's accountants.

Additional surprises lay ahead. The 93rd was assigned to one of the Canadian Pacific Princess steamers for the trip from Seattle to Skagway. Instead of sailing in a military troop carrier, the men reposed in the comfort of a cruise ship, complete with dining-room, silver service, and plenty of waiters — although the officers had more amenities than the enlisted ranks. Bud Schnurstein recalls the voyage with delight: "Great food, and we found that if we pressed the button in our cabin, the steward would come back with a sandwich and a beer. Hadn't seen anything like it! It was a long time afterwards before we saw it again, too. And this was war! What a way to go to war!"

Not everyone went first class. Master Sergeant George Burke, 95th Regiment, former engineering student at Howard University and full-time movie projectionist, received his marching orders while at Fort Bragg, Louisiana. He only learned of his destination when directed to stencil "Dawson Creek" on boxes of supplies. Like many people in the United States, Burke knew little of the area, and mistakenly confused Dawson Creek with the more famous Dawson City. For six long days, the soldiers of the 95th jostled in the train, slowly making their way toward Edmonton and Dawson Creek. Along the route enthusiastic crowds gathered to greet the trains and cheer the men on. Burke's unit arrived in late May and was assigned to Charlie Lake, just outside of Fort St. John (and, in the minds of many locals, the "real" starting point of the Alaska Highway, since there was already a rough road from Dawson Creek to Charlie Lake). Their first task was to erect a sign announcing "You Are Now Entering the Alaska Highway. Drive Carefully." As Burke laconically notes, "It really was superfluous. Nobody could drive any other way."

For field engineers such as John Mueller, the opportunity to work on the Alaska Highway was an opportunity too good to miss. Mueller had recently returned from a project in Panama and was working in a soils research laboratory in Washington, D.C., when news arrived of the highway project. Since he was dissatisfied with his office job and anxious to return to the field, he approached his boss over a coffee break and requested an assignment in the North. Approval of his request was, he says, "the fastest thing that ever happened in Washington." Within twenty-four hours, he left Washington by car for Denver, Colorado, where he picked up a truck and trailer full of the soils survey equipment his crew needed in the North.

The roads between Denver and Edmonton were not expressways, but they proved much better than the rough trail from Edmonton to Pouce Coupe. Mueller arrived at a dangerous moment. Warm weather had weakened the ice bridge across the river, but it was much too early for the ferries to be in service. Anxious to continue northward, he agreed to follow the local mailman across the thawing river. The mailman crossed on foot while Mueller followed close behind in his truck and trailer. At points, bitterly cold water ran over the ice, adding to the survey crew's nervousness. The team and equipment made it across safely, although Mueller still believes the crossing was "the most stupid thing I've done in my life." Accommodations *en route* were crude, as befit a newly settled agricultural frontier. The Pouce Coupe hotel had a particularly noteworthy feature — a two storey out-house. (The Dew Drop Inn in Dawson Creek had similar facilities. Ed Wiggans remembers: "The smell was pretty

Construction workers aboard ship, headed to the Northwest.

bad. It got worse when the management hung chicken wire below each seat to try and discourage the tossing of beer and liquor bottles into the abyss.")

Joe Garbus started his Alaska Highway adventure only a few hundred miles north of where Mueller started his. Garbus had graduated with a civil engineering degree in 1941 and had sent out dozens of applications for employment. The American government contacted him in Connecticut in the summer of 1942 and asked him if he would accept a job on the Alaska Highway. He agreed quickly and, aged twenty-three, headed to Albany, New York, to sign on. From there he travelled by train to Toronto, where he boarded the Canadian National Railroad for the trip to Edmonton. Next it was the Northern Alberta Railway to Dawson Creek, and then by ambulance, truck, and car to Fort St. John.

By the hundreds they came, women and men, civilians and soldiers. Thelma Ashby was an office worker from Edmonton, unhappy with her job and looking for new opportunities. The Public Roads Administration was hiring *en masse*, and Ashby quickly applied for one of the many well-paid jobs. She was

American soldiers arriving
in Dawson Creek, 1942.
SUTTON COLLECTION.

hired on the spot and, only a week later, climbed aboard a ten-passenger plane – her first flight – for a trip to Fort St. John. Any hopes she had of a great frontier adventure were quickly dashed, for the British Columbian town was anything but exciting. It was, she remembers, "a very small, backward town, which consisted of one street with a general store, a drug store, post office, and bank. There were no sidewalks, just boardwalks built above ground, and the mud was horrendous. More than once I got stuck and had to be pulled out of my boots and carried to the boardwalk, retrieving my boots later." The town also lacked the spirit that surrounded the highway project. Even business people did not seem interested in making the most of the new opportunities: "It was nothing to see a sign in a store in Fort St. John saying 'Gone Fishing. Back in a week.'"

Harvey Hayduck decided to join the Alaska Highway workforce because he would not have to travel very far to take advantage of the boom. When construction began Hayduck was teaching in a one-room school near High Prairie, Alberta. Wages and working conditions hadn't changed much since the Great Depression, when teachers were paid with welfare chits and irregular contributions of food from parents. He received forty-five dollars a month, more than half of which went to a local farmer for room and board. The paltry sum remaining was minimal compensation for the rigours of teaching forty-eight students, ranging from grades 1 to 10, in a single drafty classroom. Although only twenty-one years old, Harvey Hayduk was no starry-eyed idealist. When word reached High Prairie in April 1942 of high-paying jobs with the highway crews, he handed in his resignation and, with few regrets, dashed to Edmonton.

His timing was perfect. He arrived at the hiring hall just as a convoy of trucks from one of the private construction companies drove into town. Like many rural men Hayduk had considerable experience with heavy equipment and was a welcome addition to the crew. He signed on, was given control of a seven-ton Coleman truck and pointed toward Dawson Creek. The drive took four days, crawling along at twenty-five miles per hour, the trucks pounding the stuffing out of the poorly constructed rural roads. Hayduck had been promised a job only for the drive to Dawson Creek, but he soon discovered that the shortage of skilled operators there gave him plenty of opportunities. His salary as a driver was more than twice what he had earned as a school teacher – even better, his room and board was free, leaving him with more cash in his pocket than he had ever had before.

Hundreds of miles away in North Bay, Ontario, Ralph Fowler had heard stories of high wages to be had. He wrote to a friend's father who was working on the highway. When he read the answering letter describing the high wages and heavily subsidized room and board, he happily gave up his low-paying job and his "half-starved boarding house" and applied to R. M. Smith, the Ontario-based contractor. Shortly thereafter, he found himself in Dawson Creek where, to his utter delight and astonishment, he received a 20 per cent pay raise after only a few days' work in the camp.

Wages varied across the region, in proportion to the perceived unattractiveness of the work site. For Canadian workers the highway was divided into two zones: Dawson Creek, and the rest of the route. Carpenters received 95 cents an hour in Dawson Creek, but $1.20 farther up the highway; labourers, paid 55 cents an hour at the southern end, got between 70 and 75 cents an hour in the camps. To further complicate matters, Americans were paid more than Canadians. While Canadian labourers in the Yukon in 1942 were paid 75 cents an hour, American contractors paid their employees 96 cents an hour, plus free room and board. Although the different wage rates caused a few tensions along the highway, Canadian and American workers in the South all recognized a good deal when they saw one.

The deluge of promotional material circulating about this great military project ensured that the stream of workers heading northward scarcely slowed at all during the summer of 1942. Jean Waldon worked for the Canadian government in a Toronto office. As it had for many North American women, the war had thrust great responsibilities on her shoulders for which she was not properly compensated. She was on late summer holidays at a chalet in the Laurentian Mountains, enjoying a pleasant break from the pressures of the war, when the radio brought news of the death of the Duke of Kent in an airplane crash. The loss stirred her deeply, and she began to question her involvement in the Allied war effort. Earlier that day, she had picked up a copy of *Reader's Digest*, which talked about the need for women workers in the Northwest. The seed of an interest in the Alaska Highway had been sown.

Back in Toronto, and immersed once more in her office work and Red Cross classes, Waldon continued to think about the war. Her close friend, Charlotte Mens, broke off an engagement to be married and, perhaps to escape the hurt, talked of going to Alaska. Mens arrived in Waldon's office early in October and announced that she had found out about jobs for two women on the Alaska Highway. After a brief interview, both women were offered two-year contracts. Waldon's mother was enthusiastic: "You need a change. If it is good enough for Charlotte, it's good enough for you." Her father, undoubtedly disturbed at the thought of sending his daughter off to the northern frontier, balked. He was soon brought around. Waldon's boss, however, no doubt concerned about the loss of a good employee, loudly expressed the view that the North was no place for her – or any other proper woman.

Dawson Creek, starting point for the Alaska Highway, in 1943.
PHYLLIS CHURCH

Time flashed by as the two women prepared for their greatest adventure. They each bought a new wardrobe of winter clothes, including long, red underwear. After a farewell lunch given by Waldon's co-workers, topped off with a gift of an Elizabeth Arden make-up kit, it was time to go. The women received a big send-off at the Toronto train station, stopped off briefly to visit relatives in Winnipeg, and then pushed on to Edmonton. After a brief delay in Edmonton – with enough time for the "last tub," something of a ritual among workers destined for the highway camps – they rode on to Dawson Creek.

The journey quickly brought home a northern reality – there were very few women and hundreds of men. When Waldon retired to her bunk the first evening, she was confronted by a drunken officer who insisted he share her bed. She demurred politely, but with enough firmness to deter him from his objective. (A man sleeping in a nearby upper bunk later told Waldon that she had done a fine job of rejecting the drunk's salacious advances. Then he added that he had had no intention of stepping in had she been less successful. The experience taught her that she was very much on her own.) The women's excitement faded by the hour. Dawson Creek was muddy and dirty, supplies were short, and the construction camps a discouraging sight. The camps consisted of little more than hastily constructed dormitories and offices, muddy streets, and precious few amenities. In the town, hotel accommodations were spartan and hard to find. The women had to make do with temporary beds in a warehouse. Doubts about the excursion, repressed until now, burst out. Waldon wondered if her boss had been right after all.

The next day, Waldon and Mens pressed on, crossing the Peace River and bumping and jostling over the dirt road to Fort St. John. If Dawson Creek had been a disappointment, Fort St. John was a delight. It reminded Waldon of the set in a western movie: "A freshly painted Hudson's Bay store caught my eye. The town had a Bank of Commerce, a movie house of sorts, and a well-stocked drug store. The arrival at the Public Roads Administration camp just before sunset was thrilling. Old American CCC [Civilian Conservation Corps] buildings had been painted white and trimmed with green. The entrance to the camp was grass bordered with white stones and, best of all, two beautiful flags were waving in a slight breeze – Canada's flag of 1942 (my favourite still) and the Stars and Stripes. The food was good, rooms clean, and mattresses comfortable. Any fears lingering after the overland trip from Edmonton and the night in Dawson Creek disappeared. There was work to be done."

Gordon and Lorna Gibbs were living in Vancouver when work began on the highway. They had purchased a two-ton General Motors truck, a spanking-new vehicle with a van box on the back. Filled with a sense of adventure, and encouraged by visions of thousands of dollars flowing from the free-spending construction companies into their pockets, they set off for the south end of the highway. Their gamble quickly paid off. For the first few weeks, they hauled furniture and general merchandise. Then they graduated to pulling trailers, hauling steel, and delivering fuel.

For one group – engineering students at western Canadian universities – the start of highway construction was a dream come true. Shortly after the project was announced, the Public Roads Administration sent recruiters to the University of Alberta campus to sign up students for work on survey and design teams. The opportunity for many budding engineers was far too good to pass up. Bruce Willson remembers when PRA officials approached the Dean of Engineers for assistance with recruitment. To help the students make up their minds, the Dean offered to release volunteers from their final examinations, provided their term grades were high enough. Willson qualified and, together with a dozen colleagues, signed on with the Americans. Their trip by rail to Dawson Creek was notable only for its discomfort and boredom – it took twenty-four hours – and for the students' travelling companions, "a few thirty-five- or forty-year-old worldly looking types who reminded one of riverboat gamblers, but who turned out to be much gentler than initial appearances suggested." A similar recruitment effort was targeted at engineering students at the University of Saskatchewan in Saskatoon. Walter Polvi and a few others – a much smaller contingent than the University of Alberta's – agreed to terms and headed for the highway.

The highway offered Stacia Gallop a break from a tedious routine in Edmonton. Only eighteen years old at the time, she accepted a job with a construction company in Whitehorse. Although Edmonton was jammed with vehicles headed north, young secretaries did not have top priority, and Stacia waited for over a week for a northbound airplane, each delay adding to her uncertainty. "As I was sitting at home my mother was getting more and more worried, and I was thinking, am I going to leave all of this? What am I going to? It was such an unknown." She finally found a spot – up front with the pilot – on a large American cargo plane, which delivered her safely to Whitehorse.

Finding workers for the Alaska Highway in the early months of 1942 was far from easy, for thousands of young Canadian and American men had already enlisted for military service. As well, the huge demand for food and materials to supply the military effort ensured there were plenty of jobs to be found in the South. But some people saw working on the Alaska Highway as an opportunity to combine a high-paying job with a chance to contribute to the war effort. Alex Forgie of Edmonton was one of them. He first applied for military service in 1939 but was turned down because he had only a Grade 8 education. When he tried again a few years later, the air force indicated that the educational requirement had been waived. With some fanfare, he resigned his job with Massey Harris Farm Equipment and reported for duty, only to be rejected because of weak vision in his left eye. Too embarrassed to return to his old job, Forgie opted instead to sign on with the Public Roads Administration and head north.

Cyril Griffith found himself in much the same boat. Drafted into the air force in 1941, he was granted a medical discharge the following spring because of problems with his leg. He returned to Regina, where he signed on with Newman Brothers, hauling oil products from Moose Jaw, Saskatchewan, to Brandon, Manitoba, making six trips per week. In August, Newman Brothers got a major contract in Dawson Creek and moved nine of its vehicles to the area. Griffith went along, drawn by the promise of higher wages, and found himself working on the army's tote road, delivering oil and hauling equipment.

Many workers attracted to the highway camps were too old for military service. For Frank Speer, there was an added attraction – the opportunity to escape a tedious inside job, managing a MacLeod's farm supply store six days a week. Anxious for a bit of fresh air, and not deterred by the fact that he was forty-two years old, Speer took a two-week vacation and travelled to Dawson Creek. Hitching a ride with a supply truck, he went on to Fort Nelson to learn about the highway work. He liked what he saw and immediately tendered his resignation. MacLeod's management rejected his letter. Terse negotiations followed, ending with the agreement that Speer could leave his post for an indefinite term, but could return to work whenever he wished. (He was still on leave forty-eight years later!) He left his wife and children behind in Melfort, Saskatchewan, and signed on as a cat skinner (bulldozer operator) with R. Melville Smith, a Canadian contractor working on the southern sections of the highway. The work was just as promised – long hours and great pay. The standard work day was eleven hours, at a dollar an hour, and all workers had the option of putting in an additional three hours each evening. With his family hundreds of miles away, and his mind fixed firmly on the prospect of big money, Speer tackled the extra hours with the zeal of a gambler on a winning streak.

Bill Bennett, working in a hardware store in Woodstock, Ontario, when the war broke out, had been declared medically unfit for military service. But Bennett was anxious to do his part. His father had served in World War I, and his three brothers and two sisters were fighting in World War II. When he saw an advertisement in *Hardware and Metal Magazine* for men with knowledge of building hardware, plumbing, and electrical supplies, and

Army equipment destined for the highway rumbles on a train through Skagway, Alaska.

willing to work on a war project in the North, he sent in his application to the R. M. Smith Company, care of the Ontario Parliament Buildings in Toronto. He got the job.

Dozens of Americans also found themselves pulled between a desire to serve in the war effort and to take advantage of civilian opportunities, but few in as complex a fashion as William Pryor. Born in Cedar City, Utah, Pryor graduated in civil engineering from the University of Utah in 1930. He then began a long and distinguished career with the Bureau of Public Roads (later renamed the Public Roads Administration). He was working in Idaho when war with Japan broke out. Early in 1942, shortly after he had successfully applied for acceptance into the U.S. Navy, he was contacted by Thomas McDonald, Chief of the Public Roads Administration, and asked to accept an assignment on the Alaska Highway. Since the navy had not yet given him specific instructions, he accepted, and found himself assigned to the southern portion of the highway, working under Joseph Bright, district engineer for the Alaska Highway. Shortly after Pryor arrived in Dawson Creek, his call-up notice from the navy arrived. Bright, who happened to be in the office at the time, took the office notification from Pryor's hands and, following a patriotic appeal to the young engineer to stick with the important construction task at hand, offered to fix matters with the navy. Pryor accepted and, although he never learned how Bright accomplished it, never again heard from the navy.

Pryor was only one of dozens of American civil servants dispatched to northwestern Canada in the spring of 1942. Paul Warren was working for the Public Roads Administration in Boulder, Colorado, when he received instructions to head north. He and other PRA engineers joined a convoy of Dodge personnel carriers, loaded with men, survey gear, and camping equipment. They left Boulder on 10 March (before construction had been authorized by the Canadian government) and drove north through Cheyenne, Billings, and Shelby, on to Calgary, Edmonton, and finally Dawson Creek. The heater in Warren's truck blew out shortly after leaving Edmonton, just when they entered the coldest part of the journey, hardly the most welcome introduction to Canadian life.

Warren provides one of the best descriptions of travel on the southern approaches to the highway: "Beyond Smith, Alberta, travel became increasingly difficult; truck traffic had ploughed the mud road severely. I recall dodging large balls of mud, maybe up to two feet in diameter, that had been deposited as they squeezed through their dual wheels, meat-grinder style. But we fought through until we bogged down somewhere about Faust or Joussard. Mud built up in the fenders of our Dodge screen-side panel trucks until the wheels could not turn. We had to dig the mud out and sit until the mud road froze at midnight. Two other cars, of local people, got stuck in the same place, so we held a picnic. About midnight we drove on to High Prairie, found a meal and a few hours of sleep, then pushed on over frozen, rutted roads."

At Dawson Creek, Warren's travelling companions divided into small groups. His unit hurried north along a winter trail to Sikanni River crossing, carrying instructions to join a couple of engineers, a local guide, and two dog mushers (complete with teams) to work on the survey to Fort Nelson. The trip north was over a road that wasn't: "From Fort St. John the road followed a winter freight trail, packed with snow. We frequently met trucks, both civilian two-wheel drive and military six-by-six, returning empty from the freight haul to Fort Nelson. Since northbound vehicles had the right of way, all those trucks yielded to us. It was quite a revelation to meet a five-ton six-by-six and see it pull off, ploughing through one to two feet of snow and the thick growth of small trees, yielding to our little three-quarter-ton two-wheel-drive panels." The trip, 116 winding, rough miles, took over twenty-two hours.

Chuck Hemphill, unlike almost all other workers, actually had to come south to find work on the highway. Only eighteen at the time, he had ventured north in search of high adventure. A month's work as a pantry steward on the Hudson's Bay Transportation Company's paddle wheeler *Northland Echo* quickly soured him on the North. He quit his job and hustled back to Edmonton. There he ran into an old friend, Mike Bulat, who told him about the high wages being offered by the American army. The two of them signed on quickly – although the young-looking Hemphill had some difficulty convincing the hiring officer that he actually was eighteen years old. Like so many others heading to the southern end of the highway, they reached Dawson Creek and then got bogged down in chaos and confusion. After a few days of odd jobs and make-work projects, Hemphill was assigned to a survey crew and sent to Muncho Lake. The eighty-five dollars he earned each month was almost double his previous wage.

Locals with a little moxie and equipment discovered an almost unlimited demand for their services. Vera Brown and her husband lived on a small farm west of Grande Prairie, but the low wheat prices of the Depression had left them short of cash to buy the equipment and supplies necessary to farm successfully. When the highway crews first moved in, the Browns decided to cash in on the bonanza. They moved a small granary from their farm to Dawson Creek and set up house inside this unorthodox cabin. They quickly found work with Wilson Freightways, he on construction, she managing the ledgers in the office. The pay was good and the working conditions acceptable. Each

Supply depot at the south end of the highway, 1942.
NATIONAL ARCHIVES OF CANADA.

weekend, they piled into their 1930 Model A Ford and dashed back to their farm to complete a week's worth of chores. They had no intention of maintaining the pace forever, but could not bring themselves to miss out on the boom times.

The workers came from all directions, and they kept coming throughout the war. Most workers stayed only a year, and thousands lasted only a few months. From the first months of 1942 project managers were constantly recruiting new employees and arranging for their transit to the Alaska Highway camps. They came for the same curious mix of reasons that had attracted the first wave of workers: patriotism, a desire to assist with the war, adventure, money, infatuation with the idea of the Northwest, career experience, or, in the case of American civil servants and soldiers, because they were ordered to do so. For many, their trip north – rough, chaotic, seemingly disorganized, dirty, and uncomfortable – would epitomize their entire experience in the region.

For the people of the North, the arrival of more than thirty thousand soldiers and civilians was both exciting and daunting. Tiny towns, such as Fort St. John, Watson Lake, Big Delta, and Burwash Landing, had no facilities for the thousands of incoming highway workers. Even the larger towns – Edmonton, Dawson Creek, Whitehorse, and Fairbanks – had nowhere near

Fort St. John, looking southwest. J. GARBUS.

enough hotels, restaurants, and stores to handle the invasion. Nonetheless, town boosters saw much to celebrate in the frenzied crush of the spring of 1942.

The editor of the *Whitehorse Star* wrote about the Americans' arrival in grandiose terms: "The arrival of the advance party of U.S. Army Engineering Corps on Saturday last presented an unusual sight on the streets of Whitehorse. Never before had such a contingent of uniformed men been seen here. Their advent into the Territory marked a Red Letter Day in the history of the Yukon....In conjunction with our airport this highway definitely places Whitehorse in an unique position on the map for all time. The town is bound to become a great distributing centre and therefore to all intents and purposes the commercial capital of the Yukon."

The Native people of the area were initially incredulous that this peaceful invasion was happening. Virginia Smarch, a Tlingit from Teslin in the southern Yukon, remembers when a man from Carcross came to their village early in 1942 with a remarkable story. He told the villagers that hundreds of Americans with large machines and tons of equipment were pushing across from Carcross toward their town. They wanted to believe the man, for he was known to be honest, but his tale was simply too tall to accept. So they were astonished a few days later when the first bulldozers crashed through the bush into their village. The highway was coming, bringing both opportunities and risks for the Native people in the region.

It was time to get to work. The task at hand – the construction of a highway to Alaska – was mammoth and, at first sight, impractical and impossible. The North was too big, too intimidating, and still virtually unknown. There was so much to do: surveying the official route, completing the pioneer road, beginning work on the actual highway, supplying, feeding, and housing the soldiers and civilian workers, and so very many obstacles to tackle. No one said it was going to be easy.

3

Running the Line

B Y APRIL 1942 the Northwest was awhirl in a hurricane of construction activity. Trainloads of men, equipment, and supplies rattled through Edmonton on their way to Dawson Creek, the end of steel at the south end of the construction zone. Ships loaded with human and material cargo destined for the highway sailed into Skagway, Valdez, and Seward, Alaska, dropping hundreds of tons of road-building paraphernalia on the docks. The White Pass and Yukon Route railroad and the Alaska Railroad to Fairbanks nearly buckled under the weight of the continuous traffic heading north. The Richardson Highway, connecting Valdez and Fairbanks, was pressed into service in a major way as a trucking route to Big Delta, the focus of construction activity at the north end of the highway, and Gulkana, the western terminus of a spur road constructed to meet the Alaska Highway at Tok. Tent cities sprang up on farmers' fields outside Dawson Creek and Fort St. John, on the escarpment above Whitehorse, and alongside tiny, seasonal Native villages. The invasion, friendly and frenetic, had arrived.

Far from the chaos and confusion of the construction camps, a pivotal process in the building of the highway was more quietly underway. Surveyors from the Canadian Department of Transport, the United States Army Corps of Engineers, and the Public Roads Administration had moved into the Far Northwest. Their task was to take General Hoge's basic sketch of the Alaska Highway route and turn it into a formal plan for road construction.

Survey crew in the field.
PUBLIC ARCHIVES OF CANADA.

Highway surveys usually proceed at a fairly leisurely pace, with care taken to test the terrain, soils, water courses, and other environmental features that might influence construction. The pressures set by war provided no time for these professional approaches. Surveyors worked under a tight schedule. Even as the first crews moved into the North – to Big Delta, Tok, Burwash, Whitehorse, Teslin, Watson Lake, Fort Nelson, and Fort St. John – they could almost hear the roar of the bulldozers behind them. Their challenge was made more formidable by their limited geological knowledge of the region's many natural barriers, particularly the permafrost and muskeg which stood in the way. Poets and novelists, in future years, would spare few words for the surveyors. Running a transit lacked the emotional impact of bulldozers crashing through dense forest or bridges being flung over torrential mountain-fed rivers. But no highway could be built until the surveyors' work, however hasty, was complete.

To add to the confusion, the highway route was divided into sections, and, as well, two overlapping operations were under way. The military, charged with completing a pioneer road, were not overly concerned about the nuances of a professional survey. It simply required the fastest possible route north and directed its surveyors to push across the sub-Arctic wilderness as quickly as they could. The PRA, on the other hand, had orders to complete a highway to the highest civilian standards and took the assignment seriously.

As a consequence, the military and civilian crews operated simultaneously, working on roughly the same assignment but with very different agendas. Although logic – reinforced by strong hints from Washington, D.C. – suggested that the teams of surveyors follow the same general path, the military and civilian teams began working from different principles. The army's task was to lay out a basic trail for a pioneer road to Alaska. There were no provisions for luxuries or aesthetics; its surveyors were directed to work in straight lines whenever possible and to follow the path of least resistance. To the civilian surveyors fell the more daunting task of identifying and laying out a route suitable for a proper civilian highway. The army built along existing trails whenever possible and pushed across land that it knew would not be suitable for a permanent route. Civilian surveyors took advantage of the army's construction activity and kept their surveys within the general proximity of the pioneer road. They did not, however, feel constrained by the military survey and headed where construction logic dictated.

Surveying looks deceptively simple – a small group of men plunge into the wilderness, marking out a general direction and drafting a specific design for the road. The initial push, by the first army engineers, was little more than the location survey, a traverse of the route to establish the topography and controlling features of the countryside. The layout surveys were left for the PRA crews that followed. This survey involved a series of complicated and vital tasks – establishing the centre line, marking the horizontal alignment, and marking where excavations and fill were required. The survey information provided the basis for the compilation of proper highway designs.

The PRA's surveyors held the key to the success of the entire venture. They followed a fairly standard routine. A small survey party, made up of axemen, transit operators, and an engineer, would head out to its assigned section. The axemen would work ahead, clearing a line of sight through the trees so that the transit operators could do their calculations. The transit party would lay out the centre line; a level party would follow behind, dividing the road into short segments of usually 100 feet, charting elevations and cross-sections. The result, drawn with remarkable speed, was an accurate, three-dimensional profile of the terrain and the proposed road, compiled in three different charts – horizontal, vertical, and cross-section profiles of the road surface. The surveyors also provided detailed estimates of the fill required to build up the road surface and where the fill could be found in places where the highway had to be carved out of the hillsides. The surveys required careful, accurate engineering work under extremely trying circumstances.

Later in the summer of 1942, the implications of developing competing routes would become clear, and the Army Corps of Engineers and Public Roads Administration would engage in a bitter and even unseemly battle over plans for the Alaska Highway. For now, more basic considerations took precedence. Organizers had to get survey crews into the field and provide them with enough local information to complete their assignments. The latter was of vital importance, however, for precious few professional engineers had even a smattering of knowledge of the area.

Given the urgency of the surveying task, such knowledge was treasured more than warm mittens on a frigid Arctic morning. Fortunately for the American planners, they could call on a small number of professional surveyors associated with the Canadian Department of Transport who had been working on the Northwest Staging Route project. The surveyors also quickly discovered that no one knew the Northwest better than the Native people, whose ancestors had lived on the land for generations. These men could make their way across the sub-Arctic wilderness with greater ease than a London cabbie could navigate through the maze-like streets of that great city. The army and the PRA also called on non-Native trappers and traders and local bush pilots to assist them with their work.

Government surveyors in northern British Columbia and Alaska gave invaluable help. Canadian government surveyors had conducted aerial investigations of the poorly mapped area

The traditional means of transportation for Natives in the North. J. GARBUS.

northwest of Dawson Creek in the mid-1930s. Beginning in 1939, surveyors had been dispatched to assist with the layout and design of the Northwest Staging Route airfields. Knox F. McCusker had supervised much of this early work and was, consequently, highly sought after in 1942 for advice on the southern portions of the highway. Farther north, engineers and surveyors with the Alaska Roads Commission also found their knowledge of and expertise in northern construction conditions and methods much in demand.

The vast majority of the work fell to newcomers. The surveying challenge was particularly acute on the southern section, from Fort St. John to Teslin. The highway planners recognized early on the need to move men and equipment while trails and rivers were still frozen. If they started too late they would have to sit for several months, equipment and men poised for action but unable to move because of spring run-off and the mountains of mud created by the annual thaw. It was imperative that the survey crews get into the field immediately and that a preliminary investigation of the region between Fort St. John and Fort Nelson be completed forthwith. Knox McCusker played a pivotal role. He had earlier sketched out a trail northwest from Fort St. John in March 1942 and offered to lead the American survey teams into the area. He was hurriedly pressed into service and found himself escorting a number of American surveyors into the field.

Army surveyors had no choice but to work as expeditiously as possible, leaving all major design and construction obstacles to the PRA engineers to work out. Hampton Primeaux of the 1540th Engineers of the 29th Engineers Battalion, United States Army Corps of Engineers, was one of the first army surveyors into the field. Travelling north from Seattle to Skagway and then to Whitehorse, Technical Sergeant Primeaux and his platoon were directed to complete the preliminary line (basic survey) from Whitehorse to Alaska. After a short stay in Whitehorse waiting for the snow to clear, the platoon headed west. Work was intense and exhausting. They moved their camp five miles every day, and their daily surveys usually entailed twenty miles of walking, often heavily laden with equipment and supplies. Once they reached Kluane Lake, they hired two Native wranglers and twenty pack horses, using the expanded outfit to move rapidly between Burwash Landing and the Alaska boundary.

Primeaux and his platoon completed their work on schedule and returned to Whitehorse for the winter of 1942-1943. The army surveyors moved at a similar pace across the region, following existing trails wherever possible, flagging a quick route for the pioneer road. Military construction units barked close on their heels, urging them on to faster and faster work. Civilian surveyors followed close behind. Paul Warren of Boulder, Colorado, loaded his crew and its supplies into Dodge half-ton personnel carriers filled with supplies and surveying equipment. After a long and tiring journey from the American West to northern British Columbia, they stopped briefly for a breather in Fort St. John, "the last bit of civilization before the bush," before

Engineers' camp at Mile 165.
J. GARBUS.

heading north. It took twenty-two hours of kidney-jarring travelling to cover the 116 miles from the farming town to Sikanni Chief River. The men drove until too tired to continue, and then slept until too cold to stay still. At the Hudson's Bay Company's Horsetrack post at Sikanni Chief River, Warren's group divided into three reconnaissance parties and separated to examine the proposed route between Fort St. John and Fort Nelson.

Warren and his engineering partner, William Willesen, were assigned a guide, Elisha Callison, and two dog mushers, Tud Southwick and John Harold. They worked north from Sikanni Chief, travelling on three loaded sleds, each pulled by four or five dogs. Working across a landscape covered by two feet or more of snow, the surveyors attempted to develop a reasonable profile of the highway route.

The journey was not without incident. Once when Warren and Willesen climbed a small hill to examine the land ahead of them, the dog teams left below tangled in one of the North's infamous husky fights. Nine large animals attacked each other with the ferociousness of a sub-Arctic blizzard. Southwick and Harold rushed to separate their charges, clubbing the animals with their snowshoes. Harold got too close to one of the infuriated animals, which promptly bit into his hand. From their vantage point, Warren and Willesen could see Harold recoil in pain and fury, a large, enraged husky dog hanging from the musher's mitten. Harold twisted loose from the dangerous grip, and the two men were able, slowly, to restore order. Harold's finger was severely gashed, but fortunately without lasting damage.

Bruce Willson (left) and his survey party at work north of Dawson Creek.
BRUCE WILLSON.

Willis Grafe worked on the survey of the Kluane Lake section of the highway. Grafe arrived in Whitehorse in late spring 1942, after signing on with the Public Roads Administration in Oregon. Once in Whitehorse, he was assigned to work with Fred Johnson, whom he had met on the boat trip up from Seattle. A fifteen-person crew was assembled and dispatched to Burwash Landing. It was a rather mixed lot. Johnson and three others were career PRA employees, two of the men had formerly worked for the government agency, and the rest of the crew, selected more for attitude and enthusiasm than knowledge, included a few experienced surveyors, a collections agent, a Canadian prospector, and several mail-room workers. A Curtis Condor Biplane operated by Yukon Southern Air, carrying the men and their supplies in shifts, ferried the team to Burwash.

The survey team assembled, with its gear and supplies, at the trading post on the shore of Kluane Lake. The Burwash Landing store, operated by the Jacquot brothers, Eugene and Louis, one-time prospectors, traders, and big-game guides, attracted a small, seasonal Native population. Burwash Landing was not much to look at, particularly for men who a few weeks earlier had been in California, Oregon, or Washington. The post was relatively self-sufficient, with its own blacksmith shop, sawmill, store, and other facilities. The crew members were crammed into several small cabins – Grafe and five others lived in a small hut they named the Boar's Nest – and ate with the Jacquot family.

The crew began work a few miles south of its camp, making its way over the frozen lake to the work site. Grafe and several of the others had no experience in the field and received a quick indoctrination in the surveying enterprise. The crew members soon fell to their assigned tasks – the axeman cleared a path through the trees ("If they can't see, they can't survey"), transit operators took their readings, and the topographic crew developed a contour map of the highway route. Work progressed slowly, about a mile per day, and Grafe quickly cottoned on to the fact that the experienced men worked slowly to ensure that they did not finish ahead of others and thus get pressed into service cutting trees – the least attractive job on the crew. Within a few weeks, the men had worked far enough south and north from Burwash Landing that, by the time they walked to the end of the line, they had no time left for surveying. It was time to shift camp.

By this time a full complement of supplies had arrived by plane, and their two Native wranglers, Jimmie Joe and Sam Johnson, had pulled together a train of ill-tempered pack horses to move the survey team into the bush. Having prepared themselves for hardship throughout their time in the North, the men were delighted to discover that the camp outfit included proper cots, a full-sized cook tent and, although slow in arriving, a proper 200-pound cast-iron cook-stove.

The arrival of the cook-stove touched off a contretemps between Fred Johnson, the survey chief, and Eugene Jacquot, owner of the horses that were expected to carry this culinary behemoth into the back country. "A hungry and waiting crew, an anguished cook – and the whole Alaska-Canada war effort could hang in the balance," Willis Grafe jokingly recalls. "The upshot of it was that a horse came into our camp carrying not one, but two stoves. Light, boxy, sheet-metal ones with a small oven and smaller firebox each. So the day was saved, and maybe the war."

Armed with the requisites for proper life in the bush, the survey team moved north to Burwash Creek, where it repeated its performance of working both north and south from its base

One way to keep the food out of the reach of bears.
J. Garbus

camp. As spring turned into summer, the workers discovered new problems. The cold, bitter winds abated, but mosquitoes quickly moved to ensure the surveyors' continued discomfort. As the snows melted, mud, wet boots, and chilled feet became the norm, quickly removing the sense of adventure that had temporarily motivated the entire expedition.

When its work was completed in the second section, the crew pushed on once more. This time, it had to cross the Donjek River, a shallow, silted, glacial river known by the Indians to be particularly treacherous in the spring season because of its deposits of quicksand. The cook took one look at the river, declared himself fed up with the discomforts of life on the trail, and attempted to return to Burwash Landing. Only heartfelt (and self-interested) counselling by the crew members convinced him to stay for a while longer. The expedition successfully crossed the river without major incident.

Out in the bush food supplies began to dwindle, and enthusiasm declined ever further, leading to frequent complaints on the shortcomings of the military and civilian enterprise in the Northwest. Cigarettes were so rare that a few of the more addicted smokers resorted to sifting through fire pits for old butts. Clothes wore through, were patched, and quickly wore through again. The area around Kluane Lake contains a high concentration of volcanic ash, notorious for its ability to work its way through good leather boots, rendering them virtually worthless within a matter of days. Replacement equipment was hard to come by, forcing repeated adaptation and innovation in order to keep the work on schedule.

In the midst of the shortages, district engineer John MacGillvray arrived at their base, which the crew had named Starvation Camp, to see how the survey was proceeding. Fred Johnson, just returning from an unsuccessful hunting trip with the crew's wranglers, offered his superior a few choice and intemperate observations. Upon learning that Grafe and his co-worker, Jack Edwards, had carried MacGillvray from his float plane to shore, wading hip deep into the cold waters of Kluane Lake to do so, Johnson exploded, "Why didn't you drop the [son of a bitch] in the lake?"

And so it continued. The crew moved camp regularly, resupplied on occasion by float planes. The work was hard and tedious, offset partially by the beauty of the surroundings – they had, as a backdrop, the majestic St. Elias Mountains and, in the foreground, the deep blue waters of Kluane Lake – and the increasing pleasantness of the summer days took some of the testiness out of the enterprise. The surveyors continued north along Kluane Lake, past Pickhandle Lake, and pressed on to White River. They had hit their stride, having put many of the difficulties of the spring work behind them. One day, as if to torment them, a plane circled low over their camp and dropped a small object. The men searched for it, expecting that it contained important news. The message was brief and to the point – the survey crew was working too carefully and cautiously. The pressures of construction dictated that they speed up their work and worry less about details.

To make matters worse, the crew's temperamental cook learned at the same time that civilian contractors were offering better

A survey crew's pack team.
WALTER POLVI.

wages and better conditions than the PRA and demanded to be taken out. He was removed, and Grafe and Sam Johnson, one of the Native guides, were assigned to cooking duties. It was not by choice. Grafe says, "We were the only ones not given the opportunity to decline." The cooking assignment was not a favoured job, and Grafe quickly discovered why. In addition to the usual problems of camp cooking — working over a hot and smoky stove, without proper supplies, and subject to regular critiques by back-country gourmets — was one unique to their site at Pickhandle Lake. The surveyors' camp, it seemed, was a favourite "target" for American pilots flying to Alaska. The pilots took great delight in watching out for the smoke from the cooking tent and flying low, engines screaming, over the camp. The assaults were more than a little disconcerting, and Grafe's response contrasted sharply with the pilots' mirth.

Frank Johnson's crew finally reached White River, the end of its section of the highway. Grafe was allowed out of the cook tent to take part in the final day's work, which ended on the banks of the turbulent, silt-filled waters of the White. Back in camp at the end of the day, the levelman, J. H. Tucker, pulled a bottle of Scotch from his baggage, carefully protected and secreted for more than a month on the trail, and offered it as the foundation of a well-deserved celebration. There was a slight damper on the party. Several members of an army engineer regiment had passed through the camp a few days earlier. Short of food and tired of military C-rations, they had been given fresh meat. When the surveyors returned to their base camp after the final trip to the White River, they discovered their possessions had been rifled. "Nothing too good for the boys in the service," Grafe sarcastically noted.

The crew had finished its assignment. A float plane arrived at Pickhandle Lake to fly the men back to Burwash Landing. The settlement was no longer the place they had left just a few weeks before. The influx of army personnel and civilian contractors had upset the equilibrium of the small post Grafe remembered so affectionately. Liquor was now widely available, and relations between Indians and the incoming workers had became somewhat bitter. Grafe was relieved when his crew was assigned to work with the army on the location for its tote road, following a route that differed significantly from the one initially selected by the surveyors. They remained on site until October, Grafe working in the cook tent, helping out with some of the office and draughting work and, in the late fall, assisting with soils surveys. By the end of October, Fred Johnson's entire crew had returned to Whitehorse. From there, they were disbanded. Some left the North altogether, others decided to stay with the highway. Willis Grafe, surveying assistant and camp cook, was sent south of Watson Lake to work on location surveys in the Fort St. John district.

In the spring of 1942, the temperature often fell to minus thirty Fahrenheit, causing problems for poorly supplied crews from the south. When summer arrived, the day-long sunlight led workers to push themselves to the point of exhaustion in their effort to take advantage of the short but intense construction season. The men were continually on the move and had to construct temporary accommodations as they went. Vernon Kennedy, who worked with different survey crews on the southern end of the highway, describes their quarters as having been "primitive but satisfactory. We built our benches, tables, wash stands, as well as tent pegs and ridge poles — all from trees cut from the forest. Our beds were made with a pine frame, filled with spruce boughs, a canvas groundsheet and army blankets."

Kennedy's crew worked in ten-mile segments. When they had finished one segment, they leap-frogged forward, walking ahead while their equipment and supplies followed on pack horses.

The surveyors' litany of complaints became a familiar refrain among northern workers. Grumblings about cold, mud, and muskeg filled almost every letter heading south. In later years, the pristine wilderness and grandeur of the Far Northwest were uppermost in the surveyors' memories, but at the time, it was the bugs — mosquitoes, black flies, no-see-ums, and other aerial pests — and the climate that claimed their attention.

The surveyors' work, as Johnson's crew discovered, could not have proceeded as efficiently without the assistance of Native guides and wranglers. The Indians had something no other surveyor could claim: a deep personal and spiritual intimacy with the land. No Native person knew the entire route, but in the areas around their home territories, they had unparalleled knowledge of the land and its resources. Understandably, the American surveyors were anxious to recruit these local experts to put some flesh onto the skeletal plans sketched by General Hoge and his advisers.

While surveyors often had difficulty conveying their requirements to the Native guides — Heath Twichell noted in a letter home that the "Indian trappers' idea of what is needed for a road, for instance, is liable to be what is required for pack animals" — they came to rely very heavily on their advice. According to Twichell, Charlie MacDonald, a Beaver Indian, was found by an advance party "living on the sap which you get by peeling the bark off the trees. We have his undying freindshup [sic] at the cost of a sack of flour and a few supplies." Twichell was impressed with MacDonald's knowledge of the land, which the man had gained in over half a century of trapping in the area.

Billy Smith worked for the army out of Watson Lake, leading the soldiers overland to Teslin. His wife, Kitty Smith, later described his work, "They walk, walk, blaze, blaze. Two men behind them. The guide just walks. This side, one man blazes; other side, another man blazes. Keep going, keep going, that guide keeps going, you know. They end up someplace — Billy knows the name of that place. And, they make it to Teslin."[1]

David Johnston, a Tlingit, found work with the surveyors at Teslin. The Americans seem to have believed that all Indians

knew all of the land like the backs of their hands. Not one to discourage such a generous description of his talents and abilities, Johnston did not inform the Americans when they were venturing into territory he'd never seen before as they pushed to the southeast of Teslin. As Johnston later related the story, he and the other Tlingit guides kept their lack of knowledge to themselves, tried to stay in front of the Americans, and when truly confused would climb trees to get a view of the land ahead of them. The survey line, consequently, was neither particularly straight nor logical, but the Tlingits' reputation remained intact.

Johnston and his friends encountered a more serious problem when they returned to Teslin. In their absence, disease had broken out in the village, killing several people and knocking almost all the Native people onto their backs. David Johnston was particularly worried about his wife and small children and rushed into town. He was turned back by the Royal Canadian Mounted Police, who had placed the entire village under quarantine. Desperate with worry, Johnston ignored the quarantine, sneaked around the blockades and returned home. He promptly became very ill and spent several weeks sick in bed.

Disease accompanied the construction crews throughout the Northwest. When Gertrude Baskine travelled through Teslin sometime later, she was disturbed by what she found: "The whole place was under quarantine. In the Indian settlement raged spinal meningitis. These children of the outdoors, tempted by the wages paid for work on the Highway, had given up their trapping and fishing, had remained at Teslin all winter instead of going inland as was their wont. Alas, not only the high wages of the white man had they acquired, but with them many of the diseases to which they were not immune. First 'flu, then pneumonia, and now the dread spinal meningitis. For months they had been ill. Despite efforts to save them, many were dying."[2]

Surveyors' recollections of Native guides and workers is not always positive. A number of surveyors commented unfavourably on Indian work habits, confusing their need to go hunting and trapping with laziness and a lack of commitment to the work at hand. Hampton Primeaux was disappointed with the wranglers attached to his survey outfit at Burwash Landing. "These two Indians were something else. When they wanted to go to the nearest Indian village, they would cut the horses loose and pretend they were rounding them up. They would always come back though."

Not all the surveying work was as dramatic and exciting as that conducted by Watson, Primeaux, Grafe, and dozens of others in the first months of 1942. Bruce Willson, one of the engineering students recruited from the University of Alberta, passed the first months on the job at Pouce Coupe. He was sent there to work on upgrading the rough farming roads to suitable standards, but the grid pattern of rural roadways did not suit the needs of a modern highway. Willson described them as "narrow dirt grades with very little gravel in sight and, of course, no pavement or hard surfacing of any kind." The surveyors were asked to lay out a more direct route for a proper road. After less than a month in the field, working on the first forty miles of the highway (one of the only parts initially built to formal civilian standards), Willson was transferred to the Dawson Creek design office, where he spent the summer transferring data from field notes onto right-of-way maps.

After several weeks of slogging through the wet fields of the Peace River country, the transfer to the engineering office was most welcome. For two months, the surveyors worked in jerry-built facilities in Dawson Creek crammed into a small office and jostling for space on one of the two draughting tables. At the

The beginning of the Alaska Highway — the survey crews' muddy trail.

same time, work was proceeding on modern Public Roads Administration facilities. Early in July, Willson and his workmates were relocated to the new camp, which consisted of about a dozen prefabricated buildings, a well-equipped design office, and well-appointed living accommodations. The engineering students were, as Willson recalls, "hardly roughing it on the frontier!" They all stayed on site through the summer of 1942, returning to their classes in the fall. In that time Willson draughted a series of right-of-way maps, created from field notes, containing all the information required for the construction of a proper civilian "superhighway."

A great deal of the 1942 survey work was for naught. By the fall of that year, civilian and military engineers were embroiled in a major controversy about the location and design of the highway. As Frank Johnson's crew had discovered by the fall of 1942, speed, not accuracy or design quality, was the army's highest priority. At dozens of sites along the route, the army's pioneer road and the line located by the Public Roads Administration diverged widely, sometimes by several miles. Even as the army was completing its work on the pioneer road concern mounted among its commanders about the gap between the two routes and, more particularly, the cost of building a proper highway along the route laid out by the civilian surveyors. The resolution of this controversy lay several months off, and meanwhile even surveyors in the field were affected by the tension.

Working as a surveyor meant weeks of slogging through mosquito-infested muskeg, living in mobile camps, and making do with army-style dehydrated food and whatever could be harvested from the surrounding countryside. Thinking back more than forty years later, many of the surveyors remember that the land they worked through was majestic, unsullied by development – a true wilderness. Wistfully, they also recall that they were working so hard, and for so many hours during the short summer months, that they scarcely had any opportunities to take advantage of the fishing and hunting opportunities. There was little drama associated with running a transit, profiling a preliminary line, or taking a cross-section. Journalists who came north to capture the action were far more likely to photograph a bulldozer crashing through a stand of timber than a surveyor standing knee-deep in mud at a transit. In the first year of the Americans' involvement in the war, as well, there was more interest in the soldiers' work than in civilian activities.

Highway folk knew, however, that the surveys were essential to the successful completion of the highway project. Within the construction fraternity, surveyors were (and still are) an élite corps, possessing special skills and ultimate control of the highway building enterprise. Their job is to go first, to find the proper line for the highway, and then to move on before the first bulldozers and construction crews arrive on the scene. Along the Alaska Highway, the surveyors developed a strong *esprit de corps* which remains in evidence through to the present. Like an architect with a favoured building, a doctor and a unique patient, or a writer and a once-in-a-lifetime story, most of the surveyors saw the Alaska Highway as the ultimate challenge, and viewed the successful completion of the road as a vindication of their work and commitment. Even as they worked, however, the army's bulldozers were churning up the miles behind them. The construction of the pioneer road was underway.

4

The Pioneer Road

THE UNITED STATES ARMY CORP OF ENGINEERS faced a nearly impossible task – to push a pioneer road across 1,523 miles of little known sub-Arctic wilderness, and to do so within less than eight months. It was an assignment of Herculean proportions – the stuff of which legends are made. While the army's work was far from the complete story of the Alaska Highway, its work on the pioneer road was the focus of attention during what was one of the most unusual and massive construction projects of the twentieth century.

The Corps of Engineers was not new to such challenges. Established in 1799, the Corps had undertaken numerous war- and peacetime construction projects across the United States and in foreign countries. Among its many accomplishments, some of them extremely controversial, were the Washington Monument, Capital Dome, several major western dams, and flood control systems on the Mississippi. During World War II, the Corps of Engineers built airfields in Tonga and Greenland, bridges in Germany and Papua New Guinea, and docking facilities in Australia and the United States. It was an integral part of the Allied war effort, erecting the behind-the-lines facilities necessary for successful combat.

From the moment General Hoge received his orders to construct a highway to Alaska he began organizing the mobilization of a massive workforce. Within a few months of receiving the official go-ahead, Hoge had more than ten thousand American soldiers assigned to the Alaska Highway project, scattered from Big Delta, Alaska, to Dawson Creek, British Columbia. By plundering army and civilian supply depots across the United States, Hoge also arranged for the dispatch of thousands of pieces of construction equipment and materials for numerous warehouses, barracks, and administrative offices. By March 1942, even as the surveyors were making their first tentative steps, the Corps of Engineers had a logistical cannon pointed at the Northwest.

The troops began arriving in Edmonton, Dawson Creek, and Whitehorse in March 1942. They came ill-prepared for the experience. The army had little knowledge of sub-Arctic conditions, and did not properly outfit the men. Thomas Riggs, a member of the Alaska International Highway Commission, provided much sage comment on the problems of morale, isolation, and cold; he also had this to say: "Please do not underestimate the mosquito plague. I have had horses killed by mosquitoes in the country into which you must go."[1] While most soldiers disregarded such evident exaggeration, they would soon rue their lack of preparation.

From the start, immense bottlenecks developed at the key transportation points. Skagway, the Pacific terminus of the White Pass and Yukon Route railway, was snowed under by a storm of equipment, material, and military personnel. Many soldiers sat for several weeks in makeshift camps in the tiny coastal settlement. In what verged on being a military re-enactment of the Gold Rush of '98, the soldiers impatiently waited to press north, although the goal on this occasion was highway miles rather than ounces of gold.

Hoge realized that the highway could not possibly be built from a single direction, not if he hoped to come close to the target date. Consequently he divided the route into sections. Construction developed much like an underground fire emerging from the peat moss, small points at the ends and in the middle that, gradually at first, but with increasing speed, raced together.

Hoge dispatched large work crews to the ends, Fort St. John in the south and Big Delta in the north, and the middle, Whitehorse. Even this division of the construction work was insufficient, however. Speed made it imperative that other units be dispatched to other points along the highway route. Beginning in the early

The "office" of the C. V. Smith construction party on the banks of the Liard River. J. GARBUS.

spring of 1942, Hoge assigned construction units to more isolated sites. The 35th Engineers winter-marched to Fort Nelson, determined to be over the trail before the river ice thawed so that it could start work as soon as the snow and mud permitted. Army officer Heath Twichell was excited at the prospect: "It is going to be a huge job, with many hardships and adventures no doubt, but probably the chance of a lifetime. We are all pepped up, realizing fully the difficulties and perhaps dangers ahead of us."[2]

Few Alaska Highway workers suffered as much as the members of this early expedition. Twichell wrote: "The bitter cold and bitter wind combined with the difficulty of the 'road' [winter trail] to work painful hardships on many men. There were many cases of badly frozen feet since the shoe pac is not a satisfactory piece of footgear when temperatures reach 35 degrees below. Tractor operators were found along the road sitting beside their parked equipment and crying violently so great was the cold.

"Men transported in trucks could scarcely walk upon arrival at destination. Once dragged inside a tent and piled near a fire, they fell quickly asleep. Some of the officers and non-commissioned, who were determined to keep going whether or not, soon learned to keep away from fires. Truck drivers who had not earned their pay since maneuvers began to earn it again; countless are the stories of drivers who went for days without stopping and almost without food."[3]

Another unit, the 340th Engineers, travelled overland from Carcross to Teslin, while their equipment followed on riverboat up the Teslin River. From their base on the east shore of Teslin Lake, they worked south toward the units pushing north from Fort Nelson.

Two regiments, the 341st General Service and the 95th General Service, arrived in Dawson Creek and were quickly moved into position on the southern end of the highway. Work on the more difficult northern section proceeded in a similar fashion: the 18th Engineers worked northward from Whitehorse, and the 93rd General Service Regiment was directed to work south from the Yukon town. At the northern end, the 97th Engineers landed in Valdez, Alaska, in May 1942. After delays on the Richardson and Gulkana-Nebasna roads, the 97th began working south along the surveyed route toward the 18th Regiment working north from Whitehorse.

The seven regiments, each with approximately forty officers and between nine hundred and twelve hundred enlisted men, were outfitted with "20 D-8 tractors and bulldozers, 24 D-4 and R-4 tractors and bulldozers, 2 half-yard power shovels, 50 to 90 dump trucks, 12 pickup trucks, 6 tractor-drawn graders, 1 portable sawmill, 1 truck crane, 6 12-cubic-yard carryalls, 2 pile drivers and assorted small tools."[4] The logistics of moving this equipment from the southern states to the Canadian Northwest and Alaska strained transportation systems to their utmost, creating numerous backlogs and delays in the process.

There was no single construction beach-head, no single line of advance northwest. Instead, the battle against the sub-Arctic wilderness was waged simultaneously on several fronts, ensuring the fastest possible completion of the pioneer road. The sole priority was speed; as Hoge liked to say to his officers, "Your road is too good, too wide, and too short."[5]

The 18th Engineers, based in Whitehorse before moving north along the highway route, found their initial location to their liking: "We were permitted to visit Whitehorse daily, without passes. We were getting our first stiff dose of canned and powdered rations in camp, and the mediocre meals served in the three hotel restaurants and one café seemed good in contrast. Moose steaks tasted much like beef. We were on the old pay scale, but while our money lasted we enjoyed the heavy Canadian beer. We walked out to see the tumultuous Whitehorse rapids, and wondered at the gold madness that made men try to shoot them on rafts. We got a kick out of paying for a ten-cent article with a U.S. dollar and getting a Canadian dollar bill in exchange. We discovered that Mounties wear red coats only in movies. We watched the Northern Lights."[6]

Hoge's greatest problems had little to do with actual road construction. Even as construction began, it was clear that the direct supervision of the entire project was too much for one office. In May 1942, the highway project was divided in half. Hoge retained command of the larger northern section, and held four engineer regiments under his control. The southern sector, from Dawson Creek to Watson Lake, was handed over to Colonel James "Patsy" O'Connor. Hoge also had difficulties with his superiors. Brigadier General Clarence Sturdevant, assistant chief of engineers and Hoge's commanding officer, had his own ideas about road construction, and pushed ahead negotiations with the Public Roads Administration without informing Hoge of his actions. Sturdevant and Hoge would eventually come to loggerheads.

Relations with the Public Roads Administration complicated an already difficult situation. It was enough for Hoge to supervise the construction of a military highway; as the Corps of Engineers began working northward, however, the PRA was already moving into the region. Its assignment was to work under military direction, to follow the general route of the army's pioneer route, and to construct a full-service, permanent highway, up to the standards set by agreement with the Canadian government. Even as Hoge was getting his troops into the region, the PRA was organizing its civilian contractors and workers for a similar, albeit slower, assault on the Northwest.

For the Corps of Engineers, this meant that it had to work closely with the civilian authorities. For the PRA, the arrangement ensured that the military's pioneer road pulled rank on the civilian highway, frequently diverting the civilian workers from their primary task. The potential for misunderstanding and disagreement was immense, and not surprisingly, major difficulties developed. The PRA engineers were not, for example, impressed with the line selected for the pioneer road. In some cases, the civilian route deviated by several miles from the army's road. As work proceeded through the summer of 1942, army officials in

The highway emerges
from the bush, north
of Whitehorse.

Washington worried about the "appalling lack of co-ordination" between the Army and the PRA and the subsequent cost increases and construction delays.[7] Through the crucial first summer of construction, poor communications, conflicting goals, and different agendas complicated an already intricate undertaking.

For Bill Hoge, personal friction clouded the debate over construction tactics and interagency relations. Overall supervision of the highway rested with Lieutenant General Brehon Somervell, Army Service Forces commander. Somervell wanted his two pet projects, the Alaska Highway and the CANOL oil pipelines and refinery, to proceed as quickly as possible. For his part, Hoge found Somervell to be a pretentious officer; according to Hoge's biographer, Somervell's "reputation for pomp, show and grand designs was unrivaled in the U.S. Army."[8] His style was a far cry from the low-key Hoge. Following a tour of the highway in August 1942, Somervell was impressed with O'Connor's "first class construction job," but unhappy with Hoge's progress. In the last week of August 1942, Bill Hoge was fired from his post, and Colonel O'Connor assumed responsibility for the newly created Northwest Service Command, which included the highway, the CANOL project, and support services. Not everyone was pleased with O'Connor's appointment. One Canadian supervisor referred to him as a "pompous, publicity-seeking general" who antagonized many under his command by treating them as "an inefficient, bumbling bunch of hillbillies."[9]

Brigadier General William Hoge and Colonel Earl Paules, 18th Engineer Regiment, inspect the road route near Kluane Lake.
HOGE COLLECTION.

Hoge had never been particularly happy with the highway assignment. In the light of the pressing military needs of 1942, he remained unconvinced that the construction of a road to Alaska was worthy of the manpower and money devoted to it. He had, nonetheless, tackled his duty with professionalism and energy, and the highway would bear his imprint for many years. Hoge's dismissal was far from a fatal blow. He spent the latter stages of the war as a tank commander, and participated with distinction in the Normandy invasion and the Battle of the Bulge in December 1944. At the end of the war, he was in command of the Fourth Armored Division. When he retired from the U.S. Army in January 1955, he was commander-in-chief of the U.S. Army in Europe. Fittingly, Hoge was invited back to the Yukon Territory in 1946 for the ceremonies marking the passing of control of the Alaska Highway from the U.S. Army to Canadian authorities.

For the soldiers skinning the cats, driving the trucks, and moving supplies, the nuances of this prolonged administrative battle were of little consequence. Few of them knew much of the broader picture. They had small assignments, limited in geographical and strategic scope, and were more than fully occupied with these tasks. Most of them, however, were aware of the mounting tension between the army and the PRA, and wondered how much of their work would prove to be in vain. The crews' attempts to develop a construction rhythm routinely ran up against muskeg, permafrost, rocky mountain passes, and flood-

*Clearing the right of way
– the hard way.*

United States National
Archives.

swollen creeks. The primary construction impediment across much of the region, however, was the thick carpet of stunted sub-Arctic evergreens. The Corps of Engineers moved through these vast tracts, remarkable to the soldiers primarily because of the tenacity and size of the mosquitoes, with typical military efficiency – concerns about cost, environmental impact, and long-term utility simply didn't exist.

The construction pattern was straightforward.[10] Today, environmentalists would protest such a rapacious assault on the frontier, but the technique answered the requirements of 1942. A locating party led the crew into the bush, marking the centre line with axe blazes in the trees or pieces of bright cloth. Three bulldozers followed close behind. The first knocked out the centre line. The two other machines pushed the trees and brush back, clearing an opening from sixty to ninety feet wide. Smaller dozers, operating independently, tidied up, levelling off the ground and clearing away the remaining brush. If the ground was firm and supplies of gasoline were readily at hand, a phalanx of bulldozers could root through two or three miles each day. The bulldozer crews worked well in advance of the main construction units and had to be supplied by pack train or tractor-drawn sleds.

The history of the 341st Engineers describes the activities of the "Cat Camp:" "Forests of jackpine, spruce and poplar were slashed with a 100-ft. clearing. Sidehill developments requiring considerable movements of earth and rock were carried out with

Clearing the right of way – the easy way.

United States National Archives.

good speed. Patches of muskeg were eyed with much speculation. If by-passing was impossible and the muskeg was shallow, the 'dozers simply mucked it out, exposing a bottom of clay for the roadbed. In cases where the muskeg was deep, one or more of the line companies were called up from the rear to corduroy [lay logs] across the dangerous section."[11]

Several miles to the rear, the small appendage of the engineering unit worked over the swath carved out by the bulldozers. Where required, they patched together temporary bridges or culverts from local timber, dug ditches to keep the main road surface relatively dry, and, in soggy sections of the trail, laid down a thin corduroy road. Over particularly wet sections, they would build a covering several feet thick of trees, branches, and shrubs, piling tons of dirt and gravel on top of the wooden bed. Their task was simple: to ensure that the road to the bulldozers ahead stayed open and to provide a rough surface that the main construction crews could later turn into a workable military supply road.

The largest engineering unit followed as much as thirty to forty miles behind the bulldozers. They had many tasks: widening and straightening the road, eliminating steep grades (where that was consistent with the overriding need for speed), covering the often muddy surface with gravel, and packing it down ready for vehicle traffic. When their work was done – and they proceeded much more slowly than did the vanguard units – they left behind a passable road, eighteen to twenty-four feet wide,

A pull-blade carves out a ditch alongside the highway.
PUBLIC WORKS CANADA.

usable by military traffic but still far removed from the standards of a proper civilian highway. Even farther behind, bridge construction units worked quickly, replacing the temporary pontoon bridges with more durable structures.

Not all the work proceeded in such a logical fashion. Late in 1942 units were still arriving and were quickly rushed into the field to patch up sections of the highway and complete unfinished bridges and culverts. The 341st Engineers, for example, constructed a warehouse in Dawson Creek and then moved to Fort Nelson in September 1942. After a brief period working on the road south of the Liard River and constructing a bridge over the Trout River, they were assigned to a winter camp at Sikanni Chief. They passed the winter cutting timber for the bridges that would be built the following summer. In March 1943, some of the men from the 341st were dispatched north to Lower Post, where they erected a saw mill and again began cutting bridge timbers.

Field officers faced numerous problems that had not been anticipated by the engineers. In the Tok Valley of eastern Alaska, for example, one outfit wanted to leap-frog a clearing crew several miles ahead. Supplying the isolated unit posed a problem, until an officer decided to dump pontoons filled with food, camp equipment, and partially filled barrels of oil and gas into the Little Tok River. The pontoons bobbed down the stream, which was scarcely wide enough for the task, until they collected at an army-built log boom some fifteen miles downstream.[12] A touch of ingenuity had saved the army a few days' construction time.

A six-by-six mired in the mud.

This bald outline of the military construction strategy doesn't begin to describe the very real difficulties that the soldiers faced. Mosquitoes and black flies constantly swarmed around the workers, particularly those working around still water. The bugs drove many soldiers to distraction and fury – the jokes that followed in later years were a poor reminder of the persistent pests. One soldier wrote, "During the summer months the mosquitoes and another black bug which can bite like all hell gave us a bad time. Some of the men were so badly bitten their eyes were all but closed."[13] Mud, thick and stinking, covered their equipment, seeped into their boots, and rendered their clothing all but useless. The excitement of building across the sub-Arctic wilderness soon paled after several dozen sixteen- or eighteen-hour workdays. Many of the bulldozer crews worked each day until they dropped, the men sleeping in hastily constructed tents or simply on the ground alongside their machines.

Camps were established and then, just as quickly, abandoned. The chronicler for Company E, 341st Engineers, wrote, "Life during these months was really rough. We lived in pup tents all during the summer season. Types of pup tents were varied. There was everything from a common lean-to affair to an elaborate five-person bungalow constructed from any number of shelter halves and rough timber."[14] The 18th Engineers reported that the eight regimental units moved a total of 174 separate times in ten months. Such moves were far from easy: "Movements to new campsites were trials of endurance for man and trucks. In the summer we jolted over half-completed road in billows of red dust, until our faces became pink masks. Thick deposits of dust collected in the creases of our blue fatigues. Trucks went where trucks could not go. High on boxes, tents and barracks bags we rode, dirty, beaten and breathing mosquitoes. In the winter we sat stiffly under tarps, the pain creeping up our legs."[15]

Work continued non-stop throughout the week. Norman Allison, who spent the better part of a year cutting timber for the 341st Engineers, remembers working seven days a week, with only two and a half days off in the fifteen months his company spent building the highway. The men soon learned to curse the "land of the midnight sun," for the long summer days prompted the officers to urge their men to keep at their jobs, to press for another couple of hundred yards or one more culvert, before breaking for an all-too-short rest.

Many of the soldiers assigned to highway construction had little or no experience operating heavy equipment and certainly no knowledge of the specific problems of construction in the sub-Arctic. The equipment took a severe beating, as untrained operators ground gears relentlessly, ignored proper maintenance procedures, and handled the army-issue hardware with less than respect. Unskilled operators repeatedly put their trucks into the ditch, easy enough to do given the rough road surface, or otherwise damaged their equipment through poor judgement or recklessness.

Snafus (situation normal, all fouled up – to use polite language) became the order of the day. On a number of occasions soldiers arrived at their construction sites only to discover that equipment was not available. The 18th Engineers, assigned to the Whitehorse sector, were actually set to work on the highway with hand tools while they waited for their machinery to arrive from Skagway. As one of their men later wrote, they proceeded "in coolie fashion, bending pick points in frozen ground and mucking around in rivers of mud, getting nowhere."[16] According to another story, repeated by several veterans, one engineering unit was required to turn in all of its equipment while in the South. It was promised, in turn, that it would receive brand-new machinery when it arrived in the North. As the men off-loaded their supplies in Valdez, they discovered that they had been shipped, not new trucks and bulldozers, but the very same

The highway claims a victim.
U.S. Army Corps of Engineers.

equipment that they had turned over to the army depots, at some inconvenience and cost, in the South.[17]

Days of continuous battering took their toll on both men and machines. Replacement parts were hard to come by, and men were frequently forced to sit with their equipment for days on end waiting for a single small part. Equipment destined for the highway crews piled high on the ground in Dawson Creek, Fort St. John, Skagway, and Whitehorse, taunting the army officials whose task it was to get it into the field. Chronic shortages of spare parts plagued the project through most of 1942. The project was saved only by the fact that the bulk of the army's equipment was near new and did not readily succumb to the rigours of northern construction. Logistical delays cost the engineering units many days of lost construction time, and infuriated field officers cursed headquarters officials who, they were convinced, were too busy enjoying the delights of town life to be concerned with their urgent needs in the field.

Supplying troops in the bush caused many difficulties, as the surveyors had previously discovered. An American journalist described the farcical efforts in 1943 to resupply one such unit,

Constructing a wooden culvert.

stranded after the winter trail they were using turned to slush in a spring thaw: "They were supplied entirely by air, but for some time when the lakes were breaking up neither ski nor pontoon planes could land.... Finally a desperate effort was made to relieve their plight by dropping stuff from a plane. Here are the results of the first try: First pass over, the plane dropped mail, so the boys rushed out to get their long-delayed letters. Next pass the plane dropped a sack of bridge spikes. The bag broke and the spikes rained down on the mail-reading soldiers like shrapnel. The third pass was to drop an axle and several bearings, tied to a parachute for safety. The parachute ripped apart on the way down – they're still digging in the muskeg for the bearings. On the fourth pass over the camp a side of beef was dropped; the pilot went back and reported he just missed the fuel dump – what he really barely missed was the nitro (explosive) dump. The next time the plane came up a sack of mail was thrown overboard but it caught on the tail of the plane, and went all the way back to Whitehorse in that position. So the pilot figured a few weights might help and [on the next try] loaded the sack with small bearings – the weights worked just right, just enough to carry the mail sack through the top of an oil drum into a diesel fuel bath."[18]

Many of the soldiers were less than impressed by their working conditions. Harold Griffin, who travelled along the highway in

U.S. Army encampment,
Whitehorse, Yukon.

1943, wrote of the men: "They were not pioneers by choice but by the stern necessity of war and the majority of them came to hate the country. They hated it because of the loneliness of their camps in the wilderness and the monotony of the work, with only such recreation as they could devise for themselves to relieve it. They hated the rain and the mud, and when the rivers froze they hated the cold and the snow. They wanted to get back to the bright lights of a familiar city, to see their families, to jostle the crowds along busy streets and sit in the corner drugstore with a girl."[19]

Even the more accessible construction units suffered from chronic shortages of supplies and equipment. Providing oil and gasoline for the hundreds of bulldozers, trucks, jeeps, and other machines proved a constant worry. Within a few weeks of the start of construction, fuel drums were scattered up and down along the highway route. As one writer noted, "Officially it may be Alcan, but to the boys on the project it is the 'Oilcan' Highway because of the hundreds upon hundreds of gas and diesel fuel drums scattered over the full length of the road."[20] There was no shortage of military and construction supplies at Whitehorse, Skagway, and Dawson Creek, but there were bottlenecks all along the highway, where a dozen or more fully loaded trucks waiting by a washed-out section of road, collapsed bridge, or other barrier, continually slowed the movement of material to the site of construction.

The logistics of supplying a large, complex, and widely scattered workforce resulted in inevitable foul-ups. Several truck drivers reported being ordered to carry a tanker-load of oil to a certain point on the highway, only to discover that there were no storage facilities within miles of their destination. The more conscientious drivers sought out an army storage depot; a few others, resentfully following their orders to the letter, delivered their fuel as directed – dumping it in the middle of the highway.

The regular problems with supply proved a constant source of irritation for the soldiers, adding to a growing list of discomforts and frustrations. During the construction phase they lived in mobile camps, consisting of the ubiquitous pyramid sleeping tents and field kitchens in spartanly furnished canvas tents, and they existed on a steady diet of the rudely named and unfavourably remembered military field rations. Life in the tent encampments was grim: "Tents averaging seven occupants were overcrowded for men who carried two full barracks bags and the usual gear, plus sleeping bag....We slept without pillows on canvas cots without mattresses, in which condition the cot has about the same 'give' as a concrete floor. We jammed what gear we could under our bunks, the rest we hung in the air. A soldier's closet is the air and our tents were full of strings, ropes and miscellaneous rigging holding clothes, rifles, anything we wanted to keep off the ground. We found a place to hang a picture of the 'girl at home,' or pin-ups. A stove dried the ground until the floor was deep dust."[21]

The men saved their most creative profanity for the army food, which consisted of dehydrated and canned rations, supplemented only occasionally by deliveries of fresh meat and, on rare occasions, vegetables. The soldiers learned to despise the sight of Yukon shrimp (Vienna sausage) and Spam. One officer recalls the efforts made to combine army rations with local produce: "Everything was canned. Nothing fresh. We would shoot game when we could until the RCMP got onto us....We eventually scared all the game away from the road, so we didn't get that much."[22] Corporal G. S. James complained in a letter home, "I am so hungry I can hardly stand it. We are now having hash almost every meal and none of us can eat it, so all of us in my squad decided to send home and have packages sent to us. One boy has been doing this for a while and all of us have been eating it." Soldiers begged wives and girlfriends to send jars of

peanut butter, jelly, and any other non-perishable goods that
might free them from the poisonous monotony of army food. But
the food could not have been always that bad. Heath Twichell
wrote fondly of army fare: "We...eat the best of chow. They have
provided a special ration for us, which is more than adequate.
We have 80 tons of fresh meat (steaks and chops) which have
been stored in an ice house that we built. The quartermaster has
set up a field bakery, and we will have fresh bread, rolls, and pas-
try. Some of the other items in the ration include powdered milk
and eggs, dehydrated potatoes, all kinds of canned fruits, meats
and vegetables, etc."[23] Spoken like a good officer.

The soldiers complained constantly, but to little avail. The
officers, R. C. McFarland says, had a way of dealing with constant whining: "They would have an officer on what they call
mess duty. He'd come along and ask the boys, 'How's the food.'
'Fine, fine,' they'd answer. Anyone complaining would probably
end up washing dishes or peeling potatoes, so nobody complained." At least not in front of the officers.

There were few distractions from the monotony of the construction camp, and perhaps little need – at least in the frenzied
summer months of 1942. Journalist Harold Richardson wrote in
1942, "Work, work and more work was the only program – day
and night, seven days a week."[24] An American officer commented,
"It is a fact that this post, like most outposts, is an officers' paradise and an enlisted man's concentration camp. It's really tough
on the men living the restricted life they must...but everything to

break the monotony of camp life is done that is possible."[25] The soldiers were particularly avid gamblers, a questionable recreation tolerated by Canadian and American authorities so long as the professionals stayed away. A corporal with the 93rd Engineers, busted from sergeant for his persistent gambling, bragged to his wife about his "biz" and claimed to have made more than $1,100 in a matter of a few months.[26]

Although cold, isolation and hard work did much to drain the soldiers' energies, the men's sexual desires were not easily repressed. Project planners did their best to keep the soldiers away from the main communities and to keep contact between the men and the local women to a minimum. But these were soldiers, after all, and mostly young men; the Northwest reeked of masculinity. The following is a relatively mild soldier's poem about women in Whitehorse:

> Two hundred people and six thousand dogs
> Trillions of "skeeters," and millions of bugs.
> Five or six women were in the town
> (There may have been more – I wasn't around).

> A lady came out and tripped in the slush
> And seventeen soldiers were killed in the rush.
> Right down on her back, her skirts flying free
> (She made sixteen dollars before you could see).[27]

The problem, put simply, was that there were precious few women around. One of the most frequently reprinted images of the construction era was of a roughly printed message, "Help Wanted – Female." Journalists wishing to illustrate the sacrifice made by the American soldiers working in the Northwest routinely commented on the absence of women. One typical headline shouted (in words that would now be rejected as racist) "Alaska Highway Workers Treasure Pictures of Girls: Many Have Not Seen Any Women Except Squaws in 9 Months." Another journalist commented on the "low chicken count" in the highway camps, and wrote that one of the favourite pastimes was "marrying Canadian girls," and dismissed the Far Northwest as a "dreary womanless country."[28] Tents and dormitory walls were often covered with pin-ups, scarcely immodest by modern standards but the best available at the time. The *Washington Post*'s story summarized it best: "A sweater-girl clipping becomes something of a shrine...something to rest one's eyes on after a bitter day among the great groves of spruce that lead to nowhere. The chorine who has posed for some picture magazine would be proud if she knew how many good-looking young men had dozed off in a Yukon tent with her face and legs as their last waking memory."[29]

The army brought very few women with it to the North, and the Northwest Service Command tried to prohibit civilian employees from bringing their wives with them. Norman Allison says that there was "no female companionship, dances, or anything of that nature. I do remember I did not see any women for eleven months, and then it was only Indian women at Lower Post, B.C." When women did arrive in small numbers, the army instituted tough rules to regulate social contact. Female employees were not permitted to invite men into their quarters, and tight curfews were instituted for dating couples. One civilian, Richard Hislop, says laconically, "There were the usual fights related to the scarcity of women." T. E. Molyneux agrees, saying that soldiers and civilians got along well, except "when they were after the same girl."

For many soldiers in the construction camps, alcohol provided some solace, even though it was available only on rare occasions and then at considerable cost. Civilians travelling in the area quickly learned that smuggled bottles of beer or whisky sold for premium prices to the weary soldiers. According to Ed Wiggins, a mickey of whisky that cost $1.40 at Pouce Coupe sold for over ten times as much to the black soldiers working north of Fort St. John. As Wiggins remembers, "All one had to do was drive by, and they came out shaking their money at the truck." Bootleggers became extremely adept at hiding their caches: many bottles were smuggled into the camps in hollowed-out loaves of bread or in rolls of tar paper. Lake Southwick describes an even more ingenious scheme: men would "cut the bottom out of a forty-five-gallon barrel, empty it, but leave the top looking like a barrel of gas. The rest would be filled with sawdust and whisky. Then they'd put the barrel right in the middle of the load. They [the U.S. Military Police] would walk right over it. We'd have quite a few bottles of whisky in there." Another truck driver hollowed out a beam, stuffed whisky bottles into the hole, and sealed in his treasures with padding and a plug.[30]

Creativity was the order of the day in the search for booze. Cyril Griffith came upon an American soldier apparently discussing innocuous technical matters with a civilian trucker. On closer investigation, he learned that the soldier had willingly drained the antifreeze from his radiator — and traded it to the Canadian for a bottle of whisky. "The last I saw of them," Griffith says, "the army guy was on his way, tipping up his bottle, knowing full well he had just drained the radiator. On my return trip, a few miles from the spot, I saw the army truck in the ditch, the motor seized up, no doubt." In the small communities along the route, the soldiers found an honoured temple; one veteran remembers, "One of the favourite occupations was standing ankle deep in the mud outside the liquor store."[31]

Archie McEachern, a Canadian assigned to work in Whitehorse, decided to pack a dozen bottles of beer in his vehicle for a trip up the highway. Not being a beer drinker himself, McEachern placed little value on the quart bottles he'd rolled up in blankets. He soon discovered that he had, in fact, a cache of riches. With his gas gauge registering empty, he pulled into a U.S. Army Engineering depot twenty miles outside Fort Nelson and asked for some gas. The G.I. rebuffed him brusquely. When McEachern offered to trade a bottle of beer for some gas, the soldier brightened. "You got a quart of beer for gas?" he asked. McEachern dug into his car and reappeared with a quart; the soldier filled his tank to overflowing. As McEachern notes, "From then on I knew why I was carrying a dozen quarts of beer. It was the best

A military band performing for the troops.
UNITED STATES NATIONAL ARCHIVES.

legal tender a fellow could have, and it was good at any USED [United States Engineering Department] camp for fixing flat tires, and so on."

Beer binges – rare but highly prized – provided the troops with a brief respite from the rigours of work and distraction from their painful isolation. For travellers who happened upon the camps during one of these occasional flings, the scene was Bacchanalian. Harold Griffin, an author who visited the Northwest to write a book about the highway, recalls stopping in one camp where a load of beer had just arrived, and almost the entire detachment was drunk, or very much under the influence.

The army did its best to provide recreational distractions for the soldiers. In the early months of construction, they could do little other than send a few baseballs and gloves, reading materials, and an occasional film. But as permanent camps were built, full-time recreation officers entered the district, providing a comprehensive round of games and activities. Baseball games and tournaments, between military units, with the civilian workers, and with locals, were exceptionally popular; in winter, hockey and bowling replaced summer sports. The army also provided a regular radio service, which broadcast American military news, a regional newspaper, the *Northwest Newscast* and, perhaps the most popular item, first-run movies flown in from the South. As work slowed, which it did perceptibly in the winter of 1942-1943, the army made sure that the soldiers had lots to do.

To no one's surprise, the American troops found it very difficult to adjust to sub-Arctic conditions, particularly to the chill and darkness of winter. Keeping heavy equipment running in extreme sub-zero temperatures challenged the best mechanics and operators. Major Compton, in charge of transport maintenance in Whitehorse, observed: "At 70 below lubricants become solids. Grease normally used under winter conditions in the United States congeals. Motors cannot be turned and wheels lock. You can take a can of undiluted Prestone, cut the tin away and take out a solid block....At first, before we had heated shrouds to put our vehicles under, it was more difficult to keep our trucks operating. We had to thaw them out by placing a smokepot under each differential."[32] During the depths of winter, the army often kept trucks and equipment running twenty-four hours a day; even a short shut-down was sure to make restarting difficult. The *North Star Magazine* offered a more graphic description: "That first winter was a nightmare. Glyco, a fluid antifreeze used in airplane cooling systems, was kept about four feet from stoves and yet congealed. At night the men would climb into their sleeping bags, leaving just their face out; in the morning, a half-inch layer of frost would be around the opening of the sleeping bag. Metal frames of eyeglasses froze to the face. Pitchers of water (most bases had no running water then) sitting about five feet from stoves would be frozen solid. Ink in pens was always frozen. Typewriters (few of the bases had them) would freeze and had to be thawed out on a QM [quartermaster] pot-bellied stove."[33]

Consider the plight of the 19th Quartermaster Salvage Repair Platoon, which disembarked at Dawson Creek in the first minutes of 6 February, 1943. It was forty below Fahrenheit, and a stiff wind was blowing the fine, powdery snow of extreme cold around the men's feet. The scene was altogether depressing: "The small cluster of buildings, Dawson Creek, appeared desolate and deserted. For nearly thirty minutes we stood, shivering and shaking, until negotiations were completed for an overnight stay at the Casual Detachment. Morning appeared no better —

due to overcrowded conditions and lack of facilities, our Mess was late, cold and unappetizing. The imminent shortage of water resulted in dirty, unsanitary conditions and produced a general feeling of discomfort."[34]

The U.S. Army's problem, in the opinion of Canadian engineer Archie McEachern, "was largely of their own making. There were quite a number of us who knew how to dress for the cold weather and how to handle permafrost; too many directives came from too far away and there weren't nearly enough Colonel Hoges to look after a more commonsense approach to the huge task of building the highway."

The army's mechanics had the greatest problems. In the first year, before proper maintenance facilities were constructed, they did virtually all of their work out of doors. In the winter, thin canvas shrouds and small, inefficient heaters provided only minimal protection from the bitter sub-Arctic chill. Worse, it was dangerous to touch metal in sub-zero temperatures, for the skin would quickly stick; only painful extraction – by pouring hot water over the adhesion or by ripping one's skin off – would separate man from machine. Leslie "Bud" Schnurstein still admires the mechanics who were under his command: "The guys would get out there and get on those tractors and would pull them apart and do all sorts of things – with gloves on. I don't know how they did it, but they fixed them. They were good."

The cold and the frequent mishandling of machinery meant that equipment was constantly in need of repair. Replacement components were scarce, so mechanics became exceptionally adept at invention and innovation. The best ones were also skilled scavengers. Jim Sutton remembers, "If a jeep broke down we just kept it out of sight. If another jeep came in that needed repair, we always went to the one that had broken down and took the parts from it." Cannibalized trucks and equipment were a common sight during the military construction period.

Few soldiers in the Northwest faced as intimidating a winter challenge as did the railwaymen charged with keeping supplies moving along the White Pass and Yukon Route – taken over by the army from the private company early in the war to ensure the highest priority was given to army goods. The mountain passes on the railway from Skagway to Carcross routinely clogged with deep snow drifts, presenting even the most determined workers with an almost impenetrable barrier. Corporal Charles Biller offers an evocative description: "The mercury had plummeted out of sight and the piercing cold air was hanging like black chiffon. These young men who came to conquer the frozen North, and who had never before had the chance to be defeated by an Alaskan winter, were now facing defeat. They would return again and again to the water tanks, but they had returned this final time to find that the water in the tanks was frozen solid. Fire doors in snorting, straining locomotives were coated with half an inch of frost. The engineer and fireman looked like ghosts, for the steam that had sprayed over them froze quickly to their clothing."

The bitter winter of 1942-43 — soldiers were told by locals that it was the worst in two decades — presented a serious challenge to the railway crews. Buttressed by additional men and equipment, they gradually pushed back the drifts, only to have more snow dumped across the rails, forcing them back to work once more. The military railroaders played a major role in keeping the supplies moving to Whitehorse, putting a major strain on the narrow-gauge railway in the process.

Many locals commented, with evident sympathy, on the plight of the black soldiers dispatched to work on the highway. These men had particular difficulty because so many were from the American South and had never before experienced a real winter. One army officer alleged that "Our colored boys are allergic to cold weather, and it's going to be a problem to keep them well and happy I fear."[35] Gordon Gibbs excoriated the U.S. Army for sending troops from the Deep South into the Far Northwest, and then housing them in bell tents. "Now the story was," Gibbs says, "and this I saw, they all had good eiderdown sleeping bags, army issue sleeping bags. And they'd cut the bottom out and they'd wear them. Of course, the feathers kept dribbling out." Jim Sutton, an American soldier, believes that the black troops got a dirty deal. He says, "They were up here when we got up here. We were put in barracks, wooden barracks, and we had stoves and everything. These poor black people were doing the same job as we were and they had them in tents. I didn't think that was really fair."

Most of the tales about the black troops contain two elements — memories of the men as excellent workers and references to their intense dislike of the cold. One officer wrote, "During the most severe weather encountered, it is believed that Negro

troops, properly led, have accomplished more physical labour than other troops in the same area engaged in similar work."[36] Ruth Gruber, an official with the U.S. Department of the Interior, quoted the soldiers' officers as saying, "The Negroes were better soldiers and builders than the whites. They put our gold-bricks to shame. We never had a bit of trouble with them; they policed themselves. If one of the Negroes got out of line about 10 others would get around him right away and yell: Everybody's been good to us. We don't want no bad nigger spoiling things for us."[37] Today, it is clear that the black soldiers managed to perform as well as the white soldiers, despite the disadvantages imposed by a racist and discriminatory age.

In the fall of 1942, Ray Talbot and his friends were in an encampment with a number of black soldiers, most of them complaining about the bitter cold. Talbot and Rusty Johnston made themselves a stove out of a forty-five-gallon drum, and their small tent was soon toasty warm. Several black soldiers asked for directions on how to make a similar stove. Their first attempt was less than successful: "In the tent there were about six or seven soldiers trying to get warm by this stove. One guy would get the diesel fuel, one guy would open the door, and another guy would throw in the fuel. It would go *poof*, you know." As well, the soldiers had neglected to burn the paint off the barrel, and their fire unleashed noxious fumes into the small tent. As Talbot is quick to point out, the men's problems rested entirely with their lack of experience – men from Louisiana and Georgia had little reason to know how to cope with temperatures of minus twenty Fahrenheit.

There were numerous tales of a different type about the black troops – many apocryphal and often reflecting little credit on a group of men who made a signal contribution to the success of the construction venture. In the winter of 1942-43, a civilian driver came across a small group of American black soldiers waiting in their truck at the bottom of a very steep hill. After the civilians made a successful run up the hill, the soldiers decided to give it a try. Red-lining the r.p.m. on the six-by-six, the driver charged the hill. They almost made it, only to have the wheels begin to spin furiously at the top, polishing the already slick ice and stopping the truck in its tracks. As the vehicle started to slide backward, the soldiers bailed out. Driverless, the truck hurtled down the hill, smashed off the road, and burst into flames. The soldiers walked back up the hill, where they were greeted by the incredulous civilian drivers. "Why," they asked, "didn't you stay with the truck?" "Man," the driver answered without guilt, "we weren't just about to try. Uncle Sam got lots of them god damn trucks but he's only got one coloured boy like me. Going to live a long time."[38]

Another civilian trucker, expressing similar sentiments about the wisdom of the American army sending soldiers from the Deep South into the Far North, wrote that the black soldiers "became completely irresponsible. Survival was their only aim." When his truck broke down along the road, the trucker hitched a ride back to camp with a black crew. The driver pushed his truck at breakneck speed. Aware that his passenger was more than a little concerned for his safety, the driver observed, "Don't worry, boss, Uncle Sam has lots more trucks and lots more nigger boys to drive 'em."[39]

The black troops' experience of the Northwest was significantly different than that of other soldiers. Most of the officers were white, a minority of whom treated their men with disdain. One letter from an officer – stopped *en route* by military censors – gives an idea of the bitter racism of the time: "Had trouble with a couple of the colored officers who were sent up to help me. First they wanted to live in the same barracks with us. That was too much, so I told them that as long as they were working up above here with me, no colored officers would live with any whites. Have trouble getting them to work and get up on time so, just like Simon Legree, I ride them....Pretty soon I expect to be called before the Colonel but I'll be damned if I am going to live with any niggers. It's bad enough to serve with them and wash and use the same toilets."[40]

Not all the soldiers – black or white – tackled their assignments with the expected level of military gusto and enthusiasm. Alex Forgie, who worked at a PRA camp, talked about the many soldiers who would drop by to visit: "Some of the soldiers would hide their trucks in behind our camp and then spend a day or two sleeping, or would eat in our mess hall." Sooner or later, the military police would come along and haul the soldiers back to work.

The Alaska Highway extracted a grim toll. A small number of soldiers died – victims usually of drowning or car accidents. The 341st Engineers, for example, suffered a number of fatalities, several by drowning when a pontoon raft swamped on Charlie Lake.[41] The raft "was caught in a sudden squall near the centre of the lake and swamped in near-freezing water. A lone trapper, Gus Hedin, at home in his cabin a mile away, rushed to the scene of the accident in a small rowboat and at continual risk of his own life succeeded in rescuing five enlisted men from drowning. The men who sat in the boats that night searching for those who were lost will remember the display of Northern Lights – the first and the most brilliant during our 15 months in the North – which added to our already deep feelings."[42] The 18th Engineers lost one officer, who was crushed when his jeep overturned, and four enlisted men. Two of the men died in industrial accidents, the third drowned while fishing, and the fourth victim succumbed to a heart attack.[43] Many other soldiers felt the sure bite of the northern winter and took home frozen fingers and toes as a memento of their time on the highway. Truck and equipment accidents accounted for most of the deaths. In a bit of gruesome construction humour, Cale Roberts tells a story of a young man killed when he was crushed under heavy equipment. A man was perplexed about where to send the body. "Send it?" said another. "Hell, file him! He was run over by a packer!" Gordon Gibbs remembers that the troops referred to the Army's big four-wheel drives as "widow-makers" because they frequently went off the road. "When they started to go," he says, "there was just nothing on earth could hold those wheels....They lost quite a few people that way, with those big trucks."

For most of the troops, isolation was the North's greatest punishment. They were hundreds, if not thousands, of miles from family and friends, with little means of contacting them. The army began construction of a telephone line, but it was not ready until after 1943. It was hard to educate Americans – in the Northwest and in the lower forty-eight states – about the distances and lack of services in the region. A telephone operator in Edmonton tells a story about a persistent Chicago operator who wanted to put a call through to a soldier at Fort St. John – several hundred miles away. Informed that there was no service to Fort St. John, the Chicago operator asked her Edmonton counterpart to have someone contact him and have him come to the phone. Only on the fourth attempt, when a Chicago supervisor finally came on the line, did the Illinois exchange accept the Edmontonian's explanation.[44]

Most soldiers found the interminable winter months an awesome burden. An internal army report agreed that the long periods without furlough caused serious problems: "Men have been interviewed who have not seen a woman for a year. Many have wives and children – one man, a child sixteen months old he has never seen. These men seem to feel that from a standpoint of prosecution of the war and to maintain a man as a fighting soldier, he cannot be kept in complete isolation too long in an environment that at best is taxing."[45]

Despite the snow, mud – always mud – freezing temperatures, and isolation, the American soldiers were quickly moulded into a finely tuned construction machine. Cyril Griffith, a civilian truck driver who came north in the first summer, says of the soldiers: "By the time we arrived in August of 1942, they were well seasoned – having fought rivers, creeks, hills, swamps, permafrost, mosquitoes, sand flies and the roughest of living conditions. It was said that one camp of about one hundred men not far from Fort Nelson lived for over a week on only fish, as supplies were unable to get to them. They were well aware of the reason they were there and were willing to help everyone to proceed up the road any way they could."

Throughout the entire enterprise, the army never forgot that the major portion of its operation was on foreign soil. The

Ice bridge over the Liard River in early 1942.

J. GARBUS.

Canadians were accommodating hosts, but there were more than a few tensions, over everything from the location of the highway and the sale of army surplus to the different wage rates and the punishment of American citizens found guilty of breaking Canadian laws. A small number of Canadians complained about the Americans' over-bearing presence – comments usually directed at the United States military police – but most found the Yankees to be acceptable bosses and co-workers.

Most residents greeted the Americans with open arms. The arrival of soldiers in Edmonton, Dawson Creek, Fort St. John, and Whitehorse was marked by large civic celebrations. Local businesses along the highway route saw the soldiers as a great boon to trade, even though the military units were largely self-sufficient. As well, the early months of 1942 were times of uncertainty and concern in the Allied world, as the Axis powers advanced, seemingly unchecked, on all fronts, so the soldiers' presence assured residents that they were truly being defended and that any enemy invasion was sure to be repelled. Bruce Willson fondly recalls the celebrations that greeted the arrival of one troop train: One particular image lingers: "I have a vivid memory of a haunting trumpet playing the blues after a troop train pulled in one evening, the sound carrying across the open space between the encampment and the main street of the town.

To a jazz devotee it sounded like Harry James or Louis Armstrong had arrived in this remote corner of North America."

Other locals remember the arrival of the American troops a little differently. Iris Sutton, who was only sixteen when the first soldiers entered northeastern British Columbia, remembers her initial fear and foreboding as hundreds of young American soldiers flooded the region: "You heard all sorts of things about what soldiers do, and that they're wild and the whole bit. At first, I don't think they were too well accepted. But as time went on, we grew accustomed to having them on the streets all the time. They weren't criminals. Generally speaking, I think they were very nice young men."

Crowded towns, hopelessly deficient local facilities, and muddy streets greeted the arriving soldiers. F. Rainey described Fort St. John in terms hardly designed to please local boosters: "Fort St. John was the most dismal little settlement I had ever seen. The one street, lined by dilapidated and unpainted frame buildings, was a slough of mud which had the consistency of axle grease. There were no sidewalks, and the floors of all public buildings were nearly as deep in mud as the street."[46] It did not help that many Americans were gleefully ignorant about the Far Northwest. One American newspaper described Edmonton as "a village with less than 100 permanent residents...the last place to be served by railroad, and persons desiring to continue their travel north must resort to dog sleds."[47]

The crush caused tremendous confusion and chaos. Homes and hotels were crammed to capacity. Harry George recalls that the shortage of rooms extended along the highway: "Accommodation was very limited. People slept under trucks. I've seen trucks drive away in the morning and a man sleeping underneath it in a sleeping bag. Every time a trucker moved off with a load of stuff he always looked underneath in the morning in case someone was sleeping under it." Restaurants, theatres, and other facilities scrambled to keep up with a seemingly insatiable demand. Local post offices, staffed to handle a community of several hundred, suddenly had to deal with the mail sent by and to thousands of American servicemen and civilian workers. Laurent Cyr, the postmaster in Whitehorse, found himself surrounded by stacks of unsorted mail and without the necessary staff. Unable to get authorization to hire additional help, Cyr moved on his own,

The small communities of the Northwest joined in the wartime construction boom. Fort St. John in 1942.

J. GARBUS.

recruiting several workers who helped him attack the growing mountain of mail.[48]

In the chaos surrounding the importation of construction supplies, civilian materials got short shrift. Residents in Whitehorse had particular complaints. Their supplies had been assigned low priority on the White Pass and Yukon Route, leading to endless complaints about the military's command of the railway. C. A. Penner of the Northern Commercial Company complained that "During the past month we have found that fifty percent of our dry goods and gent's furnishing goods have been broken into and sox, mitts, gloves, shoes, shirts, underwear and dry goods have been taken out of the cases. The same applies to candy in which we lost twenty-two boxes of chocolates out of one case, and in the case of fresh fruit it is seldom we get a full case."[49]

The military workers were welcome in the towns, but the townsfolk soon tired of line-ups outside the restaurants, movie theatres, and liquor stores (particularly in Whitehorse). The constant flow of military vehicles through the small towns wrecked the local roads – in Dawson Creek, the heavy pounding destroyed a number of culverts. When several residents complained to the commanding officer of the American troops, a construction unit was hastily dispatched to fix up the culverts and repair the road.

Most of the towns, particularly Whitehorse, benefitted greatly from the Americans' presence. They were recipients of improved roads, water and sewage systems, a telephone network that stretched the entire length of the highway, and numerous other

Winter on the pioneer road near Trout River. J. GARBUS.

amenities. New facilities built and paid for by the army combined with the general prosperity of a region in the middle of a tremendous economic boom to give an entirely different visage to the small, isolated towns of the Northwest. Compare Knox McCusker's later description of Fort St. John to Rainey's early dismissal of the town: "At Fort St. John, in our absence, everything had changed, from a one-restaurant town where the proprietor was his own best customer, the place supported several eating places unable to handle the business. Sleeping places were almost impossible to get, with parking spaces in the feed barn loft selling at $1.00 a night."[50]

Locals had difficulty knowing what to make of the incredible construction boom. Whitehorse exploded from a population of less than one thousand to more than ten thousand within a matter of weeks. One Yukoner could not believe the transformation: "I was dumbfounded with the activity, both military and civilian. There seemed to be line-ups for everything. If you wanted to eat in a café, you lined up; if you went to the theatre, you lined up. As

The construction workers far from their base camp had to sleep wherever they could.
United States National Archives.

liquor was the only thing rationed, line-ups were 3 and 4 blocks long. If you went to a dance there were line-ups....Every shack in Whitehorse was occupied."[51] Dawson Creek's population swelled from about eight hundred people in 1941 to about ten thousand, most of them transient Americans. While it was clear that the people would not all stay, most locals still knew that their towns would never return to their pre-war state. The American army continued its building – of everything from theatres and ball-parks to warehouses and dormitories – and the towns grew like Topsy, with little central planning and little sense of permanence.

What could be built up could just as quickly come down. On the afternoon of 13 February 1943, a fire broke out in a livery barn used as a storage building on Main Street in Dawson Creek. The American army, again offering services not otherwise available in the small town, turned out its fire-fighting units to deal with the blaze. A large crowd of locals, soldiers, and civilian workers gathered, enthralled with the mid-winter distraction. Unbeknownst to the crowd, Miller Construction had stored a truckload of dynamite

Much of downtown Dawson Creek was flattened by an explosion and fire in February 1942.

J. GARBUS

and explosive caps in the building. The fire worked its way through the building and, within minutes, licked at the dynamite. The result was sudden and gruesome: "When the fire reached this cache the building and the fire fighters disappeared in a welter of smoke, burning boards and coils of telephone wire. The crowds of curious onlookers were broken like surf on a beach and debris and flaming timbers showered surrounding roofs with a red-hot rain."[52] Kaare Aspol, Fire Chief for Dawson Creek at the time, explains what happened: "They had stored some forty cases of dynamite in the livery barn, and to prevent the dynamite from freezing they had a stove there, a small stove, and it became overheated. The barn caught fire and so the dynamite, of course, caught fire as well. I was about fifty feet from the dynamite when it exploded."

Chuck and Bob Baxter were just coming into town when they heard the commotion: "Fire trucks like we'd never seen before. Hooks and ladders and great khaki-brown army command or what- ever they were. And we thought, heck, we may as well go and watch the fire. We were between 2 and 3 blocks from the blast when it went. Now several of the black soldiers, I think they were black, were up on the roof – we were close enough to see them –

Ferry crossing the Peace River in northern British Columbia. J. GARBUS.

with wet blankets, beating out the flames in the tar-paper when the blast happened. The roof just opened up on this building, and those guys were gone. I read somewhere afterward that two of them had been blown a block away and through the front of an old livery stable, and the bodies were found in the back of the stable."

An entire block of downtown Dawson Creek was all but obliterated in the resulting firestorm. R. Panter was having supper a few houses down the street from the warehouse: "There was a loud bang, and I jumped up and looked out a window and saw a mushroom cloud going up in the air." Five people were killed by the massive blaze and explosion (local accounts suggest an unconfirmed death toll of twenty-one), and more than a hundred were sent to army and civilian infirmaries, including a number of people who had climbed onto nearby buildings to watch the blaze. Kaare Aspol says, "The explosion was so heavy that it was felt six miles away. The vacuum was great. One man got killed when he was sucked into a building, right through a window. Amazing." Armed troops were rushed onto the site to guard against looting, and civilian and military authorities set to work to rebuild the downtown area. Army messes were temporarily opened to civilians to replace the destroyed cafés.

For Chuck Baxter, a young boy at the time, the event had a bizarre ending. Walking around the site of the disaster, he came across a fifty-pound box of sugar, a great treasure in times of rationing. Realizing its value, he grabbed it, only to be grabbed

The remnants of a pontoon ferry that sank in Charlie Lake, May 1942.

himself: "Here's this great big, black U.S. soldier, with a white stripe on his arm and the white helmet. He said, 'Where you all going with that boy?'" Bravado racing, Baxter answered, "I found this in the ditch." The soldier replied, "That's looting. You beat it. Get out of here." Baxter left, still uncertain of his crime but more concerned about the loss of the precious sugar.

Damage also occurred on a much smaller scale. Whitehorse residents often complained that the visiting American soldiers showed little restraint in their activities. Local citizens had, some years earlier, built a small campground at Whitehorse Rapids. In 1943 they discovered that the kitchen pavilion had been vandalized and shot through with bullets. It was, in the broader flow of events, a small matter, but one that served to heighten tensions between Canadians and Americans.[53]

The first Public Roads Administration office in Fort St. John. J. GARBUS.

There was dynamite of a different sort loose in the North. The arrival of the soldiers in the towns, particularly Dawson Creek, Fort St. John, and Whitehorse, for evenings and weekends, caused all kinds of problems. The soldiers, happy to be away from their camps and among civilians, their inhibitions occasionally loosened by drink, often caused trouble. Sometimes dances erupted into brawls; in rare instances, knives flashed, sending the slower combatant to the hospital. Sylvia Cranston, a teenager when the construction began, remembers, "There were a lot of Mexicans and darkies that came in the first bunch before they shipped them up and there were lots of fights at the dances." Cale Roberts found himself in the middle of such a ruckus: "I was dancing with a girl, trying to get her out the side door, and a guy with a knife got between me and the side door. I grabbed for his wrist and got hold of the knife. Damn near bled to death. Just when I grabbed the knife from the guy, somebody hit him with a whisky bottle. The doctor was up all night, sewing people up." The dance-hall fights led military officials to institute segregated dances – civilian and military – for the early months of construction.

Officers searched for alternative distractions, favouring carefully controlled shows over bars and dances. The USO, remembered best for Bob Hope's shows before the American troops overseas, sent small troupes of singers, magicians, and other performers on long and difficult tours of the Far Northwest. The visitors – particularly the female performers – were enthusiastically

The 18th Engineers building a temporary bridge.

UNITED STATES NATIONAL ARCHIVES.

welcomed by the soldiers, starved for entertainment in their northern outposts. Locals had something to contribute as well. Sylvia Cranston of Fort St. John helped a group of local musicians put on the Alcan Follies: "We had a good stage, and we ordered shiny materials from Edmonton and made costumes for the chorus girls. It was fun. We travelled to Dawson Creek and Grande Prairie with the show, as well."

The army was concerned that sending women into the isolated construction camps might cause "difficulties." Although reluctant to tell the women how to dress, officials nonetheless made their concerns known: "On the question of the girls wearing long or short wardrobe, it has been decided to leave it up to their own judgement. Long wardrobe would really be best, as the set-up here is much different from the States. Some of these boys are in remote places and haven't been out of the rough for a long time."[54]

There was also great disagreement about the proper tone for the entertainment. The officers wanted good clean fun – magicians, singers, and jugglers. The men, not surprisingly, desired more earthy entertainments, and particularly favoured song and dance routines and risqué humour. Comedian Russ Brown earned the ire of a few officers and an Oblate priest for singing about having "caught a cold getting out of a warm bed and going home"

Driving on the pioneer road.

and, in a parody of a famous Bing Crosby song, of "dreaming of a white mistress." Crowd-pleasers, no doubt, but a bit much for moralistic army officers who, in a wonderfully bureaucratic turn of phrase, promised to "obviate a recurrence of objectionable entertainment."

There were legitimate reasons for concern. USO unit no.100 visited Big Delta in 1943 and performed for the soldiers and other workers. After the show, Carl Mondor, the unit's manager, became concerned for the women working with him: "I sensed a situation that is quite common with some officers in that part of the world, and that was the idea to get rid of the two single fellows on the show, get the girls drunk, and force them." Warned, the female performers fled to their quarters, asking Mondor to stay with them. One of the officers, as if on cue, followed the women. He confronted Mondor, demanding that he leave; the women backed up their manager and asked the officer, described by Mondor as having "the brains and ability of a latrine orderly," to leave. The officer "shouted an obscenity about our morals, grabbed me by the arm, threw me across the room and threatened to throw me in the guard house."[55]

There were other forms of entertainment, such as the band from the 18th Engineers. Harold Richardson writes that "hearing this band play in the Arctic dusk, standing in deep snow in a spruce forest while the soldiers filed past an open field kitchen for their evening mess" was a highlight of his northern experience.[56]

Around the larger centres, particularly Dawson Creek, Fort St. John, and Whitehorse, the local women afforded the soldiers an additional distraction. The soldiers, who would be in the field for a year or more, were anxious for female companionship; the women, for their part, were more than a little impressed with the usually polite and well-behaved American soldiers. To provide a break in routine for the soldiers, the army organized dances and recruited local women as dance partners. In Whitehorse, the army sent several panel trucks into town to pick up any girls wishing to go to the dances. Finding volunteers for events in the isolated camps was more difficult. For special occasions, a few women would be flown or driven in for a night of carefully supervised recreation.

Few were surprised when love blossomed between local women and the American soldiers. Sylvia Cranston says that "there might have been a little jealousy because the girls here were certainly interested in the American boys." A number of the romances became serious, resulting in widely celebrated marriages – although project officials were not enthusiastic and did their best to discourage such romances. Rose Botsford was working as a clerk in an engineering office in Fort St. John. Her close friend, Jean Waldon, remembers that Rose's "good figure and pretty hair soon attracted a young American airman. She was the first to marry in the local church. Charlotte [Mens] decorated the church with flowers made by her mother, and we mustered what we could to provide a reception." Jim Sutton, from New Jersey, who was assigned to the 843rd Signal Corps, was dispatched to Dawson Creek. While there he met a young local woman, Iris, whom he married.

More than one northern woman had experiences of a different sort. A young female office worker succumbed to the advances of an American visitor. The man staged a mock wedding, and she thought she was married. When the "bride" became pregnant, the man suddenly remembered that he had a wife and child in the United States. The young woman's child was put up for adoption, and her parents came north to take her home. Mildred Spencer recalls a similar situation: "There was a very nice chap there who became involved with a girl. The man was married, and as a result of this his work was going all to pot. The commander just stepped in and shipped the girl right out." Charles Knott tells the story of a female office worker in Watson Lake who discovered the painful realities of wartime double standards; she was fired for becoming pregnant. The American soldier she claimed to be responsible did not, from available reports, face similar disciplinary measures.[57]

Not all of the men were content with occasional dances, chaperoned social events, and chaste night-time walks through town. A few – a tiny minority – forced their affections on women, most often on Native women. Their behaviour, rationalized in their minds by racist assumptions about Native people, left a severe mark on the women involved. Other men, unwilling to tolerate prolonged chastity but equally unwilling to have recourse to violence, found temporary romance in the arms of a prostitute. There were, in each town, a very small number of women willing to provide sexual favours for the soldiers. One local woman recalls, "I know some of the girls were quite loose, but I don't think they charged." Other women knew a money-making proposition when they saw one.

In such circumstances, it was hardly surprising that a number of prostitutes turned up in the major centres. Prostitutes – "loose women who worked for pay and fun" in the words of Hampton Primeaux – presented a particular challenge to the military police who sought to impose chastity on the more than ten thousand soldiers. For those women willing, or having no choice but, to prostitute their bodies, there was money to be made. According to one local resident, a prostitute in northern British Columbia "took on twenty-one of those niggers in a hotel one night. They

A highway convoy approaching a temporary bridge. PHYLLIS CHURCH.

paid her fifty bucks apiece. Made over a thousand dollars. Took her three hours. And the whites – there was lots of talk they were going to take her out and hang her. She put herself out of business, because the whites wouldn't touch her after that."[58]

There were a very small number of other women – the prostitutes and officials both contemptuously dismissed them as "amateurs" – who were more widely known as "party girls," who charged nothing for their sexual favours. In the more isolated regions, the only women around were Native, adding yet another element into the complex social fabric surrounding sexuality along the highway. The army took steps to control the men's access to the Native women – the Whitehorse reserve, for example, was declared off limits – but they could not stop all such interaction.

The combination of hundreds of American soldiers – aptly described by that great World War II cliché, "over-sexed, over-paid, and over here" – and a few women willing to accommodate their sexual desires guaranteed that venereal disease would develop. Most often, it was introduced by men arriving or returning from the South. The army attempted to control the diseases from spreading by offering free condoms and encouraging sexual hygiene. When there were outbreaks, however, it was usually only the sexually active women who faced the brunt of

An army camp.
WALTER POLVI.

officialdom. A special ordinance in the Yukon, for example, gave the government the authority to hold any person with venereal disease until he or she was healed; this provision was applied almost exclusively against women.

A number of the soldiers found other recreational opportunities in the vast northland. The highway passed through rich and varied hunting grounds and past many fishing holes, and Canadian officials did little to regulate the soldiers' hunting. As one private arrogantly wrote, "We get a lot of fresh meat up here. The fellows shot two moose & a mountain goat here last week. We ate all of it. The meat tastes pretty good. The Canadian Govt. has put out orders that we are not supposed to do any hunting or fishing up here. But who are they?"[59]

Following requests from military authorities, the American soldiers were permitted to acquire resident hunting licences in the Yukon and Alberta; British Columbia was reluctant to change its regulation as was, surprisingly, Alaska. The soldiers quickly overhunted the areas immediately adjacent to the route; as one Canadian official observed, "very few men will wander far from the beaten track without a guide owing to the fear of being lost." In the southwest corner of the Yukon, the intense pressure on the local wildlife convinced Canadian authorities to set aside a large area west of the highway as the Kluane Game Sanctuary in December 1942. For many of the Americans, hunting and fishing was a welcome combination of recreation and respite from army

*Staff of the Ordnance
Spare Part Depot, Dawson
Creek, in September 1943.*

UNITED STATES NATIONAL
ARCHIVES.

food. Moose, caribou, goat, sheep, bear, game birds, and other wild fare showed up frequently on the army mess tables.

The soldiers' desire to hunt provided officers with a built-in incentive scheme. The men could not head out into the bush without a vehicle and supplies, which were provided only to soldiers who were in their commanding officers' good graces. In the Dawson Creek area, the army added the extra requirement that the soldiers be accompanied by a local resident, familiar with the territory. Hunting permits, therefore, served as an effective reward system: "As a reward for long hours of work men were sometimes given a day or two's leave and allowed to go hunting; as a punishment for any infraction of Army discipline or of the Game Ordinance, their leave was automatically cancelled, and their hunting activities, of course, restricted."[60]

The hunters were not always successful. Jim Sutton and three mates went hunting one Sunday. While driving back to camp, one of the men spotted a brown object in the ditch and called out to Jim to stop. Two of the men chased after the animal and, with well-honed military marksmanship, brought the animal down. The men hot-footed it back to the car, and told Jim to drive on. "Well," Jim asked, "what about the moose?" "It wasn't a moose. It was a farmer's cow," was the mournful answer as the brave hunters packed themselves back into the car. The farmer had witnessed part of the event, and confronted the company commander with a request for compensation. Sutton and his pals had to pay for the cow. But when the farmer attempted to hold onto the carcass, the hunters insisted that they now owned the meat. They collected the dead animal and hung it in the cooler – fresh meat, albeit of a different variety than they had anticipated.

The North quickly produced its share of great fishing and hunting stories. Ray Talbot remembers one of the better ones, involving a soldier working near Muncho Lake. The man was returning from a successful evening's fishing, carrying a gunny sack of grayling over his shoulder. His friends, always looking for a chance to play a practical joke on him, watched from a distance. As the man walked on, a bear came up behind and tugged on the bag. Not looking back, the fisherman kept going, calling out, "Go on, I know it's you fellows there." Talbot continues the story, "A couple more steps and another tug. 'Go on. I know it's you.'" He turned around – and found himself face to face with a bear that wanted his fish. He surrendered his catch enthusiastically, but he did not stop fishing. Talbot says, "He went back down there the next day. When he came back home at night he walked backwards and looked around."

With dozens, if not hundreds, of soldiers hunting occasionally, the animal population along the highway corridor dramatically decreased. Wartime over-hunting has been the subject of many inflated rumours – a favourite has American fighter planes strafing caribou and moose, leaving their carcasses to rot in the summer sun. There is no question that a great deal of wildlife was driven away from the immediate highway area, as much by the equipment noise as by hunting activity. One observer commented, "local Indians...stated that they had observed moose moving northwest through Lake Creek valley [through which the highway now passes] in droves for three weeks before the first Army caterpillars arrived on the scene."[61] For the most part, however, over-hunting was limited to the highway corridor.

For enterprising locals, the American invasion presented most welcome opportunities. Hotels opened up in spartan facilities, many homeowners took in boarders, and numerous businesses sprang up to meet the soldiers' many and varied needs. Chuck Baxter, the young lad from Dawson Creek, demonstrated a fine capitalist touch. A troop train derailment in the summer of 1942

Highway workers in 1942.

– no fatalities – presented a superb opportunity that he quickly seized. The soldiers were, for reasons known only to the officers on board, ordered to stay on the train. They soon began to complain openly of thirst. "I knew where to get water," Baxter says. "I raced into town, got a couple of cream cans, chopped up a bunch of ice in a local ice house, threw it in the can, went to the well and pumped it full of ice cold water, went flying down the road, six inches off the ground, down to the train wreck, and the soldiers just gathered around. I didn't charge them, but I got a nickel a cup, something like that. I got American dollars left and right. I got, I don't know, twenty dollars a can for that water. My pants were hanging down, loaded with money from these rich American soldiers, who were just delighted with a drink of ice cold water."

Baxter did not lose his touch. A platoon working on the telephone line close to his home provided a second opportunity. He quickly signed on as their unofficial water boy. Early in the morning, he would collect the men's canteens – twelve to sixteen each time – fill them with water (often mixed with army-issue lemonade powder), and tie them to his belt. He'd struggle back to the work site, the water bottles threatening to pull his pants down to his ankles. He perfected his delivery technique, learning how to fling the full bottles up to the soldiers working on the telephone poles. Baxter made quite a bit of money in all, often gleaning a collection from a crap game held at the end of the day's work.

The soldiers were not always so laid back. This was a military operation after all, and a certain amount of regimentation and ceremony was called for. Still, some civilians, both Canadian and American, found the occasional American military pomp and circumstance to be somewhat out of place. Lake Southwick, who lived in the Fort St. John area at the time, described the arrival of military dignitaries: "There was a lot of respect shown when the brass came down, like a brigadier or something. There'd be maybe two or three cars, flags would be flying on the one the big boy was in. We saw that all the equipment and men were in the very best of order and working. It might not have been what we did every day, but we sure showed it the day when they came through."

Not everyone was so deferential. Karl, a "wispy Scandinavian barber" from Minnesota and head waiter at a civilian construction camp 150 miles northwest of Whitehorse, stopped a party led by Lieutenant Colonel Campbell, section chief, from seating themselves in the mess hall. When Karl found three chairs together in the middle of the hall, he turned to the officers and, in a loud voice, hollered out, "Okay, Shorty," referring to the stout Campbell, "I can fix you up now."[62] While not destined to impress, Karl's actions characterize the civilian response to the American military brass who, after all, were paying for the enterprise. Cale Roberts, a civilian who was in military hospital recovering from meningitis, failed to show the proper deference to a visiting officer: "Saturday morning, all the soldiers were standing up to attention at the foot of their beds, all the ambulatory patients. I guess I was supposed to stand up, too. I was standing at the foot of my bed, just kind of half sitting on the foot of it. This guy with a big moustache, eagles on his shoulder, came up to me and said, 'How long you been here?' 'Oh, about three days.' He said, 'Do you know what these are on my shoulder?'

'Nope.' 'Well, I'm a colonel.'" "'Well,'" Roberts answered, "'I'm a civilian.' They all walked out and never said anything."

The reverse was also true – the soldiers were not always thrilled with the appearance of thousands of civilian workers on "their" project. Enlisted men were particularly distressed to find that the civilians were receiving five times (or more) their wage for doing exactly the same work. One officer could not hide his bitterness: "It's too damn bad the government has to have civilians doing the same jobs as soldiers. The civilians make as much in two days as the soldiers do in a month. I wonder what type of suckers they think we are."[63] The soldiers' anger at the civilian workers extended to those in the lower forty-eight states who were striking for better conditions and wages: "No press agency will make these kids forget the racketeers who called strikes when we were wet, cold, hungry, and in fear of our lives. These boys are coming home though to slug it out with the bastards who have been forcing honest Americans to pay tribute to a union before they were permitted to work, even in war plants."[64]

Surprisingly, the highway project was not surrounded by any real sense of imminent danger. The Japanese forces were far away, defeated at Kiska and Attu in the Aleutians in 1943 by a combined force of American and Canadian troops. The project was not formally guarded, and most of the soldiers operated as

Construction starts on the Fort St. John-Fort Nelson sector.

though they were on safe turf, far from the front lines. For the first year the race to push the pioneer road through to Big Delta drove the soldiers on, but in 1943, as the highway project was steadily downgraded by U.S. military authorities, even the soldiers had difficulty convincing themselves that they were at the forefront of the Allied war effort. Many soldiers silently celebrated the fact that they were far from the battle lines, but others wished for a more prominent role in the war. While there was no overriding sense of fear, comparable, say, to that felt by people in London during the blitz, there was, in Muriel Collip's words, "a singleness of purpose." Thelma Ashby, a civilian working at Fort St. John, remembers, "We didn't really feel close to the war and never thought of a Japanese attack. It was said, jokingly, that we were building a road for the Russians to march down." Agnes Brewster, a Canadian nurse, recalls "an army officer saying that perhaps a time will come when we will need this highway to fight Russia."

Slowly, inexorably, the gaps on the construction maps narrowed. With units working furiously north and south on each of the main sections of the pioneer road, it was only a matter of time before the army crews completed the task at hand. By the end of August, a rough road had been constructed between Dawson Creek and Fort Nelson. The 340th Engineers working south from

An army convoy driving over the rough pioneer road.

Teslin Lake and the 35th Engineers pushing north from Fort Nelson met at a site they named Contact Creek in northern British Columbia on 24 September 1942. By the end of the month the pioneer road was complete through to Whitehorse. Only the toughest section of the road – through eastern Alaska and the southwest corner of the Yukon – remained under construction.

Finally, on 29 October 1942, only seven-and-a-half months after work began, the 18th Engineers and 97th Engineers met south of Kluane Lake. Malcolm MacDonald, British high commissioner to Canada, described the final seconds of the work: "The final meeting between men working from the south and men working from the north was dramatic. They met head on in the forest. Corporal Refines Sims, Jr., a negro from Philadelphia...was

Cutting the ribbon to celebrate the completion of the pioneer road at Soldier's Summit, 20 November 1942.

driving south with a bulldozer when he saw trees starting to topple over on him. Slamming his big vehicle into reverse he backed out just as another bulldozer driven by private Alfred Jalufka of Kennedy, Texas, broke through the underbrush. Jalufka had been forcing his bulldozer through the bush with such speed that his face was bloody from scratches of overhanging branches and limbs. That historic meeting between a negro corporal and white private on their respective bulldozers occurred 20 miles east of the Alaska-Yukon Boundary, at a place called Beaver Creek."[65] The first phase of the Alaska Highway – the one that would become the stuff of legends and stories for decades to come – was complete.

But no construction project is finished until the officials place their mark of approval on the operation. The United States Army Corps of Engineers hosted the official opening of the Alaska Highway on 20 November 1942. It was a fête befitting the completion of a major international construction project – although in bitterly cold weather and an isolated setting – at Soldier's Summit, a short distance south of Kluane Lake in the western Yukon. Journalists from across North America attended, and the ceremonies were broadcast live by radio. A formal dinner was held the evening before, with a suitably northern menu – St. Elias mountain sheep, Takhini corn, Tanana potatoes, moose milk, and sourdough bread with bulldozer butter. Lunch the following day followed a similar theme, with the visitors being served up moose steak à la Donjek, Kluane salad, and horse-camp pudding – fancy names for a combination of local fare and traditional army food – and a substantial improvement on the normal offerings for the soldiers and construction workers.

The ceremonies had a decidedly egalitarian flair. Captain Richard Neuberger wrote, "Everyone slept that night dormitory style. The blue-printed programs were given out and privates traded autographs with colonels. A Negro soldier asked General O'Connor for his autograph, and the General climbed out of his sleeping bag, put on his spectacles, and signed the soldier's program. 'That's the epitome of democracy, isn't it?' Bob Bartlett asked Ian Mackenzie as they watched."

The program, aired over U.S. military radio and by the Canadian Broadcasting Corporation, took place on a blustery day, in temperatures of fifteen below Fahrenheit. An invocation by Father Charles Hamel got the proceedings started. The dignitaries were out in force: Major-General George Pearkes of the Canadian armed forces; J. S. Bright from the Public Roads Administration; the Honourable W. A. Fallow of the Alberta Government; the Honourable Ian Mackenzie representing the Canadian government; Dr. Charles Camsell, Commissioner of the Northwest Territories; the Honourable E. Bartlett for the Territory of Alaska; and Brigadier General James A. O'Connor, commanding officer, Northwest Service Command. A detachment of Royal Canadian Mounted Police – "Their feet must have been as cold as anvils, but they stood as straight and rigid as signal poles"[66] – provided a colour guard.

The formal ceremonies were, by all accounts, quite moving. Four enlisted men – Corporal Refines Sims and Private Alfred Jalufka (the two bulldozer operators who had finished the northern section), representing the Whitehorse sector, and Master-Sergeant Andrew Doyle and Corporal John Reilly, from the Fort St. John Sector – held the ceremonial ribbon. Captain Richard Neuberger described the highlight of the day's gathering: "The ceremony moved toward a natural climax. At its end Mackenzie and Bartlett were given a pair of scissors. These scissors had been especially engraved in Alaskan gold by William Osborne, pioneer resident of Juneau. Fittingly, Mr. Osborne's daughter is Mrs. Joe Crosson, the wife of the Arctic aviator who has saved so many lives. Mackenzie took one blade of the scissors, Bartlett the other. The crowd became tense. Then the

Admiring the view along the Alaska Highway.

blades closed and the red, white and blue ribbon across the road was severed."[67] After the speeches, spirited if somewhat chilled renditions of "God Save the King" and "The Star Spangled Banner" and a benediction by Captain E. May, U.S. Army Chaplain, brought the ceremony to a close.

Neuberger provided an eloquent summary of the event, directed to the press: "It was an episode which will not soon be forgotten by those who participated in it. My own vivid memory of it is the playing of our national anthem by the band at Soldier's Summit. As the music faded away and I looked around me at the stern faces of the American soldiers and at the grim countenances of the Mounties, I felt sure that in such a scene lay the future of the United Nations — that in the ability of us all, Canadian, Americans and Alaskans, white and black, civilian and soldier, to fuse together our efforts in such a project as the Alcan Highway rests the hope of free peoples throughout the earth."[69]

As many workers on the project knew only too well, the events at Soldier's Summit were more show than substance. The highway was not, in a practical sense, really finished, as the next spring would prove. A real highway remained to be built. Even as the dignitaries gathered for speech-making and back-patting, engineers, administrators, and civilian construction crews were working on the upgrading of the Alaska Highway to a proper standard. Archie McEachern turned down a chance to attend the opening ceremonies: "I knew the opening was purely a propaganda effort as there was no way anyone could go more than a very few miles past Soldier's Summit. It was at least 1945 before White River was bridged with any degree of permanence." Lorne Fizzell worked for Greyhound, which had a contract to carry American soldiers between Dawson Creek and Whitehorse, and north to Fairbanks "when roads permitted." Remembering the state of the southern section in early 1943, Fizzell comments that "at that time most of the road was on a temporary road and bridges."

The opening ceremonies were not the only Alaska Highway events subjected to media coverage. The army allowed journalists to interview the soldiers and to document the hectic pace of construction. Clearly, American and Canadian authorities were anxious for the general population to know that everything possible was being done for the defence of North America. Newsreels, radio programs, and numerous newspaper and magazine articles appeared throughout 1942 and 1943, describing the sacrifices and efforts of the soldiers in the North. Richard Finnie, a well-known northern writer, photographer, and filmmaker, produced an hour-long documentary on the Alaska Highway — one that was classified by the U.S. Army and not formally released until well after the war. The journalists' stories were often shrouded because of military secrecy. A CBC story began with the disclaimer that the journalist was "somewhere in the Canadian Northwest," at a location that could not be disclosed lest the enemy learn about Allied activities. The reporter punctuated his pronouncement by thrusting his microphone into the baffle of a bulldozer exhaust — an Alaska Highway variant of the "sounds of freedom."

If there was one damper on the excitement it was the Canadians'
concern about American long-term designs on the region. One
U.S. diplomat observed in 1943, "The only cloud on the horizon
is that the extent of our War Department expenditures and activities in western Canada has been so great in connection with the
war effort that some people in Canada have privately expressed
apprehension. In other words some people feel that we may have a
vested interest there and be reluctant to leave when the war is
over. That is of course nonsense but not all Canadians realize it. I
don't think this is particularly serious. We have done everything
we can to dispel any apprehension on that point."[70] The concern
continued, however, particularly when British High Commissioner
Malcolm MacDonald touched off a diplomatic storm when he
warned the Canadian government about America's "manifest des-
tiny" in the Far Northwest.

The people of the area were more interested in the condition of
the highway than in diplomatic niceties. Descriptions of that early

pioneer road abound, which make note of its temporary nature. C. E. "Red" Anderson, a Canadian engineering student working on the southern portion of the highway, says the pioneer road, "may be compared to present-day seismic lines with a lot of corduroy over the soft muskeg areas, log bridges and sliding, gumbo hillsides where one never knew whether the road was in its normal location or had slid several hundred feet down the hillside. In winter, some of the steeper hills became very hazardous due to ice and snow. One particular hill on the southern end of the road was called 'Suicide Hill' because of the number of wrecked trucks that had gone out of control." It was hard to miss Suicide Hill; a plethora of signs with such *bons mots* as "Prepare to Meet Thy Maker" provided better warnings than did standard highway signs.

Cyril Griffith, who worked closely with the American army during the summer of 1942, has vivid memories of the pioneer road that are a far cry from the prosaic descriptions offered by wartime propagandists. "In dry weather, it became near impassable because of dust that hung for miles between the trees. Night became the best time to travel, as the lights of oncoming trucks would show up around the numerous blind corners and seemed to show through the dust a little better. Farther up the road you got the more natural obstacles. There were wash-outs and slides, and in late June and July numerous bogs would show up in places that the army had got through the year before by corduroying long stretches at a time, or were able to get through on just plain permafrost, but when it was disturbed it would melt down, leaving a trough of mud. We would have to be pulled through by large cats operated by the army personnel, and some of those operators were not too sympathetic with the Canadian civilians."

Portions of the pioneer road were excruciatingly bad. Tight switchbacks, particularly around Steamboat Mountain in northern British Columbia, intimidating hills, and narrow roads carved into the banks of Muncho and Kluane lakes presented truck drivers with innumerable challenges and ensured that the army traffic seldom advanced beyond an aggressive crawl. Most drivers left winter chains on their tires until the chains wore out. On steep hills, drivers worked in tandem with their passengers to inch their way up the incline. While the driver rode the brakes and toyed with the clutch, the passenger would jam wooden blocks behind the tires, stopping the vehicle from sliding back

The first truck to drive from Dawson Creek to Whitehorse. Opening ceremonies at Soldier's Summit, 20 November 1942.

down the hill. On the map the Alaska Highway looked complete; in reality it was anything but.

There were signs all along the Alaska Highway. Watson Lake's sign posts became permanent – and the most famous – but collections of direction signs had sprouted in almost every camp. The signs included the obvious – distance to the next maintenance yard and to the larger centres in the Northwest – the nostalgic – mileage to hometowns and large cities in the south (rarely Canadian) – and the military – mileage to Tokyo and, occasionally, Berlin. At the Alaska-Yukon border, in addition to a small marker denoting the international boundary, a sign informed travellers that they had just left Kansas and were entering Los Angeles city limits. A third sign observed that Tokyo was only 4,289 miles away.

The U.S. Corps of Engineers has long received formal credit for the completion of the pioneer road in record time, but the highway formally opened in November 1942 was also a civilian creation. According to one careful estimate, of the 1,619 miles of the pioneer Alaska Highway, 246 had been built entirely by the PRA, and another 979 miles had been significantly improved by the contractors working for the civilian agency.[71] (The road has been called the Elastic Highway for the simple reason that mileage designations have been inexact and contradictory from the beginning. The pioneer road was longer than the finished highway, which in turn has been significantly shortened by reconstruction since World War II.)

Work on the highway was far from finished. The soldiers stayed on through the winter of 1942-1943, a bitterly cold experience that helped gild the legends of the military construction phase, but most of the units were pulled out the following spring. That winter the bell tents of 1942 gave way to semi-permanent Quonset huts and army-issue barracks. By the spring of 1943, the vast majority of the soldiers had been reassigned – some to Alaskan postings, others to Europe or the South Pacific. A few – quartermaster units, engineers, and support personnel – remained behind to assist with improvements to the Alaska Highway. For the most part assigned to headquarters camps, these workers escaped the hardships and tribulations endured by the early construction units.

The Canadian government had exerted virtually no direct influence over the army's construction activities. The task of keeping a friendly eye on the Americans had fallen primarily to C. K. LeCapelain, an official with the Department of Mines and Resources who was liaison officer between the federal government and the United States Army. LeCapelain's task had been daunting as he struggled to keep up with the military's multifaceted activities. He proved to be up to the challenge, sending a stream of succinct and informative reports to his superiors in Ottawa and providing them with well-informed commentaries on many aspects of highway construction.

On 5 May 1943, LeCapelain's duties were absorbed by Brigadier-General W. W. Foster, who was named special commissioner for defence projects in the Northwest, as the Canadian government

The completed pioneer highway, constructed in a record seven-and-a-half months. J. GARBUS.

scrambled – after most of the important decisions had already been taken – to establish a formal presence in the area. Foster brought a unique background – military veteran, northern traveller, construction engineer, and former deputy minister of public works in British Columbia – to the formidable task at hand. He was, according to one historian, "unofficial guardian of the northwest" from the time of his appointment until 1945.[72]

The soldiers who left took with them from the North indelible memories and a great pride in what they had accomplished. The historian of the 341st Engineers wrote: "It was a privilege to have been on the Alcan. In time of war and in the midst of destruction and ruin, it was interesting to have had a part in the construction of a project that may serve this country well in this war and open new frontiers in the years of peace that follow."[73] The soldiers left behind on the highway, disgruntled at being so far from vital military action, took a dimmer view. With the continual downgrading of the Alaska Highway, from a highest military priority to a project of marginal significance to a political football between the United States and Canada, the remaining soldiers lost much of the sense of urgency and commitment that had sustained them through the hard work of 1942-1943. General F. S. Strong, commander of the Northwest Service Command, could scarcely summon a noble sentiment in his Army Day message to his men: "The mission of the Northwest Service Command to maintain and operate a supply line for the defence of Alaska against the Japanese is no longer of prime importance, so we find ourselves today serving as a 'standby unit,' but we are nevertheless an integral part of the war effort and it is our duty to carry out the instructions of the War Department to the fullest extent of our abilities and I call on you all to continue to give your very best to your job while in this Command."[74]

Most of the soldiers, their minds filled with memories of the chaos and confusion at the railheads, the frenetic advance through the evergreen forests, the baffling engineering and logistical challenges, the bitter winter weather, marvelled at what they had done. Norman Allison, with the understatement that is characteristic of many of the American soldiers, said simply, "I don't believe there are very many people who could comprehend what we did or the times we put up with to accomplish this project." The history of the 18th Engineers summarily rejects the many laudatory pronouncements made about the construction of the 1,619-mile pioneer road: "The highway project was not a miracle. It was, however, one of the outstanding demonstrations of the fortitude, perseverance and indomitable spirit of the American soldier. Long hard hours of work under the worst possible conditions of living were the primary reasons for the accomplishment of the mission. All possible credit for the task should go to the soldier in the field, who, without complaining, often not too well-fed or clothed and with no means at his disposal for ordinary comforts, cooperated with his fellows in hewing out the highway by brute strength."[75]

By the summer of 1943 theirs was now just another behind-the-lines assignment, far from the battles, without the glare of publicity or public interest, all but forgotten by the rest of North America. The army's days of glory along the Alaska Highway had ended; it was now the civilians' road.

5

A Permanent Highway

THE CONSTRUCTION of the Alaska Highway broke dozens of engineering conventions and traditions. Wartime urgency ensured that the standard procedures were tucked in a back drawer and ignored for the duration, and the decision to proceed simultaneously with construction of the army's pioneer and the Public Roads Administration's finished highway created a logistical morass that threatened to engulf the entire project.

The civilian construction phase has traditionally been ignored in highway lore. Legend has it that it was the army that pushed the highway through and conquered the sub-Arctic wilderness. The truth, without detracting from the army's vital contribution, is that the PRA and its civilian contractors and workers were equally responsible for construction. Former civilian workers, somewhat hurt by the constant neglect of their effort by chroniclers of the Alaska Highway, have repeatedly insisted that the full story of the construction phase remains untold.

The Public Roads Administration (widely known in the United States by its Depression-era name, the Bureau of Public Roads), through its able manager, Thomas H. MacDonald, was involved in highway preparations from the very beginning. Its task was to use the pioneer road as the basis for a year-round civilian highway, to be completed by the end of 1943. That it was given this assignment reflected no ill-will toward the U.S. Army Corps of

Public Roads Administration Camp, Fort St. John.
MARION (AMBROSE) CLARK.

Engineers. The Corps had been given a limited assignment, and it had done well. But the major work remained unfinished. It fell to civilian authorities to turn the twisting, muddy, unfinished army route into a straighter, wider, more solid road, with proper bridges and culverts. Its job, less dramatic than the army's, was not the stuff for myth-makers and propagandists, but it was central to the construction of the Alaska Highway.

The highway was far from a normal assignment for the PRA. Historian Heath Twichell has observed: "Many of its best engineers and management personnel from districts throughout the central and western states were quickly diverted from less essential wartime tasks and given new assignments: survey the proposed route; find the best sites for bridge crossings, gravel pits, sawmills and work camps; requisition usable office and storage facilities in the vicinity of the proposed route; scour the United States for unused prefabricated buildings, furnishings of all kinds, tools, construction equipment and winter clothing, and make arrangements to ship it all. Last but not least, they were to select and place under contract the more than fifty construction firms needed to do the actual work."[1] They tackled these jobs under the same wartime manpower and supply shortages that had inconvenienced the Corps of Engineers.

The PRA got off to a racing start. Equipment from the Works Projects Administration and Civilian Conservation Corps was loaded onto trains and shipped, helter-skelter, to Dawson Creek, Skagway, or Valdez. Everything from dormitories to office equipment, aging construction equipment to bedding, was loaded into boxcars and dispatched north. The precipitous action gave every appearance of decisiveness, but it visited a plague of confusion and mismanagement on those in the field. The North had inadequate storage space for the vast quantities of supplies that fell on the region from all directions, and much of the equipment was ill-suited for northern work or was simply not needed. The lack of planning created enormous backlogs at the main trans-shipment points, where civilian material competed with army supplies for space on trains, ships, airplanes, and in the warehouses. Amid the mountains of supplies lay the raw materials for a professional highway project. It just had to be extracted from all the junk.

The government agency had no intentions of actually building the highway. The PRA maintained supervisory responsibility for the project and, under the direction of J. S. Bright, chief engineer, brought a staff of 1,800 workers into the field. With divisional offices in Edmonton, Fort St. John, and Whitehorse, and sub-offices at locations along the route, the agency provided surveys and design and kept close tabs on the construction activity.

Construction work was contracted out to private firms. The highway was divided into four sectors, with a primary contractor assigned to each sector. R. Melville Smith, an Ontario-based company and the only Canadian contractor among the four, was assigned the sections between Dawson Creek and Fort St. John and Fort Nelson and Watson Lake. Okes Construction of St. Paul, Minnesota, was to build the stretch between Fort St. John and Fort Nelson. Dowell Construction in Seattle held the largest contract: 627 miles between Watson Lake and the Alaska border. C. F. Lytle and Green Construction in Sioux City, Iowa, received the contract for the 306 miles of the highway in Alaska. The PRA hired the E.W. Elliott company in Seattle to organize transportation and camp construction. Each of the main contractors, in turn, hired its own sub-contractors to complete specific segments of the project. Most of the sub-contractors came from the same state or province as the principal

The work of construction was dwarfed by the grandeur of the Far Northwest.

contractor; many of the workers, not surprisingly, were likewise hired in Ontario, Minnesota, Iowa, and Washington State.

The contractors faced intimidating tasks. They had to locate and coordinate a number of sub-contractors and manage a difficult construction project hundreds or even thousands of miles from home. They had to build their own headquarters facilities – R. Melville Smith at Dawson Creek, Dowell Construction at Whitehorse, Utah Construction at McCrae, E.W. Elliott at Kluane Lake, and Lytle and Green at Tok Junction – and smaller maintenance and management stations throughout the region. They also had to supervise and look after hundreds of employees; in 1943, at the peak of civilian activity in the Northwest, there were 10,000 Americans and 3,700 Canadians in the area. Cumulatively they unleashed the construction equivalent of several tank regiments on the Northwest: a total of over 11,000 pieces of heavy equipment were active in the region in 1943, including 2,800 dump trucks and 900 tractors.

The civilian contractors worked on a cost-plus basis. Time pressures, combined with the difficulty of properly estimating the cost of sub-Arctic construction, precluded the PRA's normal tendering process. The companies, all managed by men with extensive construction experience, were assured that all of their legitimate costs – wages, food, material, and equipment – would be covered. The company profit would come from the "plus" portion of the equation, for each contractor was guaranteed a management fee for its work. By the end of the war, fixed-fee payments to the contractors had run to more than $5 million. The consortium managed by R. Melville Smith of Ontario, for example, received a total of $817,000. More than $100,000 went to the main company, while its fifteen sub-contractors received less than $50,000 each for their work. Dowell Construction, similarly, received a fixed-fee payment of $150,000; its seventeen associated firms gathered a total of $980,000.

The cost-plus arrangement, the only one possible under the circumstances unless the PRA opted to undertake the entire operation in-house, was a contractor's dream. Any expenses that could get past the project engineers were acceptable; there was little motivation to economize or control expenditures. In addition, initial estimates were rendered meaningless by the lack of knowledge about northern circumstances. To the surprise of few engineers – but to the great consternation of American politicians – massive cost overruns, more than twice the original estimate in the case of R. Melville Smith, were commonplace. Wartime urgency shoved all frugality to the background, at least temporarily.

Project managers quickly discovered that the plans laid down in Washington early in 1942 failed miserably in the field. The army's work had not proceeded as smoothly as anticipated, and the PRA had to redirect substantial resources to the highway through the summer and fall of that year to ensure that the pioneer road was finished more or less on schedule. There were particular problems over route selection. The army's preoccupation with speed took it over the line of least resistance as it pressed northward; the PRA assumed that it was to follow the line best suited to a permanent, maintainable highway. In several places, such as through the Liard River valley, the army and civilian highways diverged by several miles.

Engineers' tempers flared as disputes arose over route selection and construction priorities. The PRA employees were concerned about the standards of design and construction and operated under the original terms of reference, which called for a thirty-six-foot-wide road, and a twenty-four-foot graded surface – the typical, two-lane country road that had become the PRA's principal legacy to rural America. The army's priorities changed constantly as the military urgency to build the road faded in 1943. Original plans and promises were scrapped as increasingly limited American resources were dedicated to new and different tasks.

Brigadier General O'Connor offered a biting assessment of the PRA's work, which reflected the tensions between the two organizations through 1942: "The Public Roads Administration has been a hindrance to the execution of the completion of the Highway. There seems to be no question as to the ability of the PRA employees, but their attitude is such as to slow up the work....They cannot divorce themselves from the idea that their mission is to construct a finished highway of the highest peace time standard. Consequently, they do not push the contractors with the idea of putting through a road suitable for present requirements in the shortest time possible."[2] The army's reassessment of the Alaska Highway created a scramble for the PRA. A finished road would be built, but new directives made it clear that it would follow the army's pioneer road as closely as possible, and would not be up to the formal civilian standards.

Already impressive barriers to construction of a good road were further complicated by weather conditions. The spring thaw of 1943 ravaged the army's road, washing away large sections and knocking out numerous bridges and culverts. The problems had been anticipated. Civilian workers set to work rebuilding the roadbed, culverts, and bridges. However, just as the work was nearing completion, on 9 and 10 July 1943, torrential rains hammered the south-central portions of the highway. Dozens of bridges were washed away in the two-day storm, setting back construction plans by many weeks. One worker heard "boulders bumping their way down the small river that passed near our camp."[3] Huge mud slides, in July and again in August, further hampered reconstruction efforts.

The turbulent waters of the Northwest presented a major challenge to the bridge builders. The Kiskatinaw River.

J. GARBUS.

The civilian contractors also faced huge problems. Their workloads were not evenly distributed, and several of them had difficulty completing their work on schedule. Lytle and Green, which spent much of its time in Alaska, finished early and moved into the Yukon to help out with the northern Canadian sections of the road. E. W. Elliott completed two small sections near Burwash Landing, and Utah Construction of Salt Lake City was drawn in to complete the final sector of the road between Kluane Lake and Beaver Creek.

The PRA engineers worked closely with the civilian contractors, developing a relationship that mixed professionalism, commercial competitiveness, and the strains of northern construction. When she visited a PRA camp in Alaska, Gertrude Baskine observed: "A Public Roads Administration employee always had to stand a lot of gaffing in the camps. More than the Army even, the PRA men were the natural subjects for complaint, ridicule, and wisecracking by that crowd of hard-pressed and hard-ridden sub-contractors, by that mob of hard-living and hard-working men. But the chaffing was only a veneer; it hid real admiration for a job well done, for a system of administration colossal in itself, colossal in the problems it had to face and solve. And, when necessary, the wisecracking quickly became deference."[4]

The army, already concerned about the high cost of a project that more and more analysts were admitting could not be justified, ordered the PRA to pull back further. In April 1943, Brigadier General L. D. Worsham ordered a reduction in the construction standards, to ensure that the all-weather road would be completed by the end of year. Under the army's direction, the agency ordered its civilian contractors to downgrade the quality of the finished surface and to build less permanent wooden structures over streams and rivers. Heath Twichell summarized the lengthy debate: "Most of these orders, particularly those halting major relocations, produced angry confrontations between the army and the PRA. Bright and his subordinates usually took the position that not finishing such improvements was not only wasteful of resources already expended, but shortsighted as well. But the army's argument made equally good sense: why build a better road than you need, particularly when other wartime construction projects now had higher priority?"[5] Major construction halted by the end of October – the highway as of that time would, for the war period at least, be the finished road.

Since it was the army's road, the Corps of Engineers' wishes almost always prevailed. The Alaska Highway that was officially completed in October 1943 was very different than the road promised with so much fanfare the year before. In November 1943, the PRA shut down its basic operations, closing its Edmonton office and retaining only a skeletal staff in the Northwest to deal with the wind-up of construction activity. Like the Corps of Engineers before it, the PRA had done what was asked of it. It had relocated and improved hundreds of miles of the army's pioneer road and had built more than 450 miles of the highway on its own. PRA-directed contractors had constructed at least 130 bridges along the highway route, including the long span across Nisultin Bay at Teslin and the impressive Peace River bridge, which caused considerable wonderment when it was finished in the summer of 1943. Thelma Ashby and some of her co-workers on the southern end of the highway used to visit the site to watch: "While building the Peace River Bridge, which collapsed some years later, the work went on day and night by use of floodlights. We used to sit in trucks on the ice and watch the work, and I, for one, felt very bad when I heard that it collapsed. I felt that I had had a part in building it."

The withdrawal of the PRA and the civilian contractors by the fall of 1943 did not, of course, complete wartime work on the Alaska Highway. Maintenance crews, working under the direction of the army but with PRA assistance, remained on site and kept the highway open year-round for the rest of the war. Each spring and summer brought more wash-outs, necessitating bridge replacements and other repairs.

Several technical points remained to be cleared up: where did the road start and end, and what was its name to be? The initial recommendation of the Permanent Joint Board on Defence had called for a highway from Fort St. John to Big Delta; that was subsequently amended to extend from the terminus of the Edmonton, Dunvegan, British Columbia Railway, and amended once more to Dawson Creek in early May 1942. This minor point had been discussed at some length to ensure that the American military had the authority to maintain the road from Dawson Creek to Fort St. John.

There was also considerable discussion in 1943 of the matter of the name for this road. One name in common usage was Alcan, for Alaska-Canada Highway, a name much favoured by the American authorities for the statement of international cooperation implicit in the title. In the Far Northwest, among Canadians and Americans alike, however, the name Alaska Highway was also commonly used. After the usual careful consideration of such seemingly trivial but potentially volatile matters, Canadian and American officials agreed, through a diplomatic exchange of notes – and not, at Canada's insistence, through the passage of congressional legislation – on 19 July 1943 formally to call the road from Dawson Creek to Fairbanks – and both places were explicitly named in the notes – the Alaska Highway. Alcan did not immediately disappear from the travellers' lexicon and would show up from time to time on tourist maps and advertisements, but it was not the official name.

From the early days of construction, it was obvious that the cost-plus arrangement with contractors was causing headaches. Complaints arose that the arrangement ensured that some of the

companies were less than careful in spending government money. A description of one firm's operation indicates the potential for abuse: "When their trucks and equipment reached our camp, it pretty well all had to be towed there. They then had to order in motors and parts to completely overhaul the units before they would do any work. Ten men were hired to do one man's work."[6] An American civilian complained that a Canadian contractor brought in a wrecked heavy shovel and rebuilt the machine at PRA expense; when the company finished its contract, it attempted to take the refurbished, and now-valuable, shovel back south.[7] Bob Baxter, echoing an opinion of the contractors widely held across the Northwest, says, "The more they wasted, the more they made, apparently. It didn't matter. The truck would break down. They wouldn't bother fixing it; they'd just get a new one in." A Canadian worker was furious about one particularly egregious act of waste: "It occurred in the campsite area when a realignment project meant relocating the fuel pumps and their associated underground tanks. I was elected to free up my cat to pull the tanks out of the ground (after they had been evacuated free). Cables were duly threaded around a tank and attached to my cat. Once the tank was pulled free of its hole, it was allowed to roll onto its side and its remaining contents (hundreds of litres of fuel) cascaded down the slope! The waste seemed atrocious to me, especially when I

The permanent Sikanni Chief River bridge.

UNITED STATES NATIONAL
ARCHIVES.

considered how difficult it was for my father, out on the prairies, to get enough fuel to keep his farm tractor going."[8]

Several workers singled out the Peace River ferry-bridge for particular criticism. Cyril Griffith still questions the operation of the ferries on the Peace River: "There was the Peace River bottleneck in the spring of 1942 I will never forget or understand. We were being ferried across after the breakup as the half-mile-long, crooked and wobbly temporary bridge of the fall and winter was washed out. The ferry was a small barge type pushed by a paddle-wheel, riverboat style, that took about one hour to make a trip. It held six trucks at most. They would go upstream about a quarter mile close to shore then cut out into the current. Then they'd drift down current with full power, cutting across all the time, then come back up current along the other bank. They were working night and day on the bridge and had a huge barge that held about twenty-five trucks at one time and was suspended on cables anchored to the foundation of the new bridge and was powered by the current – an ideal set-up. Before that was ready, in order to get fuel up the road to keep things going all the way along, they ran a pipeline across, temporarily hung on the not-yet-completed bridge, and pumped gas into a small tank on the other side that we loaded out of for about three weeks. Then the big barge or ferry was ready to use. It relieved the bottleneck immediately and the pipeline was discontinued. The big ferry ran for about one week. I made one trip across on it, then the bridge was ready for use. I will never understand the expense or rush to get the big ferry going as the pipeline was a big help to keep the gas moving."

Harvey Hayduck also remembers the Peace River ferry operation. The approaches to the small ferry were tough, particularly during the rainy season "because of the grade and the gumbo." On one occasion, the ferry's motor cut out halfway across the river. Hayduck and the other passengers sat helplessly as the ferry floated downstream for several hours. Finally, a second ferry came and pushed it to shore, where the crew lashed it to some trees. The motor was eventually restarted, allowing the ferry to make the long, slow trip upstream against the strong Peace current.

The contractors' lack of control over expenses extended to the use of construction workers. A Denver man recruited to work on the highway returned with a bitter tale – the accuracy of which it is impossible to gauge – about his time in the North. According to a politician who picked up his cause, the man "worked less than half the time but was paid time and one-half for overtime plus regular time all the time he was there. One time they laid idle for twenty-one days without reason. He made about $1,000 per month without much work but he says the men would rather work as the monotony of killing time ... wears them down and they can't take it long. He quit in disgust and came back here."[9] A Canadian equipment operator agreed: "I do know the contractors were quite happy to have us operating the equipment in order to be able to put in for hours of operation compensation." Some contractors apparently knew how to squeeze a few more dollars out of the U.S. government.

Under such circumstances, it was occasionally difficult to motivate the workers to put in a full day's work. Alex Forgie was responsible for checking progress by civilian contractors: "On one occasion I stopped at the next camp north of ours to find a crew of men either sleeping or playing cards in the maintenance shop. I instructed the timekeeper to dock all of them a day's wages. Six of them called at my office, and I thought they were

Contact Creek, the site where two sections of the pioneer road first joined in the southern sector of the highway. J. GARBUS

going to beat the daylights out of me. After I explained to them they were cheating the taxpayers in the U.S. four of them went back to work and the other two went to the States."

The civilian workers themselves, many of whom reached the field in 1942, had their critics. Soldiers working alongside them quickly discovered that their pay and working conditions were far from equal. Fred Rusk, regimental historian for the 18th Engineers, puts it succinctly: "We were beginning to be annoyed by the presence of civilians whose pay was about ten times our pay, whose work was the same as our work, whose food was better than our food, and who could quit when they felt like quitting."[10]

The end of construction occasioned an accounting of the highway project. The army's pioneer road had, according to official estimates, cost U.S. $19.7 million, or $17,221 per mile. A year after its work was formally completed, the PRA estimated its total expenditure at over U.S. $135 million – the cost of the pioneer road, plus $60.3 million on the Fort St. John sector, $38.3 million for the Whitehorse stretch, and a comparatively paltry $16.1 million for the Alaska sector, for a final cost of $66,160 per mile – well over the $80 million estimated in 1942.

In keeping with the general lack of attention to the work of civilian employees, the completion of the all-weather road was not celebrated. Two construction crews met in the twilight of 13 October 1943 two miles north of Dry Creek. Filmmaker Richard Finnie was on site and filmed the non-event for posterity. Contrasting this event with the Soldier's Summit celebrations held a year earlier, Finnie remarked, "The record should be set straight with a marker or tablet where the Alaska Highway as an all-weather road was finally linked up nearly eleven months later – the work of more than eighty Canadian and American contracting firms."[11]

This bare-bones description of construction costs and processes scarcely does justice to the chaotic and exciting times had by the civilian workers drawn north to work on the Alaska Highway. For thousands of men and hundreds of women, work on the road to Alaska promised high wages, an opportunity to assist with the war effort, and an unparalleled sub-Arctic adventure. For many, it delivered just what it promised; for others, their time in the North was one of hardship, isolation, and frustration, more likely capped by a quick departure than happy memories of a frontier exploit.

Even the seemingly simple task of finding workers for the civilian contractors created massive headaches. The war economies of Canada and the United States were in high gear by the summer of 1942, and there were plenty of job opportunities in the South for skilled workers. Other proposals were temporarily bandied about – using German prisoners of war as labourers and temporarily enlisting civilians into the U.S. armed forces to ensure "positive control" over the workers – but they were dropped like political hot potatoes. To get men and women to go north, however, civilian employers had to offer something special. They could, and did, sell the idea of directly contributing to the war effort, and made much of the allure of the "land of the midnight sun" and the wartime variant of the "Trail of '98." Neither helped much. What got the workers' attentions was the prospect of money – lots of it – and long hours of overtime work. The contractors threw in room and board or charged only a nominal fee for them, meaning that a stint of highway work was nearly all cash in hand. The prospect of big bucks, dangled in front of civilian workers across the Canadian and American wests, was enough to get people on the move.

Cyril Griffith describes the workers as "the adventurous, hard-working type, who could see a few dollars and at the same time help the war effort. Most were in the thirty-five- to fifty-year-old range, as the war had most of our young people overseas at that time. In general they were a good hard-working lot that had just come through the Depression of the 1930s and knew how to work." Gerry Pelletier agrees; speaking of himself, he writes, "I was young at the time and was not scared of work. And I had a lot of bush experience, so for the first time in my life I got paid for what I knew, and I did real well under very tough conditions." For workers still feeling the lingering effects of the Great Depression, which had left many out of work for years on end, the prospect of gainful, remunerative employment – and more than a tad of adventure – was too much to pass up.

The pay was indeed handsome. A worker could assemble a sizeable stake with only a few months of hard, continuous work on the highway. Alex Forgie saw his $70 per month from Massey Harris more than double to $165 per month while working for the PRA. Harvey Hayduck happily surrendered a teaching job – $45 per month for looking after forty-eight children – for twice the wage on the highway.

Many workers came north with a company and remained with the firm for the duration of the contract, but others bounced around, following the best opportunities. The highway contractors soon earned reputations as free-spenders, much to the annoyance of other civilian employers in the area. From Edmonton to Fairbanks, local construction and transportation companies lost labourers and equipment operators; hotels and restaurants had their waitresses and cooks lured away by the boom-time wages offered in the camps. The labour shortage in Dawson Creek was severe: "It was impossible for the village to hire anyone because they only worked for the Army. And that's the reason that if we had any breakdowns, we had to resort to the Colonel for help to do any work in the town."[12] C. J. Rogers of the White Pass and Yukon Route complained bitterly, "Our Labour and Wage situation is all snarled up here on account of the arrival of American contractors who are competing for local labour and paying a wage scale way in excess of that prevailing for any similar kind of work as on [an] airfield here....If this scale for local labour is maintained it is going to disorganize all work in the territory, government or private."[13] Such practices caused serious problems in the mining industry; several Klondike dredges had to shut down for want of skilled workers.

Finding bodies for work on the highway was relatively easy. Locating men and women who could properly handle the assigned tasks was something else. The haste to hire workers meant there was no time to check references or qualifications. Many applicants, anxious to earn one of the legendary pay cheques being offered on the highway, gave themselves instant credentials, and learned how to operate the equipment on the job. A number of drivers and equipment operators had little direct experience with the equipment they were being paid to operate. Frank Speer, who was in this situation himself, comments that "at the start men were sent to do work that was really out of their element. Road foremen were building latrines, jewellers trying to operate shovels and draglines, and, I might add, store managers trying to operate bulldozers. There were very few accidents although some very close misses."

Rumours soon spread – rarely more than that, but then rumours make the best stories – that work on the Alaska Highway had become a prime refuge for draft-dodgers. The Royal Canadian Mounted Police in the Yukon investigated the accusation and concluded that the number who might have been avoiding military service was "extremely small."[14] Duncan Bath, a Canadian heavy equipment operator, says: "On the highway, though not particularly in our camp, there were quite a few men with shaven heads and big, bushy beards. It was generally accepted that they were more or less in disguise." It made a good story, and there may have been a few such cases, but the American official's comment that "Every American citizen we bring north is 4F [unfit for active service, a military classification] or over thirty years of age" was pretty much on the mark.[15]

The construction crews comprised the young and old, skilled and rookie, reliable and questionable. Gertrude Baskine, who travelled along the Alaska Highway during its construction, describes the group assembled for dinner at a camp in Dawson Creek: "There were at least twenty men to one woman – these latter so scattered as to be completely lost. Most of them, if not realizing the ideals of Rubinstein or Arden, were clean and tidy. The men were of every size, shape, color, age, humour, expression, state of

*Army payroll staff in
Whitehorse, March 1945.*
PHYLLIS CHURCH.

cleanliness or slovenliness, imaginable. Next to a nice young fellow shaven and white-collared, would be an old patriarch with bearded face and exposed chest; next to a dignified elderly man spic and span in flannels and clean sport shirt sat a young squirt – red beard sprouting in a circle from chin to temple, suspenders slack over gray sweatshirt. I had heard that the North was the land of democracy; one could have said that with regard to raiment and personal appearance it was that of anarchy."[16]

The problems the army had encountered over the absence of women were magnified as the civilian workers poured into the region. The soldiers could, reluctantly and with much complaining, accept chastity as one price of patriotism; the civilian workers were more reluctant to tolerate prolonged absences from wives and girlfriends.

Several hundred female employees joined the workers' migration to the Far Northwest, drawn by the prospect for adventure, high wages, or a startling change of venue. They came to work for the army and for civilian contractors, particularly in the headquarters offices. The more adventurous found jobs in the offices, laundries, and kitchens of the highway camps. Nurses found work in the principal towns and the larger camps. A few women successfully challenged the male stereotype and proved their abilities as truck or jeep drivers. But, while American and Canadian women elsewhere across the continent were successfully tackling a full range of "men's" jobs, the vast majority of the women in the Northwest had to be content with more traditional employment. There were precious few Rosie the Riveter types along the highway, although this reflected more the men's unwillingness to be innovative than the women's abilities.

The women faced other forms of discrimination. They were not always well-received by the residents. Thelma Ashby says that the people of Fort St. John looked askance at the women workers. "I was the thirteenth girl to be hired by the PRA and at that time there were two hundred men in the camp, so, of course, we were wide open for gossip." Women also received less pay than their male counterparts – even if they were doing exactly the same jobs. According to Muriel Gwen Collip, black women were not welcomed by other Americans in the construction camps. One such worker arrived at Collip's nursing station, escorted by six or seven black soldiers, and asked to be put up for the night. She had apparently been made to feel so unwelcome she was leaving. Collip pointed out that the "office working girls from the American Deep South actively verbalized their unwillingness to live or work with black people." In other camps nationality, not race, established the dividing line. Colleen Bafford remembers: "There were some Canadian girls living in our dorm, but we didn't have much to do with them. They seemed to stick together, and we did the same. There were five of us American secretaries who spent most of our time together."

The camps where most of the women workers were employed were markedly different from the construction stations stretched out along the Alaska Highway. The administrative centres had ready access to the pick of the supplies, from office equipment to food, and had large, semi-permanent barracks and offices. The engineers, office managers, secretaries, and other staff also had access to excellent recreational facilities, including skating rinks, ball diamonds, and movie theatres. There were few of the outpost hardships that characterized life in the construction camps.

Accommodations for highway workers, men and women alike, were spartan.
MARGARET (PERCIVAL) STUART.

The women were, as an unofficial part of their duties, expected to add some spice to the lives of the highway workers. The many dances, parties, and social gatherings lost their lustre if the women were not present. A newspaper account describes a dance at the Melville Smith camp at Fort St. John: "The first dress-up affair of its kind in the wild, rugged country through which the road stretches brought thanks from the soldiers who really appreciated the 'all-out effort' of the girls to make the occasion a gala one." The women in this case were five office workers from Toronto – Dorothy Brown, Laddie Davidson, Kay Huff, Charlotte Mens, and Jean Waldon – who passed many hours talking with the American and Canadian workers: "But most of all the boys like to talk – talk about home, their best girl or the latest letter they received. The girls are good listeners, but if the boys are shy, well, there is always Chinese checkers or dominoes!"[17]

At the height of construction in 1943, there were 39,606 civilians working on defence projects in the area, more than 30,000 of whom were Americans, who were treated quite differently from the Canadians. Americans working within Canada were subjected to various medical and security checks; Canadians faced the even tougher regulations imposed by the War Labour Board, which governed all aspects of the workplace, from wages to recruitment of workers. As well, Canadians and Americans worked on different pay scales – the Americans', unregulated, was considerably higher – and the imposition of wage zones

Highway workers provided most of their own entertainment – a production of "The Shooting of Dan McGrew," Muskwa camp, 1943.

MARION (AMBROSE) CLARK.

meant that people working in more northerly and more isolated postings were paid higher salaries.

Canadians frequently complained – under their breath, in good Canadian fashion – about the Americans' higher wages. One union official pulled no punches: "The Canadian has no chance here, all the best of the jobs are taken by the Yanks and the difference in wages is too great. The Yanks get away with almost murder....I know of cases where they took Yanks and put them over the top of Canadians that were fully qualified for the advance and paid them more money."[18] Another Canadian unionist, Gerald Belanger, said: "Through a padlocked income that is already heavily taxed, the Canadian worker finds himself in a position where he must, not by choice, but by forced necessity, adopt a much inferior position in the society, as well as in the economical life of the community, a position much inferior to that adopted by his American co-workers who are performing the same duties for a much higher wage."[19] Alex Forgie was "not too happy about making a lot less than the Americans." Frank Speer, on the other hand, wrote: "We envied them the higher pay, but that caused no problems." Speer must have been an exception, however, as there were numerous official and informal criticisms by Canadians about being paid less than the foreigners. The numbers certainly support the critics: the average hourly wage for Canadian workers, reported in April 1945, was 86¢ an hour; Americans received, on average, $1.57.

Canadians repeatedly asked for comparable pay scales, but were turned down by the War Labour Board for fear that workers in the South would demand similar increases. For this, and other reasons, many American employers tried not to mix Canadians and Americans. One official with the Northwest Service Command justified the decision to keep the two apart: "We didn't feel they [Canadians] worked like our people, or thought like our people....It created a lack of harmony in an office to have two different scales of wages for people doing the same work."[20] Workers on the highway, in contrast, almost unanimously declared that they got along very well with individuals from the other country.

Most of the workers stayed only briefly in the North, discouraged by the isolation, cold, and hard work, they quickly retreated southward. A few were angered by their harsh treatment at the hands of foremen. Ray Talbot recalls: "Coming out of the hungry thirties, the bosses in Canada held a big whip over the men, and they used it. They figured they could use it on the Alaska Highway all the way through Canada. All of a sudden a lot of men quit because they wouldn't take any of that abuse." Cale Roberts concurs, describing one particularly hard-driving boss: "I know I got fired because I refused to work on Sunday. The foreman came along on Saturday night and told me to be there at seven in the morning and I said, 'I don't think so.' He said, 'Why?' I said, 'I got a date.' He said, 'You keep your date. But don't come back on Monday.' That was that. But that was after working a sixty-hour week." "Contractors," one official wrote, "had three crews, one working, one going and one coming to the job."

Those who stayed disdainfully referred to the evacuees as "termites," and chided them for their lack of fortitude. And workers left in very large numbers. The turn-over rate among Canadian workers was almost 20 per cent per month, just under twice the rate for Americans.[21] Once back home, the termites revelled in telling exaggerated stories about northern hardships – the cold got colder, the hours of work longer, the mosquitoes larger, the black flies more persistent, and the bosses more intractable – making it that much more difficult to recruit replacements.

Contractors made concerted efforts to stem the hemorrhage of workers. They encouraged a "cooling off" period, in hopes that the enticement of continued high wages would overrule memories of hardship and deprivation. Okes Construction and its sub-contractors had a more pragmatic solution. Employees had ten dollars deducted from each pay cheque, until a pot of fifty dollars per worker had been set aside to cover the costs of "repatriating" a former employee to the United States. Such was the movement that the company operated a regular shuttle service, three times per week, from Fort St. John to Dawson Creek; the departing workers then travelled by train to Sweetgrass, Montana, or Noyes, Minnesota. The company gave each man ten dollars to cover the cost of food on the journey.[22]

It is difficult to capture the plodding, unbroken work experience of most of the highway workers. For the majority, one day melded into the next, as they completed the same task over only slightly different terrain. Few travelled very far along the highway; most saw only a stretch of a few hundred miles. Working ten to twelve hours each day, the men clambered aboard their machinery early in the morning (or late in the afternoon if they had drawn the evening shift) and stayed there throughout much of the day. Duncan Bath remembers, painfully, "having a pretty raw posterior from sitting side-saddle on the armrest of the cat, so as to be able to operate the LeTournear – the cat bumping and clawing its way along. That armrest was in constant and, often, violent motion."

The civilian workers faced the same extreme conditions – mud, cold, voracious pests, and long hours of hard work – that the soldiers had encountered before them. At the time, the workers had few words of kindness for their circumstances, but in later years, the men would make light of the privations. Surveyor Willis Grafe says there was only one way to deal with the bugs: "The only reasonable remedy when at work was to wear two thicknesses of clothing and head nets. That way each time you moved your body it would torture their beaks and the face was protected." Comments at the time, not surprisingly, were far less polite.

Living conditions were primitive at first, improving slightly over time as proper dormitories were erected at the major camps. Telephone workers based in northern Alberta, who were wiring the telephone service connecting Edmonton and Fairbanks, found themselves encamped in railway boxcars.[23] Robert Black, who worked north of Fort Nelson, remembers: "Our first lodg-

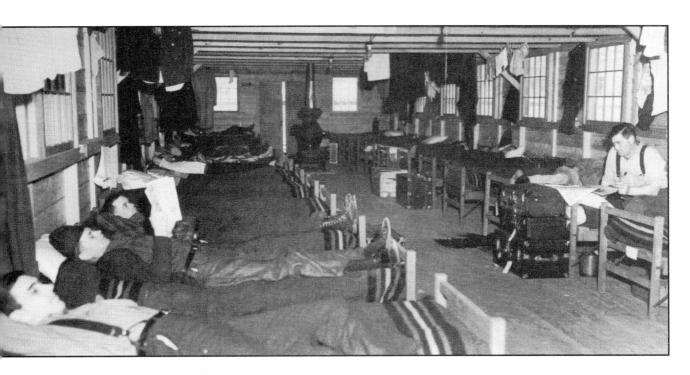

A workers' dormitory.

ings were soldiers' tents with flaps, dirt floors, green wood in the camp stoves, in thirty- to forty-below weather. Our company set up their own saw mill, so gradually the camp site took on better living conditions, framed buildings, dormitories with flooring, a large dining hall." Even when improvements were complete, the workers tolerated less than ideal circumstances. Duncan Bath was stationed about a hundred miles from Fort Nelson; his description of his camp strips away any illusions of grandeur: "We lived in bunkhouses. The one I was in had, I would say, twelve to fourteen bunks in one room. The bunks were iron-frame single cots with a 'mattress,' top and bottom sheets, and a grey blanket with a pillow. Nothing happened to any of this over the four months I was there! My belongings were under my cot. There was a small area at one end of the bunkhouses where one could take a bath in a round, steel tub. We ate at long bare wooden tables in the central cook shack." The isolated camps were the least attractive, as Joe Garbus recalls: "Away from headquarters, the construction camps were insulated, tar-paper constructions with wood stoves for heat. Generators provided electricity and also served to heat the privies."

Camp facilities were rustic at best. Ray Savela says this about the washing facilities: "The bullcook heated water in a barrel on a campfire for us. We dipped a bucket in the barrel for wash water in our tent. We had only a wash basin to wash in; a bath was not

A MacKay Construction camp. J. GARBUS.

easy to take. I was too shy to strip down in front of the guys in my tent for a sponge bath. I tried washing better when I was alone. Being in the service later takes all this shyness out of you." Paul Warren experienced the whole spectrum of conditions, from "spreading my bedroll in the shelter of a lean-to tarpaulin, to a canvas cot in a wall tent, to a steel cot with a mattress pad in a warm, waterproof building. The latest accommodations were in a group of office and shop buildings, bunkhouses, and a mess hall, equipped with pit latrines and showers."

Conditions were somewhat better in the larger camps, but only after the contractors had time to complete the quarters. In the crowded towns, where rooms were at a premium, living accommodations were basic, at best. A group of American "girls" – so-described in the press – in Whitehorse lived "in a private house, in an unheated room, and the temperatures were already hitting 20 below. The house had no running water, no bath, and canvas cots for beds. They made a deal with a man at the Public Roads Administration barracks to take a bath in his quarters while he was at work."[24]

For some crews, assigned to specific tasks and not tied to an individual site or section of the highway, work on the road meant almost constant movement. John Mueller, who worked with a mobile soil laboratory, had a markedly different experience of the highway, closer to the surveyors' than the construction workers'.

The crew's assignment was to find the valuable pockets of gravel and fill needed for highway construction in the area between Fort Nelson and Watson Lake. Working out of tent camps, Mueller's crew encountered the worst of the sub-Arctic winter. To his amazement, he even came upon a river that froze from the bottom up. Under conditions of extreme cold, ice forms on the rocks and twigs on the river bottom. It expands quickly, leading to the unusual circumstance of a flood in mid-winter, with the thermometer reading forty below.

Mueller and his crew often had to move their camp on short notice and at times of extreme cold. Doing so presented exceptional challenges, even danger, particularly as there was not enough room in the truck's cab for all the men. Showing the kind of enterprise that marked highway workers, they erected a tent on the back of their truck, leaving parallel poles sticking out behind the vehicle. A wire frame and asbestos pad were attached to the poles, and a stove, with a fire burning inside, was lifted onto the structure. The aerodynamics of the truck ensured that the heat – and unfortunately most of the smoke – was drawn back into the tent, keeping the men bundled inside relatively warm while driving along the highway.

The cold was the workers' most bitter enemy. Winter temperatures often dropped to fifty below, cold enough to freeze the equipment and kill the unwary. Strict regulations, including the establishment of relay stations at fifty-mile intervals along the highway to keep tabs on all traffic, headed off most serious problems. On rare occasions, however, drivers whose trucks broke down on the highway ignored the standard injunction to stay put, and pushed on on foot, believing that they could reach the nearest camp with relative ease. Many of those who attempted this foolhardy manoeuvre paid a severe price, measured in frozen toes, fingers, or faces or, in a few cases, death by freezing at the side of the Alaska Highway.

Cold interfered with even the most basic of tasks, such as keeping the equipment operational. Vehicles and bulldozers left unheated could freeze solid in no time at all. Truck drivers soon learned to carry extra generators to ensure that the electrical systems worked steadily, and a spare axle because they broke with startling regularity. Some drivers kept warm in their cabs by heating large rocks in a fire and placing them by their feet.[25]

Construction slowed to a crawl during the winter months. J. GARBUS.

Wood alcohol was mixed with the gasoline to keep gas flowing through the lines, although this was not always effective according to one highway driver: "Going down hill for long distances at a time our motors would cool right down until the alcohol would thicken, and then would not circulate when the up hill came." Even with these precautions, rear ends and transmissions would routinely seize in extreme cold. Cyril Griffith described the standard solution to this perennial problem: "In those temperatures it was common practice for us to carry at least four tin cans – tomato cans or suchlike – to put fuel oil or gas in. We'd light it and put it under the rear end and transmission every time we stopped, as the heavy grease that we needed to use for that type of extreme work would freeze solid if left to cool off – a practice the insurance companies of today would frown on I am sure. However, I saw relatively few fires caused from that practice."

Chuck Hemphill's crew had a different solution to the problem of slow-starting vehicles. They worked on the assumption that only one truck had to be kept warm. The men dug a trench in camp and covered it with sheet metal, keeping both ends of the trench open. A fire was built underneath the metal, and one truck was parked over the heater and left there for the evening. In the morning, the truck was sure to start easily, allowing them to jump-start the other vehicles in camp.

J. Garbus recalls that men often slept in camp with their hats on, it was so cold inside the cabins. "With the tin stove in the middle of the room glowing, red hot, each roofing nail used to attach the sheeting to the studs had a button of ice that never melted from November to June." Thelma Ashby's accommodation in Fort St. John, in one of the ubiquitous Quonset huts, was little better: "Each person had a small bedroom, walls built to within two feet of the ceiling. There was a coal-oil heater at each end of the building and in the middle, and the heat from these was supposed to pass over the walls and heat the rooms. Not very satisfactory!"

A few workers had quick, if not necessarily safe, ways of dealing with cold. Cyril Griffith remembers: "One cold morning Wally [Newman] came into the bunkhouse in the early hours where I and two or three others were sleeping to wake us with a yell. Someone yelled, 'Light the fire,' so he did just that, with a tin of gas, blowing the lid off the air-tight heater and sending flames half-way to the roof – very effective for getting men out of bed quickly." Chuck Hemphill, living in a small three-person tent near Muncho Lake, packed moss around the bottom of the tent walls to cut the draft. Even then, the men made careful preparations each evening for a quick fire the next morning. The ingredients were basic: a pile of kindling and a can of diesel oil. Hemphill says, "Come morning, the idea was to leap out of bed, throw the kindling in, dump the diesel oil in, toss in a match, and jump back into bed. Within short order the lid on the stove was whoofing up and down, and there was a great roaring as the sides of the stove became cherry red, then white hot. Lo and behold, the tent became very cosy in spite of the temperatures outdoors."

Construction engineers and contractors devised effective means for dealing with the extreme cold. Charles Knott was assigned to work on the Beaver Creek bridge, near the Yukon-Alaska border, in the winter of 1945-1946. Pouring concrete at sub-zero temperatures proved difficult; the work site had to be covered in tarps. A heater was placed under the tarp, and kept running continuously to ensure that the concrete did not freeze before it set. Even such innovations could only go so far. When the thermometer registered minus eighty-two Fahrenheit at Snag, and close to minus seventy-five at Beaver Creek on one bitter day, work mercifully halted.

Spring was, in other respects, almost as bad. As the winter snows melted, the ground turned to mud, which the workers carried

with them into the trucks, cook sheds, outhouses, and living quarters. It was so thick that, in Elizabeth Golata's wonderful phrase, one soon "had a quarter-section on each foot." Fatigued by long hours behind the wheel of a truck or at the controls of a pull blade, few workers had the time, energy, or inclination to deal properly with the mess.

If there was a saving grace to the rustic camp life, for many it was the food. The contractors, protected by cost-plus contracts, and realizing the importance of keeping the workers as happy as possible – if only in their bellies – spared little expense in providing the best meals possible under the circumstances. There were, inevitably, shortages, and the produce and meat was not always fresh, but the cooks did their best. Alex Forgie remembers that this was one area where "we lived like kings. Our cook used to be the chef of the Brown Derby Restaurant in Los Angeles. We had plenty of steak; the camp would get as many as fifty sides of beef in one shipment. There was plenty of fresh fruit, dehydrated potatoes, powdered milk. No ice cream." The better places, such as the Campbell Construction Company's camp north of Fort Nelson earned an enviable reputation among the truckers, some of whom planned their daily journeys so as to ensure supper at the station. Walter Nelson remembers one camp, where he had his first experience with real southern

Hearty highway fare!
U.S. ARMY CORPS OF ENGINEERS.

cooking. "One man had been a chef in a big southern hotel, and it was just beautiful. Sweet potatoes and molasses. I'll never forget it. And ham. Boy, could that man cook!"

Not all the memories of Alaska Highway food are positive. One cook's experience making hotcakes still leaves Roy Talbot shuddering: "She made hotcakes in the morning. Big bowl under her arm and throwing them on the griddle, saying, 'Oh dear, oh dear.' She kept making the cakes and saying 'Oh dear, oh dear.' One of the other cooks said to her, 'What's the matter with you?' She said, 'Well, I've got a hell of a head cold and my nose has been dripping in the hotcakes.' But we never found out about it for months." There was a saving grace: "But, you know, she was a good cook; a real good cook, and a fancy cook." Just not when she had a cold.

Transportation delays along the Alaska Highway caused annoying food shortages. One spring, the temporary bridge across the Peace River washed away in the run-off, and bad weather prevented planes from making it through to Fort St. John. The workers lived on Spam – "breakfast, lunch and dinner. When a plane finally came, it brought us several cases of mustard pickles, which we attributed to government efficiency."[26] A number of camps suffered through shortages. Duncan Bath says, "The quantity of food was down, as was variety. And, of course, once one person started complaining, there was an epidemic." Others avoided the army camps whenever possible, preferring the better fare available

The highway truck drivers were an intrepid and resourceful lot. J. GARBUS.

at the contractors' cook houses. One breakfast at an army camp lingers in Cyril Griffith's memory: "On one occasion when it was quite cold, myself and another driver were on the end of the line. We had to pull frozen pancakes out of the way to get to cold ones, and break the ice on the syrup container."

For another group of workers, the independent truckers who began moving supplies along the highway as early as 1942, there were no camps or proper facilities. They could stop in the highway stations while on the road, but were on their own in Fort St. John or Dawson Creek. A group of truckers' wives operated a small restaurant in Dawson Creek for the drivers: "It held about ten people if it was full – and it was most of the time. It was stools around a counter and was very good and well run – a kind of home for us poor bachelors."[27]

The civilian workers and the small U.S. military staff remaining along the highway after 1943 benefitted enormously from the recreational facilities constructed for the army. The bowling alleys, theatres, hockey rinks, meeting halls, and libraries left behind by the Corps of Engineers in the larger camps provided a full range of recreation for the remaining workers. Even so, innovation was still essential. The civilians in Fort St. John had a recreation hall but no other facilities. They chipped in ten dollars each and bought a Wurlitzer; the five-cent-per-play machine soon returned the investment. Thelma Ashby and her boss, who had put himself through college teaching ballroom dancing, would go to the recreation hall on Sunday afternoons and dance. Soon twenty other couples would join them.

The Peace River bridge.
PHYLLIS CHURCH.

The list of activities was impressively long, including hunting and fishing for the more adventurous, competitive sports, bus trips to outlying "beauty spots," religious gatherings, card games, picnics, hikes, and dances. One enterprising truck driver had a trapline that ran the length of the highway to Whitehorse. R.C. McFarland remembers it as the longest trapline in the world. Along the southern portion of the highway, the noted Anglican evangelist Monica Storrs provided spiritual solace, and William Brown, a Protestant chaplain who worked out of the Whitehorse area, preached the length of the highway. His trademark was a small chapel built onto the back of his truck.

In the isolated construction camps, there were fewer facilities. One civilian camp a hundred miles outside of Fort Nelson had only a gymnastics high bar and a horseshoe pitch for the workers. The absence of better facilities was scarcely noticed. According to Duncan Bath, "With twelve-hour shifts, one did not have a great deal of time to do other than eat, sleep, and work." Leisure activities in camp consisted of letter-writing, walking (although seldom far from camp), and card-playing. Gambling was popular in both camps and towns, and was tolerated by Canadian and American authorities so long as the stakes stayed small and no full-time hustlers tried to muscle their way into the business. One worker, returning south after three months on the highway, stopped off at Dawson Creek. He had the bad luck, and poor judgement, to fall in among professional gamblers. He lost all of his money and had to return to work on the highway. When news of the man's misfortune reached authorities, they moved in quickly to close the gambling shop down.[28] One equipment operator had much better luck and wisely avoided the gambling joints. He saved all his government cheques and carried them with him back to Colorado. Within a short time he purchased a gas station, store, and restaurant, paying cash for them all.[29]

The civilian workers, like the soldiers before them, found temporary distraction in drink. Liquor rationing remained in force throughout the region, limiting supplies and giving a big boost to the bootlegging industry. The British Columbia government's liquor store in Pouce Coupe was a popular destination for workers on the southern portion of the highway; Whitehorse and Fairbanks – described by a 1944 visitor as "a frontier town with a façade of modernity"[30] – were the drinkers' Meccas on the northern section. The B.C. store seemed to have a constant line-up: "It was a little bitty building and room for very few inside so when we went...for our monthly quota, there was a line-up out of the building, down the front of it, and all the way down the side of the building."[31] One of the resident engineers near Fort St. John was a successful gambler, and when he had accumulated a sizeable sum, "he would take off for Pouce Coupe where the closest liquor store was and spend it all on liquor. The camp didn't get much done for a couple of days." He had another, less palatable, means of meeting the demand: "He also had a still in the back of our office where he made alcohol from dried fruit he got from the kitchen."[32]

One camp foreman brought whisky into camp, and quickly got into his cups. Ray Savela witnessed the resulting unprofessional display: "In the morning I went to have breakfast in the big tent, our foreman was standing on the table challenging anyone to fight with him. He was singing, 'I am Jesus, little man, yes by Jesus Christ, I am. I am safe in the arms of Jesus.' As fate would have it, who should be standing at the door of the tent witnessing this escapade? None other than Mr. E. W. Elliott and the head man of the Bureau of Public Roads. The BPR man wanted to fire him on the spot. Mr. Elliott talked him into letting him stay, only demoting him to dumpmaster."

Liquor had another important function: it was accepted currency in the Northwest. In a time and place where money, parts, and equipment were plentiful, it was the rare item – a bottle of alcohol – that held the greatest value. Cyril Griffith remembers: "Whisky became the only medium of exchange – a bottle with the seal still intact, no matter what size, was worth a new motor or whatever you needed from the army."

The men suffered tremendously through the abstinence enforced by prolonged separation from wives or girlfriends. Some found solace in the arms of prostitutes, although Joe Garbus's sharp answer to a query about "soulless love" along the highway says a great deal: "Prostitution? With whom?" The regulations imposed during 1942 remained in place, but the increased number of civilians travelling the road and the decision to allow women into the highway camps made policing illicit sex more difficult. One man, travelling with his putative niece, was turned back a short distance up the highway when army officers decided he was really a pimp. One camp waitress discovered how profitable a sideline prostitution could be: "She went up and waited on tables, and she also sold herself to some of the officers and contractors. In three months' time she made enough money to go back and get married."[33]

Most men were content with the companionship and friendship of local women. In each of the larger centres, teenagers and young women socialized with the workers, adding a bit of spice and diversity to an otherwise all-male environment. Harvey Hayduck says, "I was young then, and in a short time befriended quite a few girls – some very pretty, I must say. We were just friends, spending spare time together, enjoying each other's company, nothing else. But there was no serious attachment to anyone." Ray Savela had similar experiences at Fort St. John: "I met two nice young girls, a little younger than me, where I brought the cook's laundry. I wanted to get better acquainted, but their mother never let them out of sight, and we were too shy anyway. I did enjoy their company and looked forward to laundry day."

Dora Easto and her friends were inveterate horseback riders and hikers and constantly explored the hills and valleys around Fort St. John and, later, Whitehorse. One day, she and three women friends were off hiking and stumbled across a small log cabin, with a sole male inhabitant. Unbeknownst to them, the man had been advertising for a wife in the newspapers. When they knocked on his door, he met them with a mixture of delight and surprise: "I asked for a woman, but I didn't expect so many!"

A picnic along the highway.
PHYLLIS CHURCH.

For the workers in the larger camps, once the urgent pressures of construction lifted in 1943, life settled into a very pleasant routine of manageable amounts of work, virtually no sense of the immediacy of war, and abundant recreational opportunities. The Whitehorse publication *Northwest Newscast*, in the cheery, friendly prose of military publications, urged the remaining workers to take advantage of a once-in-a-lifetime opportunity: "You will find here much of interest and much of value that you may recall in some distant future with pleasure and not a little regret. For here, as in few other parts of the world, there is much for the nature lover to gain in relaxation, sport and social benefit. You can, in your leisure moments, visit famed Lac LeBarge, take that week-end jaunt to Carcross at the head of Lake Bennett, or fish in the Lewes River and its tributaries. And when it's all over and done with, and you have returned to your pre-war status, there will be for many of you regrets that you did not have a longer time to savour the many keen delights of this fabulous country. So, a final word of advice to you newcomers; make the most of this land in the fleeting time you are here; take advantage of the scenic beauty and this real down-to-earth outdoors."[34]

The construction of the Alaska Highway represented more than the simple carving of a trail through the vast expanses of the Far Northwest. By bringing thousands of civilians into the region, and disrupting long-established social and economic relationships, the highway signalled a clash of the old Northwest and the new. It became, within a few months of the start of work, a symbol of the modernization of the North. But modernization meant forcing a region once relegated to the past to come face to face with its future.

Native people, many of whom found work as guides in the early stages of highway surveying and construction, found new work with the civilian construction crews. Frank Speer says the Indians around Teslin "had been trappers before the road started, but quite a few worked with us as labourers or truck drivers. The Yukon Indians were good people." Some women hired on as camp helpers, or found employment in the service industries in the larger towns; others sold handicrafts to the visiting soldiers and workers. Hampton Primeaux, working with the army in the Burwash Landing area, discovered that the Natives knew how to capitalize on a fast-developing market: "Natives would make caribou coats, mukluks, moccasins, and caps decorated with sequins. And their prices were very reasonable as we went north. On the way back, though, prices had gone way up. They learned fast." Kitty Smith, from the southern Yukon, was one of the women who sold beaded garments: "You know how we bought that truck? Sewing! One pair of moccasins is worth twenty-five dollars. I got a hundred muskrat skins. I wanted to make blanket for myself, but I made mitts. Fur mitts! Soldiers buy them for twenty-five dollars. Mukluks sometimes fifty dollars. Everybody helped sew. Then my son-in-law, Dick Craft, takes a boxful to the airport. He sells to soldiers when they're leaving. He takes three boxes."[35] Most Natives continued to hunt and trap for food and income, but the equipment and hunting by the workers had scared game away from the highway corridor. They were forced to find other livelihoods.

Contemporary portrayals of Native people's reaction to the construction activity suggest, inaccurately, that the Natives were guileless primitives, struck dumb by the majesty of modern engineering and the scale of construction. Numerous stories, told by Natives and non-Natives alike, have the Natives fleeing in horror and disbelief at the sight of bulldozers and trucks. Knox McCusker offered one such tale: "One place an Indian coming down his old pack trail met a cat coming up. Just as he came into view the Negro operator rolled his old white eyes, shoved in the clutch and three jack pines flew into the air and rolled over the bank. The savage left and tarried not in the leaving. When he finally reached the trading post he was only able to gasp, 'Big black devil him come.'"[36] Alex Forgie recalls, "We ran across some that had never seen a motor vehicle or been in a

A Native family uses the highway. J. GARBUS.

town. They came wandering into camp and were trying to open the door to the mess hall. I guess they hadn't seen a door handle and didn't know you had to turn it." Kitty Smith told of her grandchild being disturbed by the arrival of black troops in their village: "'Mamma! Some kind of man. He's got a black face.' She runs to her mamma. 'What kind of man?' 'Oh, just some kind of white man. He won't bother you.' Then she wasn't scared."[37]

Most of the northern Natives, particularly in northern British Columbia, had little to do with the highway construction, and many workers spent months in the region but had virtually no contact with them. Occasionally, Natives would pass through the construction camps while hunting or trapping. Robert Black remembers them well: "Our camp was on the road where a tribe of Indians crossed spring and fall, passing from their winter home to their summer one. It was interesting noticing the order in which they travelled. The old grandfather would walk ahead, well-laden, followed by his sons or fully matured men on horseback. Following them were women with papooses and bundles, smaller children, and the dogs, and everyone strong enough would have a young one on his back. Occasionally grown boys would come into the kitchen. The cooks usually were glad to give them some food to get the strong scent of the Indians out of the kitchen." Joe Garbus's one encounter with the Natives was

The arrival of Southerners sparked a series of epidemic diseases, which proved fatal for many Native people.
J. GARBUS.

similar: "This occurred at the Beaton River Bridge. A group of twelve to fifteen natives, two or three males on horseback, with the women, children, and dogs following on foot, stopped at the bridge. The men dismounted and approached the concrete structure. They felt the concrete, tapped it, and evidently discussed the product. After a short while they mounted and continued on southward toward Fort St. John."

The construction of the highway also opened the eyes of the non-Native population in the region, who recoiled at the discovery that the Americans had established effective control over the Northwest. While there was widespread acceptance of the military projects, many nationals were upset with the scale of the American "occupation." Complaints were directed to the U.S. Army Military Police, described by George Black, Yukon member of Parliament, as the "U.S. Army Gestapo,"[38] and by an American soldier as "HORSES' BUTTS."[39] Constable J. Gunn of the B.C. Provincial Police, parked alongside the road and visiting with a friend, was "reprimanded and insulted" by the military police, who added to the injury by declaring, "As long as we are controlling these highways law and order is going to be kept."[40] Few were as furious at their treatment by the military police as T. H. Callahan, a Canadian civilian working near Fort St. John. He was stopped in the fall of 1943 for exceeding the posted thirty-five m.p.h. speed limit. He was taken before an American military court, charged, found guilty and ordered to pay a ten-dollar fine. When, over his protests, he tried to pay with Canadian dollars, he was told that the fine was in American funds. When he insisted on paying in Canadian funds, he was charged an extra dollar.[41]

As the construction activity peaked and then rapidly declined, the highway communities experienced the inevitable shake-down. Dawson Creek saw its population shrink from a high of ten thousand to a more sustainable four thousand. Fort Nelson had experienced many changes, not the least of which was the development of two squatters' settlements, Dogpatch and Teeterville, built largely by American personnel anxious to bring their families north with them but unable to convince authorities to provide married quarters.

Whitehorse found in 1945 that it still had more than five thousand residents, a far cry from the halcyon days of early construction, but a huge gain in population over the pre-war era. Housing shortages had forced extreme measures: a squatters' area developed along the banks of the Yukon River, and Martin Berrigan constructed several log "skyscrapers" as rental units, catering to a seemingly insatiable market. The chaos of 1942 had given way to a more settled, permanent air. Ronald McEachern, an editor with the *Financial Times*, described the new Whitehorse: "Disappointing though this may be to lovers of high adventure and low rowdy-dow, Whitehorse is today a dull and prosaically well-behaved city – for all of its vigorous history, the loud and determined figures of its storied past, the youthful, adventurous and relatively rich members of its invading army, civilian and military."[42] George Jeckell, Controller of the Yukon and a long-time supporter of Dawson City's aspirations, said of Whitehorse near the end of the war: "The town has a deserted appearance compared with the hustle and bustle of former years....There appears now to be a feeling of uncertainty as to the future growth of the town."[43] The future would, of course, hinge on the fate of the Alaska Highway.

Whitehorse during the construction boom.
PHYLLIS CHURCH.

Some communities in the Northwest had not benefitted at all from the economic boom. Dawson City, capital of the Yukon Territory and famed centre of the Klondike Gold Rush, was bypassed by the Alaska Highway, despite its pleas for a re-routing of the road. Powerless to alter its fate, the community had little choice but to watch as government officials, the RCMP headquarters for the Yukon, and numerous small businesses packed up and headed for Whitehorse, now the centre of activity in the territory. Dawson's downward spiral toward ghost-town status seemed all but assured.

By 1943, it was already clear that the permanent highway society was going to be very different from that of the boom-time days. The civilian contractors began bringing more female employees into the area to handle the increasing amount of office work, changing the nature of camp life dramatically. The higher numbers of female workers was taken as a positive sign, but the official decision to cut the regular hours of work – from the 1942 standard of sixty or seventy hours per week to the more normal eight hours per day, six days per week, was a sure indication that the construction boom was over. The reduction in hours and consequent decline in income sent hundreds of workers fleeing to more lucrative jobs in the South.

Once fired by patriotism, war urgency, and the prospect of a nicely inflated pay packet, the remaining highway crews now settled into a less frenetic pace. A. W. Klieforth, an American consular official, was distressed by the work habits of men along the highway when he travelled the route in the early fall of 1943: "They drop their tools on the minute of closing time, and within two minutes after quitting time the work places are as empty as the North Pole....The contractors informed me that there was not the slightest chance of having an audience listen to a War Bond talk, unless the speaker was either President Roosevelt or a well known movie star." Klieforth had pushed ahead despite the warning. The results did not warm his heart: "I had to speak to them while they were eating, starting on the dot as the soup was served and stopping as the last bit of pie was washed down with coffee....At a recent war relief contest, the first prize was a bottle of whiskey; the second, a dozen of beer; the third – a $100 war bond."[44] The workers' priorities were painfully obvious.

The contractors' decision to allow wives and children into the camps, particularly in the major maintenance camps, was a welcome shift in policy. This had certainly not been the case early in the construction period; at several sites along the highway, particularly Dawson Creek, Fort St. John, Fort Nelson, and Whitehorse, men who had brought their families north had been responsible for finding housing – a near impossibility that had led many to erect ramshackle quarters. And still some families came into the region. On one bitterly cold winter night, Bill Bennett met the train in Dawson Creek, intending to collect some supplies. Instead he discovered a woman travelling with five children. Her husband, who was expected to meet them at the train station, was based two hundred miles up the highway. Bennett, with help from the Salvation Army, arranged to put them up in a vacant hotel. Three days later the woman's husband arrived and arranged to return his family to the United States.

Rumours of changes emerged as early as 1942. S. N. Long, who worked for Lytle and Green Construction, wrote to his wife in the South: "I heard today that they want all the guys that can stay till the first of December. Then they'll pay us $3.00 a day for every day when home if we will come back next year. We can bring our wives along if they are willing to work and they will get $4.00 a day. Such as office or kitchen work. Don't tell any- body but I am making $20.80 per day. Just think every 5 days a $100 bucks."[45] Robert Black brought his wife, Dell, and their eighteen-month-old son John, north in March 1943. He picked them up in Dawson Creek and set out for their camp: "A non- stop trip except for gasoline and a carry-out snack. We made camp in a little over thirty hours." The reasoning behind this dif- ferent policy was very simple. Soldiers could be ordered to stay in the Northwest, but civilians were free agents and would quick- ly leave if conditions were not right. R. A. Gibson noted in 1944, "Canadians are being engaged and quarters have been fixed up for married men in the hope of getting a better class of men who will stay with the job for a reasonable length of time."[46]

As construction wound down and maintenance operators took over, a determined effort was made to recruit married couples to work in the camps. Most were young and childless, both partners working to accumulate a stake for when they later moved back south. Robert and Dell Black transferred from their civilian employer, whose contract had ended, to the U.S. Engineering Department, and worked out of the maintenance camp at Mile 177. Lorna and Gordon Gibbs remained on the highway, but they, too, knew that the end was near: "You didn't feel like you were putting down roots at all. There was always the feeling that maybe next week or next month we won't be here. The war, by this time, was beginning to look as though it would end soon, and we felt that the American army would certainly start to shut down everything along the highway because the threat wasn't there any more." By December 1944, there were 175 employees with families living along the highway, over half of them in Fort St. John, Fort Nelson, and Watson Lake.

Alcan (Alaska) Highway control station.

U.S. Army Corps of Engineers.

The American withdrawal began as early as 1943. Army units pulled out *en masse* by the summer, leaving behind a skeletal quartermaster and maintenance operation. The civilian contractors wound up their work by the fall and quickly moved their men and equipment to wartime projects in the South. General F. S. Strong of the Northwest Service Command later recalled, "From the start of May in 1944, everything in the Northwest Service Command looked to demobilization, so with authority to write orders sending officers and men back home, we soon began to shrink, especially units with not really much if anything to do."[47]

For the Canadians who worked for, and around, the U.S. Army and the American-funded construction projects, the return to peacetime work brought its own difficulties. Chuck Baxter, who as a young boy grew up surrounded by the American workers on the southern end of the highway, "came out of that with something of a Canadian inferiority complex. Because after working with these U.S. construction people – the way they spend money, the type of food they had – [it was hard] to go back the following year and go to work in a Canadian sawmill, where you'd grudgingly get two bucks a day, maybe, and cheap sort of everything. The material was cheap. The trucks were cheap. Everything was cheap compared to the Americans'. Once we had a taste of that U.S. life, it was pretty hard to go back to the farm."

The complicated disentanglement left a bitter legacy. The army left without completing the road it had promised. Although residents of the Northwest accepted the military rationale – there was a war on, and the resources were clearly needed elsewhere – there was great dissatisfaction that the highway was not up to the anticipated standard. The promised legions of tourists that had long fuelled commercial fantasies throughout the Northwest were hardly going to make their way up the rough, incomplete road that was in such poor shape that it was not, even in 1946, accessible to civilian traffic.

Adding to the residents' distress was the reverse of the flood of supplies into the region in 1942. The army and civilian contractors took much of their equipment with them, but locals still complained bitterly about the apparent waste of thousands of dollars of useful material. Stories abounded of usable equipment bulldozed into the ground, of gravel pits filled with office equipment and other supplies, and of bonfires of army surplus. One particularly graphic account told of the destruction of material near Whitehorse. The witnesses saw "a barracks between two and three city blocks long, packed with winter clothes, parkas, pure wool blankets, comforters, chairs, office desks, and almost everything you could imagine. They stacked them up, poured gasoline over them, set them on fire. Guards stood over them with fixed bayonets so nobody could get anything."[48] Lake Southwick, a civilian driver from the Fort St. John area, offers a similar story: "All the Americans' supplies, like motors, tools, what-have-you, everything was taken and buried in those trenches. Seemed like a hard thing to do at the time, burying big motors, brand new, wrapped in wax and processed for shipping overseas in wartime. Complete motors that they could take and slip into a machine in the battlefields. It seemed hard to bury that stuff." Robert and Dell Black recall, "The only excessive waste we knew of was in breaking camp. No one was allowed to remove *anything* – blankets, dishes, foods such as jams – but they were all piled and either burned or bulldozed over."

When the contractors pulled out, again a few took advantage of their paymasters. An American engineer accused a Canadian company of ordering in dozens of sets of new tires and other replacement parts for its aging equipment. When the contractor prepared to ship out his machinery, he replaced worn-out parts and rubber with brand-new tires and equipment. The engineer reported the abuse. The contractor's equipment was stopped at Edmonton on the way out of the region and the new parts, including the tires, were stripped off. Paul Warren says: "As the construction contractors moved out it became necessary to monitor their activities to control active theft of spare parts and supplies. I remember one contractor who filled the drum of a sheepsfoot roller with tools and parts, but the racket resulting from moving it aroused suspicion and he had to unload." Not all such abuse was identified; nor, it must be added, did all the contractors seek to take advantage of the situation.

Most of the tales were rumours, greatly enhanced in the retelling and by the passage of time. Chuck Baxter, who did not see much direct evidence of waste, knows one such story: "There is evidently a place out of Whitehorse where they abandoned great rafts of trucks and things. In later years the trees grew up through the hoods and have just destroyed everything. They rusted away sitting there, and there's acres of them somewhere."

General Strong of the Northwest Service Command attempted to address the repeated criticisms: "Mattresses or chipped enamel, condemned by a medical officer, are destroyed, and some poor settler seeing the action thinks it looks like pretty good material and doesn't realize that it is being destroyed under army regulations. A stove is condemned because it is not considered fit for issue to troops, and it is thrown on the dump. Some settler sees it and finds it is not badly damaged and discovers he can make it like new by taking a part from another stove and he starts offering to go and salvage them for his neighbours. The junk business may be a profitable one but we're not in it."[49] In a region on the verge of returning to the pre-war depression, the abundant waste was a cruel blow – and a sorry aspect of the American military legacy in the Northwest.

Not everything was destroyed. Elizabeth Golata recalls: "Things were stolen and resold at bargain prices to locals. The army boys dropped truck loads of supplies in the bush rather than take them to the dump, informing people where they were. The army then put guards on the trucks. All along the line there were horror stories of food, material, and equipment being bull-dozed and covered. Hardly a family exists that even today does not have something that was 'rescued' from the dump. My share was sheets and pillowcases, and my neighbourhood had enough winter boots to last a decade." Stories about the private distribution of American supplies abounded: "There was quite a bit of black market along there for a while. But apparently some of them got quite high-handed, you know, about grabbing some of this stuff and burying it away, hiding it until after the war was over. But towards the last that I heard, they were checking everything that came out of that country."[50]

Complaints about official waste and the destruction of useful supplies rubbed only a little of the lustre off the genuine goodwill that surrounded the American "occupation" of the Far Northwest during World War II. The U.S. Army Corps of Engineers, followed by legions of American and Canadian civilian workers, had flooded into the North to build a highway to Alaska. In so doing, they had truly and permanently transformed life in the Northwest, providing reliable land access to Alaska, creating and recreating settlements and way stations, altering Native life in what had long been an aboriginal homeland, and ushering in modernization and rapid change.

The Alaska Highway of 1943-1946 was far from a complete civilian road; strict regulations governed all non-essential traffic on the highway and all vehicles had to report to the checkpoints established the entire length of the route. The men and women who built the highway had great stories about actually driving the road – although only a very small number travelled more than a few hundred miles from their work site. Most of the tales highlight the fact that this was, even in 1946, no ordinary road, and could be handled only by extraordinary drivers. The drivers quickly became the road's greatest critics, for they soon tired of the miles of wilderness vistas and became, understandably, fixated on such mundane concerns as safety and reliability.

When Duncan Bath returned to Fort St. John at the end of the summer of 1943, he marvelled at the skill of his chauffeur. The man played his gears masterfully, shifting up and down at critical moments and exercising total control over his vehicle. Bath soon learned of the necessity for his virtuosity: "After a few hours of this, we made a stop and I noticed that he geared down to first gear and then turned the engine off. It turned out that the truck had no brakes!" Alex Forgie heard that a number of trucks had been dispatched without proper brakes: "They were

Winter travel along the highway. J. Garbus.

loaded with soldiers and did not gear down going around a curve. We had posted a sign warning of a steep hill. As a result, the trucks all piled up on top of one another at the bottom. I never did hear what the death toll was. Military Police would not let anyone near the area." Gordon Gibbs remembers one driver who quickly had his fill of the highway: "He got down to the bottom of the Peace River hill, unloaded his load, came back down and said, 'If that's the highway that I have to drive on, goodbye. I'm going back to the States.' He just took off."

Harvey Hayduck's closest brush with death came while he was driving a gravel truck on the southern section of the highway. Men working near the top of a hill had been draining a slough, allowing the water to flow over the road, turning it into mud. Hayduck's vehicle kept sliding to the left, coming to rest on the edge of an intimidating 300-foot drop. The engine died; Hayduck froze with fear, worried that the slightest move might send his vehicle over the edge. Two cats were nearby. One hooked onto the side of Hayduck's truck, holding it in place, while the other tied on in the front and pulled the grateful driver to safety.

Many drivers recall, with a mixture of good humour and residual fear, the dangers of driving along the highway in winter time. Muriel Coates worked at Johnson's Crossing late in the war. She remembers the time-honoured tradition of looking out for other drivers: "Sometimes if you were driving somewhere in a bus or truck, you might see a vehicle stranded along the road. The driver would always stop and look around for the driver of the stranded truck. If he was smart and knew the ways of survival he would be in his Arctic bag buried in a snow bank. He would come out smiling and warm, as a rule." Gordon Gibbs says that the major trouble spots were "pieces of road that they hadn't improved. There were sharp pitches. I recall one at [Mile] 109 was a real dirty little one. You just came onto it almost in second gear and then all of a sudden you had to go straight up. A lot of trucks met their Waterloo there. They'd just slide right back. If they didn't go off the road, they'd just try and run it again." Eugene Wilkinson wrote a poem about driving along the highway, saving several verses for one of the most feared sections of the road:

> The next was the wide-famed Sikanni Hill
> 'Bout seven miles down-grade
> An orange sign on the last steep hill
> This ominous warning gave –
> "DANGEROUS HILL – USE LOWEST GEAR
> BEWARE OF SLIDES AND ICE"
> The chills chased up and down my spine
> Like a pair of frolicking mice.
>
> My heart would leap with every slide
> As she struck the icy spots
> The exhaust was popping out behind
> Like the crack of rifle shots.
> With an ice-cold motor and red hot brakes
> I rolled up to the pump –
> My right leg ached and trembled
> And my heart went thumpty-thump.[51]

Truckers moving supplies along the Alaska Highway before 1946 quickly developed considerable skill – or else they found a new occupation. In places the original single-lane road had not been widened, causing regular bottlenecks at steep hills or one of the dozens of small bridges. The treacherous combination of steep hills, sharp and blind corners, slippery, muddy surfaces, and

Highway worker Howard Burrell wrote, "I counted 72 trucks ditched from Dawson's Creek [Mile 0] to Anderson's Camp at [Mile] 107 west of Fort Nelson."

HOWARD BURRELL.

mountainous clouds of penetrating dust, challenged even the best driver. Travel was painfully slow, and it took more than two weeks to make the journey from Dawson Creek to Big Delta or Fairbanks. A popular highway jingle said it all:

Winding in and winding out, leaves me no doubt
That the dude who built this road
Was going to hell or coming out.

The route was littered with wrecks – army vehicles left to rust on the side of the road, civilian rigs turned over in the ditch, most cannibalized down to their frames. "By spring there was hardly a steep hill that did not have a few boards or a barrel of gas or other goods; broken-down army trucks littered the bottom of the hills and ditches and even over banks."[52] Owner-operators left their machines only under duress or for fear of their personal well-being, in case a subsequent traveller would help himself to any and all movable parts. Earl Gingrich recalls, "One chap woke after a sleep, put his truck in gear but it would not move, on investigating the cause, found that his rear axles had been pulled and taken by someone, while he slept. On another occasion a fellow hitch-hiked back to Dawson for repairs and on returning found that his engine was missing, and so it went on the Alaska Highway."[53]

The highway was not opened for general use at any time during the war – a decision designed to give priority to military traffic and to reduce wear and tear on the road. Residents could obtain permits allowing them to travel along the road as required, and outsiders could apply to the U.S. Army for permission to drive along the highway. George Black, Yukon member of Parliament, observed, "Some people are inclined to complain at the restricted use of the highway. I always remember it is an American Army road, built in a fit of hysteria brought on in the 'home of the brave and the land of the free' by the Japs at Pearl Harbor, built at an enormous cost and with shocking waste and until after the war it is not a Canadian possession, and our dear cousins have the exclusive privilege of using and paying for it."[54]

In the midst of the debate over the future of the Alaska Highway, the war ended. For the Northwest the war had ended in 1943. Nevertheless, when the fighting ceased, first in Europe and later in the Pacific, the soldiers and civilians remaining in the area joined residents in a wild, intemperate celebration. Charles Knott, who worked at Watson Lake, recalls that "the place went wild. All the U.S. men were quite drunk: racing jeeps, weapons carriers going up and down the runways, tearing off each other's clothes." The men and women who worked along the highway might have felt distant from the war, but the emotional release that occurred when the fighting and dying finally stopped proved that they were spiritually very much a part of the war effort.

And now, the world-wide conflagration over, the highway more or less complete, and the Northwest successfully defended from a military threat that had never materialized, the Americans withdrew. The army retreated to Alaska. A new confrontation – the long and ugly staring contest across the Arctic expanses that we know as the Cold War – was already brewing, ironically with the former ally that had been supplied by Alaskan airfields. In the Canadian Northwest, the American military prepared for the final farewell. The Americans tried, several times, to get the Canadian government to take over the Alaska Highway before the mandated transfer date, six months after the end of the war. Canadian authorities refused, citing more pressing commitments and inadequate resources.

The Canadian government's real reason was simple. It was decidedly unenthusiastic about the prospect of taking over responsibility for its stretch of the highway. As early as 1943, C. K. LeCapelain of the Lands, Parks, and Forest Branch offered sage warnings about the problems with the road: "When the Alaska Highway is finally turned over to our government to maintain, it is likely to get considerable of a liability....There are other sections extending over most of the length of the Alaska Highway where the road was located as a tote road and in a great hurry by inexperienced men....Due to poor location and that many of the bridges are being built of untreated native timber, the highway over these stretches is likely to prove a decided liability."[55]

Charles Camsell put it even more bluntly: "Canada is going to have some explaining to do when it is found out that the Alaska Highway is not to be a tourist highway but merely a serviceable road connecting airports."[56] Others disagreed. Ma Murray, the flamboyant editor of the *Alaska Highway News* in Fort St. John, declared: "The Alaska highway has moved history ahead a century for northern B.C. and the Yukon."[57] Time would tell.

A few officials actively considered shutting down the Alaska Highway. They had already decided to do so with the costly and poorly-conceived CANOL oil pipeline and refinery project, much to the dismay of American politicians, who wondered aloud how planning and financial controls could go so awry. When Thomas Riggs visited Ottawa in 1943, he found "that in all probability . . . the Canadian government will not even attempt to maintain the highway when it shall be turned into the public road system of Canada."[58] Ernest Gruening, Alaska's governor, agreed: "It is evident that the Alaska Highway will have little or no value after the war. All the evidence that I have been able to gather, which appears to me conclusive, is that the Canadians will not maintain it – certainly not as a whole – and that as far as its being a traffic artery for tourists and others to Alaska, it will cease to be."[59]

The pessimism was misplaced, but not by much. The highway opened enormous tracts of the North for potential development and provided secure road access for many small settlements. The American and Canadian public, subjected to numerous newspaper accounts and magazine articles on this wonderful highway being built through a vast and scenic frontier, would hardly countenance the abandonment of such a favourable route, built at such great public expense.

But in 1946 it was simply not much of a highway. Maintenance had been kept to a minimum in 1945 and 1946, leaving the road in rough condition. A Canadian report offered a succinct,

Signpost at Tok Junction, Alaska, December 1943.

if emotionless, summary: "The Highway on take-over was found to be generally in fair shape, but it was quite apparent that it had not been completed to the original specifications in many places. Furthermore, weaknesses were beginning to develop, especially in the muskeg area south of Fort Nelson and in the North. Many of the wooden bridges and original culverts required urgent repairs."[60] Griffith Taylor liked the highway, but wondered about the cost of keeping it opened: "The splendid road called the Alaska Highway brings up the question of the possibility of important tourist traffic. I do not see clearly what is to justify keeping this in running order after the military necessity has passed away."[61] Paul Seddicum, the American consul in Edmonton, agreed. "I may be prejudiced but I feel strongly that there is no attraction connected with the Highway great enough to make the discomfort and possible danger worth the effort."[62] *Maclean's* magazine added its voice to the chorus, warning Canadians not to get their hopes up about the highway and wondering about the value of extensive reconstruction.[63]

There were good reasons for concern. Outside the main centres, there were almost no facilities for travellers or tourists; even the hardy truckers and construction workers recognized that the few

Thawing a frozen culvert at Mile 814, December 1943.

places to eat and sleep, beyond the maintenance camps, left a lot to be desired. One of the first roadside stops along the Alaska Highway was at the Prophet River: "There were two elderly trappers that had been in there for years getting their supplies in by pack horse when the road went right by their log shack. Lum and Baner they called themselves, and were in their late sixties or early seventies. They were just so happy to see people, they started serving pancakes any time of the day and a lot of the night. Their menu hung above their stove and it read 'blueberry pancakes, raspberry pancakes.' There were about six different kinds and they all came out of the same bowl of batter, but they were happy and we were happy to be there." Facilities were basic – a tiny table in the middle of the shack, around which as many as eight people would crowd. There were no chairs; blocks of wood served in their stead.

Despite concerns about the standard of facilities and of the road itself, Canada agreed, albeit reluctantly, to keep the Alaska Highway open after the war. Canadian official J. A. Glen warned at the end of April 1946, "We may look for increasing pressure that Canada should build and maintain the kind of road that the United States promised but did not construct."[64] Substandard as it was, the highway had still been expensive to build. Some U.S. $135 million had been spent on highway construction and related projects, such as the road to Haines and the telephone system that now connected the Northwest to the rest of the continent.[65] The highway was passed over to Canada ostensibly without financial strings, but the federal government did agree to compensate the Americans for the telephone system and the airfields built and improved during the war.[66] One analyst observed that the Canadian government "concluded that the highway, though a liability, had to be retained, more for political than economic, military or strategic reasons."[67] The one condition the U.S. government insisted on was that the highway would be maintained with "the understanding that there shall at no time be imposed any discriminatory conditions in relation to the use of the road as between Canada and United States civilian traffic."[68]

The Alaska Highway was about to change hands. It was time to applaud what the road stood for. Above all else it was a tangible symbol of unprecedented Canadian-American, military-civilian, cooperation under wartime conditions. It was also a testament to what was possible under very trying circumstances, and it is here that much of the mystique and excitement about the Alaska Highway is to be found. And despite the nay-sayers, gaining in number and audience in the South, there was an honest to goodness highway in the Far Northwest. If it was less of a highway than had been promised in the first months of 1942, it was nonetheless an improvement on the few roads, pack trails, and water routes of the past. Gertrude Baskine, having finished a difficult trip from Edmonton to Fairbanks, had this to say to the critics: "And all the people who haven't done this road, who haven't been anywhere near this famous Highway and yet who insist on telling me that it is made up of impassable holes, impassable stretches of water, impassable bridges and impassable mountains – in other words there is no road – please read this. THE HIGHWAY IS THERE."[69]

The Alaska Highway was also more than a real road or a symbol, it was an unforgettable experience for the men and women who built it, including the civilian workers who, for years and much to their dismay, have been largely ignored in highway lore. For most of the people involved – men and women, Canadians and Americans, short-term workers and permanent residents – the construction period was a time of personal discovery, a testing of personal limits, of growth and adventure, hardship and fear, loneliness and new friendship, of discovery of one of the continent's last great frontiers. Even as they complained about the cold, resented the isolation, barely tolerated their bunkhouses and cookhouses, swatted mosquitoes and scraped mud from their

Civilian highway workers.

boots, the workers knew they were engaged in a historic project. The road they had built crossed hundreds of miles of sub-Arctic wilderness, opening vast river valleys, mountain ranges, and lakes to development and settlement. Not since the transcontinental railways were built in the nineteenth century had workers participated in such a monumental enterprise.

Not surprisingly, the men and women of the civilian workforce remember their highway days positively, the passage of time dulling some of the sharper memories of hardship and discomfort. Duncan Bath writes, "I would still have to rate my summer on the Alaska Highway as a very significant event in my life. There was challenge, a lot of hard work, achievement, and adventure." Robert and Dell Black went north to make money, but came away with "more perhaps than we shall ever realize." For Joe Garbus, the Alaska Highway "was a text-book example of what two countries could accomplish by marshalling all their efforts toward a common goal. The army, the civilians, the railroaders, the contractors and their managers, the blacks, the natives and the whites all together built 1,500 miles of roads and bridges in record time." Harvey Hayduck agrees: "The Alaska Highway Project was a colossal undertaking at the time as the U.S.A. was also fighting a terrible war for which it was not prepared. They are admired deeply for their perseverance and determination as well as the speed in which the task was done....What a project!"

6

The Post-War Road

ON 1 APRIL 1946, dignitaries gathered in Whitehorse to witness and celebrate the transfer of the Alaska Highway to Canadian hands. The occasion, held at a less scenic location than the first highway celebration at Soldier's Summit, was also decidedly less electric, the publicity considerably reduced. There was the appropriate pomp and circumstance – the playing of the "Star Spangled Banner" and the "Missouri Waltz," "O Canada" and "God Save the King." Major General Bill Hoge was back on the highway he had started; he was joined on the platform by such dignitaries as General A. G. L. McNaughton and Brigadier G. Walsh of the Canadian Army, Hon. Ray Atherton, U.S. ambassador to Canada, and other military and civilian officials. There were the usual speeches and declarations of international affection and goodwill. Lieutenant-Colonel J. R. B. Jones formally accepted responsibility for the Alaska Highway from Major Bernard Zohn of the Northwest Division, 6th Service Command, U.S. Army. The Alaska Highway – or at least 1,220 of its eventual 1,523 miles – was now in Canadian hands.

To call the Canadian army's assignment daunting is to understate the case. According to one of the army's highway engineers, who had arrived in the North early in 1946 to arrange for the formal transfer, "We took over a strange unknown ribbon of road covered with snow. We knew the vehicles and equipment left us were old and worn and needed immediate replacement. We had no married quarters and I, like most of the army up there, had been home only a few months after 5 or 6 years separation. It looked grim. We read the records of how the rivers rose suddenly in the spring and took out dozens of bridges. We were told of flash floods that sprang from mountain slopes to wash out miles of highway. It looked grimmer. We took another look at the old and decrepit road machinery, the tremendous task of sorting out warehouses full of unlisted tools and spare parts, and the way our proposed establishment had been pared down. It looked hopeless."[1]

The entire Northwest bore the signs of a region invaded, conquered, and then abandoned. Scores of army-issue buildings – Quonset huts, maintenance yards, warehouses, and the ubiquitous barracks used for offices and dormitories – dotted the Alaska Highway corridor. Many of them now sat empty, unused, unwanted, and rapidly surrendering to the ravages of sub-Arctic conditions. When the writer Pierre Berton visited Whitehorse in 1954, he found a town still recovering from the heady days of war: "The town that now greeted me...was a cluttered hodge-podge of wartime jerry-building, a wild mélange of tar-paper shacks, outhouses, bunkhouses, Quonset huts, corrugated-iron lean-tos, false-fronted frame structures, log cabins from an earlier day, a few trim little bungalows, and a few square blockhouses disguised by imitation brick – all mingled with piles of salvaged lumber and piping, rusted hulks of trucks and bulldozers, and scattered heaps of old oil drums. This was the mess left behind by the army of forty thousand soldiers and construction workers....Whitehorse was still cleaning up."[2]

The task of maintaining and improving the highway – and of otherwise cleaning up after the American "invasion" – fell to the Northwest Highway System of the Royal Canadian Engineers. There was something curiously fitting in having a military unit take over a highway that, in its early stages and in the public's imagination, was a masterwork of soldier-engineers. But, in contrast to the first military advance northward, there was little mystery and excitement surrounding this post-war assignment, no cheering crowds along the train and road routes north, and little public attention paid to what most perceived as the mundane task of highway maintenance and reconstruction.

The highway passed into the hands of the Canadian Army on 1 April 1946.

COATES COLLECTION.

Residents along the Alaska Highway, many of whom saw the rapid improvement of the road as the economic panacea for the entire region, were perplexed by the decision to turn the project over to the army. The military had little direct road experience except, like the U.S. Army Corps of Engineers, that of constructing military roads and facilities. Why, some wondered, was the British Columbia portion simply not turned over to the provincial government, as the Alaskan section had been handed to the territorial authorities? The answer, found in the minutes of numerous civil servants' meetings, was that the B.C. government had no desire to take over the road, whatever its apparent constitutional obligations in this area. If the federal government was prepared to look after the highway, because of lingering commitments to the United States, that was fine with the B.C. government, which was in no mood to tackle the costly assignment. Besides, as provincial highway department officials realized, the reconstruction of the highway to civilian standards would take many years and millions of dollars. Why not leave the task to Ottawa? The Yukon government was in no position to assume responsibility for the more than six hundred miles of road that passed through its territory. The tiny territorial civil service lacked the personnel and financial resources to tackle major assignments, and had no desire at this point to saddle itself with such massive obligations.

The B.C. government was more interested in access to the Alaska Highway than in the highway itself, which, after all, tied northern B.C. to Edmonton, rather than to southern B.C. The provincial government decided to construct a feeder road to the highway. Beginning in the last year of the war, B.C. started work on the John Hart Highway, from Prince George to the Peace River country. This new road greatly improved access from the South, but did not help those coming to the Alaska Highway from Alberta. The problem of the poor quality of feeder roads persisted. As one American diplomat observed in 1949, the highway was actually in decent shape, but "the real problem lies in the connecting roads at the southern end. One stretch between Edmonton, Alberta, and Dawson Creek, British Columbia, is of low grade and becomes nearly impassable during the spring thaw and the early summer, although cars do get through even then."[3] Immediately after the war, there were two access routes from Edmonton to Dawson Creek, one through Athabasca and a more southerly road through Grande Prairie. Neither was in particularly good shape. Iris Woolcock travelled the latter route in 1948, and had few kind words for the journey: "That is a terrible stretch of road at any and all times – an absolute disgrace. You'd think, in all these years since the United States built that marvelous stretch of road from Dawson Creek to Fairbanks, the Canadian government would be frightfully ashamed of themselves and be unable to find any excuse for not having built a good piece of road over those few hundred miles from Edmonton to Dawson Creek."[4]

But in 1946, the Canadian government's major headache was the quality of the highway itself. Alaskans and Canadians along the highway wanted the road improved and rebuilt where necessary. Their demands could not be ignored; there was still too much mystique and excitement surrounding the road. The government faced three options: keep the road open, with minimal improvements, and thereby satisfy the basic requirements of residents and travellers; begin a slow program of reconstruction and relocation; or undertake a quick and massive rebuilding of the Alaska Highway to bring it closer to civilian standards. Ottawa chose the first option, and assigned the Royal Canadian Engineers to the task.

The Royal Canadian Engineers had the requisite technical and professional skills; also, having them tackle Alaska Highway maintenance could be sold as something of a training exercise. The chill winds of the Cold War had begun blowing over the Northwest soon after World War II, and Ottawa realized the strategic advantage of having a military establishment in the region. The highway was used for various military exercises through the 1950s and 1960s, providing a valuable test of the army's capacity to defend the Far Northwest. The government did not declare publicly that using the army was also cheaper than civilian alternatives. The RCE's efforts were clearly intended to be a stop-gap measure while the federal government negotiated with the B.C. government and decided on the future of the Alaska Highway.

The Royal Canadian Engineers were in a thankless situation. They were commissioned to maintain a highway that was not as good as many people expected or desired, but were denied the financial and other resources necessary to modernize and improve the road. As late as 1960 the minister of national defence, George Pearkes, is said to have commented that the Alaska Highway would remain a "jeep road"; the following year, Pearkes's replacement, Douglas Harkness, suggested that Canada had done its share by maintaining a "military highway to Alaska." The message was clear: the Department of National Defence was not in the road construction business.

The initial highway maintenance team comprised military engineers imported from the South and a solid core of civilian employees, both from the area and from outside. Employees such as James Quong, Don Bakke, Harry George, Walt Williscroft, Matthew Young, Walter Wonga, John Wesley, Albert Tophma, Mo Solodan, Hector Rail, and George Nelms transferred from the American-run highway establishment and hired on officially on 1 April 1946 (and were still there eighteen years later when the Department of National Defence relinquished responsibility for the highway). Their knowledge of the highway and skill in dealing with sub-Arctic conditions proved vital in keeping the highway open.

The entire operation was under the control of Brigadier-General Geoffrey Walsh, first commander of the Northwest Highway System. Lieutenant-Colonel J. R. B. Jones, senior highway engineer, headed the operations wing, which had responsibility for road and bridge design. The Northwest Highway Maintenance Establishment, a largely civilian operation working under military direction, looked after highway maintenance. An additional military unit, No. 1 Road Maintenance Company of the Royal Canadian Engineers, undertook road and bridge repairs and tackled emergency assignments that could not be handled by the regular maintenance crews.

In an attempt to control the skyrocketing costs of maintenance, remedial reconstruction of key bridges and particularly poor stretches of the road was undertaken. But the army lacked the resources to handle even this basic work properly. The RCE had been allocated many fewer workers than they had requested; when the army arrived, their key No. 1 Road Maintenance Company was short 86 of its authorized 114 military and civilian employees. Crews gradually came up to strength, but not before the army discovered how difficult its highway assignment was.

The biggest problem facing the RCE was the absence of a substantial body of engineering information about the highway. The U.S. forces had not been in the area long enough to produce detailed studies of ice formation, spring run-off, river flows, the effects of permafrost, the significance of ice lenses on the road surface, and the many other unique features of sub-Arctic road maintenance and repair on a road that had been hastily laid out and had major defects in design and construction. The Engineers quickly recognized the problems; dealing with them properly was another matter, particularly when the Canadian government could not see its way clear to providing the funding necessary for a substantial reconstruction. The north end of the Canadian section of the highway, near the Alaska-Yukon border, had been left in rough shape at the time of the American withdrawal; Canadian army engineers and maintenance crews relocated lengthy sections, replaced bridges, and improved the road surface. (Through a very liberal definition of the relocations necessary to effect proper bridge repair, the army was able to rebuild whole sections of the highway near bridges.) But these were only stop-gap measures and did little to address the larger problems.

Few civilian travellers gave much thought to the daunting engineering challenges facing the maintenance crews. They noticed only the potholes, clouds of dust, and all-too-frequent wash-outs, and seldom missed the opportunity to complain about the trauma of navigating the rocky, rough road to Alaska. There was little sympathy for the highway workers, even though something as fundamental as keeping the gravel surface on the road required countless hours of work. Bob Brant, who worked at Prophet River, Wonowon, and Summit Lake from 1953 to 1961,

After the war the temporary bridges of the pioneer highway were gradually replaced with permanent structures. Here the new bridge is visible in the background.
PUBLIC WORKS CANADA.

noted that he "would work all summer digging the gravel back out of the ditches with the graders and putting it back on the roads so we could conserve materials. Backsloping we called it. Just rebuilding the grade on the road each summer."

Highway crews quickly found out about the unreliability of the sub-Arctic climate and constantly battled sudden summer floods, erosion through spring run-off, and the numerous complications of having portions of the highway laid over the unstable blanket of muskeg and permafrost. In the summer months, the road-bed over such stretches would soften and sag, creating rhythmic undulations and sharp pot-holes, both of which claimed a fair share of oil pans and gas tanks. In other places, particularly on the southern portions of the highway, the roadway had been carved out of unstable hillsides; landslides were commonplace, repeatedly blocking traffic and adding to the hard work of road maintenance.

In this era, wash-outs and travel delays were routine. Marvin Armitage recalls that when he was working at Mile 245, the rains came like clockwork early in July. The rainfall combined with the summer melt coursed off the mountainsides, washing out culverts and damaging the road. Maintenance crews would rush to the scene and make temporary repairs to allow traffic to proceed. Brigadier-General H. W. Lowe, commander of the Northwest Highway System from 1951 to 1955, says that during the summer of 1951 "when all but skeleton crews were away from the maintenance camps, we experienced as bad a flash flood as ever recorded along the highway from the south to the north ends of Kluane Lake. There were seventy wash-outs in this stretch of about sixty miles. Every small bridge disappeared, streams changed their courses, and about a hundred tourists were stranded in between breaks in the road." Under such circumstances, the work crews – including many single men drawn specifically by the high wages and long work hours of summer maintenance – would work around the clock; if they were close to camps, the cook or their wives would bring up sandwiches and coffee.

Much of the summer work fell to seasonal roving crews, which handled a variety of tasks, from bridge repair to road rebuilding. Most men hired on in the late spring and departed in the fall, just as cold weather set in and interfered with road work. The arrival and departure of the roving crews became something of a highway ritual, marked by celebrations. Frank Peters, who worked on the summer crews on the southern highway, says, "We always kind of looked forward to being hired on in the spring of the year. All of us would get together and have a big do, and then the next morning we'd pack up and take all of our stuff and start moving out to our locations." The fall closure brought a similar celebration: "Freeze-up time, they'd pull you all into Fort Nelson, and then they'd put on a great big dance and do, all before the break-up. Really good."

The crews had much to do. In 1948, the Testa River bridge and about one mile of road surface washed out; the area from Kluane Lake to the Alaska boundary was a constant source of trouble, as was the two-hundred-mile stretch north of Fort Nelson. In July 1963, the most treacherous combination of weather – rain and warm temperatures that increased snow melt – caused a total of forty-two wash-outs along the highway between Mile 300 and Mile 482. Amazingly, traffic was delayed only two days, and travellers moved over detours and temporary roads for a few days until repairs were made.

Not all of the highway troubles were attributable to the ill-temper of Mother Nature. Hugh Devitt, a senior highway engineer in the late 1950s, was inspecting the highway near Coal River, around Mile 581, when he came across a substantial lake backed up behind a beaver dam. Deciding that disaster would follow if the beaver dam broke without warning, Devitt dug out one end of the dam, allowing water to flow down to the road and from there, he assumed, through a culvert and out the other side. He drove on to a nearby restaurant and had just settled down for beans and toast when camp foreman Cliff Stringer burst in: "Some clown has opened a beaver dam back at 581, and I'm going out to rustle up some of my road crew." "Well, I'm the clown, Cliff, " Devitt sheepishly acknowledged. Recognizing his responsibility for the mess, which had quickly gouged out one-third of the road surface, Devitt dug in with the rest of the work crew to staunch the flow of water. They spent the entire evening sandbagging the road, managing to save enough to allow one lane of traffic through. The site became widely known as Devitt's Folly.

Winter presented its own problems, particularly those of road glaciers. Work crews battled relentlessly against the constant formation of ice blankets over the road, which made driving treacherous or even impossible. Bob Brant recalls, "We had a steamer on a truck and, of course, the roads up there were flooded badly in the winter time because of the springs in the side of the hills. That was at least a three-day-a-week job just keeping them thawed off and then, of course, diverting the water so it wouldn't get on the road."

Drifting snow was another major winter hazard. It was not enough to just clear the snow off the road. Unless the snowbanks were pushed well back from the sides of the road, strong crosswinds would create tremendous drifts across the road. When the snows fell, then, the grader operators had to clear a wide swath for the wind-blown snow to pass through. Hugh Devitt, who claimed with pride that there were no snow-caused road closures during his time on the Alaska Highway, says "The key was when snow starts to fall you started clearing it; you didn't wait until it has snowed you in to go out. We had one rule: you started clearing snow when the snow started to fall. So it never really got ahead of you."

Winter brought benefits as well as hazards. When the road froze solid it was capable of carrying much larger loads than during the summer season. Early in 1945 the CANOL oil refinery in Whitehorse was dismantled and shipped south to the Leduc field near Edmonton. For much of the winter heavily loaded trucks, which would have demolished the road surface in summer,

The Alaska Highway along Muncho Lake.

J. GARBUS.

moved south along the highway. Paul and Marion Greenan, who operated a lodge at Muncho Lake at the time, had an unexpected bonanza when the truckers stopped for gasoline and food at their restaurant.

Many drivers, including truckers, preferred the winter season: "The roadbed smooths out, with a surface of fine powder snow as dry and grainy as sand. There's no flying gravel and rarely a flat tire. The dust is long gone under the snow and the mosquitoes are dormant until late spring. And you have the whole highway to yourself." Others had less pragmatic, more poetic, reasons for preferring winter travel: "the peculiar magic of a luminous white winter sky, of rivers silenced under ice and of barren mountains lifting in fold upon fold of silent white majesty."[5] But few travellers experienced these delights, for highway traffic dwindled to a trickle in the winter season.

The RCE quickly developed important new techniques for dealing with highway construction and maintenance. In wet, swampy areas, the standard procedure is to dig substantial ditches to keep the water away from the road surface. Such an operation has the opposite effect in areas of permafrost and muskeg. The ditches serve as a conduit for summer heat to reach the permafrost under the road's surface and melt the frozen ground that provided a base for the road. Rather than digging deeper ditches, the crews instead built the road up higher. This process —

they learned as well that they had to use loose, large rocks on the bottom, building up gradually to the more dense road surface – created an insulating blanket over the permafrost, stopping it from melting.

The summer brought forest fires, ranging from small brush fires started by a casually discarded cigarette to raging conflagrations that threatened to engulf entire communities. In 1958, when drought covered the Northwest, fires crossed the highway around Swift River and south of Fort Nelson. The main battle was waged around Whitehorse. Army and highway crews hastily cleared fire-breaks around Camp Takhini as the winds twisted and turned, first pushing the fire toward the town and then pushing it back into the hills. Hugh Devitt, who was the senior officer in camp at the time, had a train standing by to evacuate residents. When he came home at lunch during the blaze, his wife asked if she should put the carrier on top of the car. His reply, showing the burden of leadership, was simple: "By no means, dear. That would give everybody an indication that we know more than they do and that we're going to bail out. So just play it cool."

Devitt himself was nearly trapped in the fire. He ventured into the burn area to do a quick inventory of highway equipment in the area. When he came across a crane, he sent his driver back to town to bring back an equipment operator. After trying to start the crane himself, Devitt began to walk back down the highway. Suddenly, the wall of fire turned toward him and advanced along the road. He dove into a culvert, finding temporary safety. Shortly after, again back on the soot-covered road, he came across an RCMP officer, dispatched to find a missing American driver. The two continued on, fire raging around them, until they found the lost traveller who, panicked by the fire, had driven into the heart of the blaze. The man had survived by remaining in his pick-up. His equipment showed the scars of the inferno: the rubber hoses on his oxygen acetylene equipment had melted and fused, providing mute evidence of his near-death.

Post-war reconstruction proceeded on a more leisurely basis than had wartime construction. The shortness of the summer season, however, injected a certain urgency into the construction activity. Crews worked long hours during the short summer months; rock crushers, for example, usually ran double shifts all summer long. Other work, particularly bridge construction across rivers noted for high summer run-off, was designated for the winter months. Bridges across the rivers flowing out of the Kluane Range – especially the Donjek and Slims – were rebuilt largely during the winter, when low water made foundation work possible.

Bridges continued to cause problems along the length of the highway because of their vulnerability to wash-outs and human-made disasters. In 1958, a trucker pulling a low-bed trailer inadvertently broke the braces of the Takhini River bridge. As one commentator laconically observed, "The driver later claimed ignorance of the fact that he had left the scene with bracing members hanging in all directions."[6]

More traumatic, by far, was the collapse of the Peace River bridge in October 1957. This bridge, opened to much fanfare during the war, was the engineering masterpiece of the southern Alaska Highway, a majestic structure in a strikingly beautiful setting. The foundations however, had been placed on unstable soil, so the bridge required constant vigilance and regular maintenance. The north end shifted early in the morning of 16 October, opening a gap on the bridge surface. Ten hours later, as the Herculean power of the shifting landscape worked on the powerful cables and concrete of the bridge, the structure collapsed in a twisted, mangled mass. Ferries were brought in to carry trucks and cars across the river, and a temporary road deck was built on the Pacific Great Eastern Railway bridge. Construction on a new bridge – the old structure was demolished and removed – began in 1958. Seasonal delays, including waiting for the ice to freeze sufficiently to support the heavy equipment and a labour strike, slowed work. The new Peace River bridge – a modern, more secure and, to date, permanent structure – opened for traffic in January 1960.

(Rumours about the collapse of the Peace River bridge have persisted for many years. Among the most prevalent is the story that the bridge was built from steel salvaged from the famous "Galloping Gertie" bridge near Tacoma, Washington. The rumour is baseless – all the steel in the Peace River bridge was brand-new and not a bit of it could be traced back to the legendary Tacoma structure. But the story remained – and remains – in circulation.)

The original bridge at Nisultin Bay.

COATES COLLECTION.

By 1964, the Royal Canadian Engineers had replaced more than a hundred bridges along the Canadian portions of the highway. Many of the structures were quite remarkable affairs. The Donjek River bridge was built in stages between 1948 and 1952, as engineers struggled with the dangers and difficulties of building across the unpredictable river, which constantly changed its course. The Slims River bridge, situated near the mouth of the Kaskawulsh Glacier, had been built on the soft silt of the Slims River. It was replaced in the early 1950s with a bridge built on solid ground. Work crews on the bridge battled with uncertain foundations and the irritating, dusty winds that billowed and blustered at the head of Kluane Lake. The original Nisultin River bridge – 2,300 feet long and hastily built by the U.S. Army – did not long survive the ravages of sub-Arctic conditions; in 1946, a heavily loaded tractor-trailer plunged through its deck. The Canadian government commissioned the construction of a new bridge, this one built by a Canadian civilian contractor.

There was, of course, more to the Alaska Highway than the 1,220 miles on Canadian soil. The highway ran on for another three hundred miles, from the Alaska-Yukon boundary through Tok Junction, the initial site of the U.S. customs station on the road to Big Delta, where the Alaska Highway joined the much older Richardson Highway, and on to Fairbanks. Alaska had benefitted greatly from the construction of the highway, and stood to gain even more by its upgrading. As Alaskan historian Claus-M. Naske observes, the principal effect of the highway was psychological: "Having missed the last boat outside and not having plane fare no longer meant spending the winter in the North. Now it would be possible to drive south." Tourist traffic, the vast majority destined for Alaska, increased from slightly over 18,600 in 1948 to almost 50,000 only three years later.[7]

The Alaska Highway was perhaps the most important road in the Alaskan system, but it was not given any special status by the territorial authorities. In 1944, the army passed over responsibility for maintenance of the highway to the Alaska Roads Commission, which became part of the Bureau of Public Roads (within the Department of Commerce) in 1956. Four years later, after Alaska became a state in 1959, responsibility for the highway system passed to the new Department of Highways. These organizations had to maintain all of Alaska's many roads, trails, and highways; the Alaska Highway was only one portion – albeit a significant one – of its many obligations and duties. The commission had, in 1947, responsibility for 2,785 miles of roads – including the Richardson, Glenn, Steese, and Tok Cutoff highways. The Alaska Highway and its branches made up only 210 miles of the total. (The discrepancy between this total and the distance from the Alaska-Yukon border to Fairbanks, the end of the Alaska Highway, arises because the last portion of the highway, from Big Delta to Fairbanks, was originally built as part of the Richardson Highway – hence Big Delta's not unreasonable claim to being the *real* end of the Alaska Highway.) Alaska, believing that its highways were vital to regional success and buoyed by an economy funded by federal transfer payments and Cold War military expenditures, paid considerable attention to them.

The commission began paving its principal road network – a series of highways linking Fairbanks and Anchorage which expanded eastward from Anchorage to Tok and south from Fairbanks along the Alaska Highway – shortly after the war. The paving of the Alaska Highway, which began with work on a section outside of Fairbanks in 1949, was only one piece of a broader enterprise. It was not, as well, given the highest priority. The road system from Valdez north to Fairbanks and between Fairbanks and Anchorage took precedence over the Alaska

Highway, as did preliminary work on the establishment of a ferry system along the Alaskan panhandle.

By the late 1950s, however, shortly after responsibility for the highway passed from the Alaska Roads Commission to the Bureau of Public Roads, substantial reconstruction work commenced along the Alaskan portions of the highway. The fact that Alaskan interest in improving the highway was not matched by Canadian federal authorities, however, restricted the prospect for a full-scale reconstruction effort. In a number of its Alaskan sections, the highway was not significantly relocated or rebuilt; asphalt was, instead, laid over the top of a slightly improved preliminary road – the road was paved but fell somewhat short of regular standards on other accounts.

The Canadians moved much more slowly on improving their vast stretch of the road, although there were a few optimistic signs. A road from Dawson Creek to Fort St. John had been built before the war; the road was, in 1946, in substantially better shape than most of the Alaska Highway. (Hence, to further complicate matters, the claim by Fort St. John that the *real* start of the Alaska Highway was in their community, or more accurately at nearby Charlie Lake; using the criteria applied by the residents of Big Delta, the claim is reasonable.) Local traffic was considerably heavier than on other sections of the road, adding pressure on the government to improve and pave this forty-seven-mile stretch. The work was completed in stages through the 1950s. In the early 1960s, the federal government handed over the first eighty-three miles of the Alaska Highway – improved and paved – to the British Columbia Highway Department. The book-ends – paved sections at either extreme of the Alaska Highway – provided a false introduction to the Alaska Highway, for in between lay more than 1,200 miles of unpaved and only partially improved road.

Residents and would-be northern travellers were first perplexed and then angered by the handling of the Alaska Highway. Wartime publicity had boasted of the scenic beauty of the route, of miles of wilderness teeming with wildlife. Stories sent south during the war had described, inaccurately, a completed civilian road that was destined to be the foundation of regional prosperity. Local business people spoke confidently of the thousands of tourists about to flood northward, and of the countless new commercial opportunities soon to develop along the highway route. The post-war era was to be the Northwest's coming-out party – the opening of the Alaska Highway to civilian traffic was to mark the start of the celebration.

With the exaggeration of wartime rhetoric still ringing in their ears, travellers interested in the Alaska Highway expected that the road would be quickly opened to them. They were greatly disappointed. Wartime highway restrictions remained in place. Travellers required permits to use the highway and were provided with a daunting list of equipment and material that they had to take with them. Even the most determined travellers could not fail to be intimidated by the stories of dangerous curves, treacherous hills, unreliable bridges, and mile upon mile of isolation. Canadian officials also maintained the U.S. Army's check-points along the highway. People wishing to use the road therefore did so initially under strict controls, which in turn reflected the poor quality of the Alaska Highway. The soldiers, Paul Greenan remembers, required all would-be travellers to state their name, employer, and business on the highway. Those without legitimate reasons for travelling (tourist traffic was not deemed acceptable), or without the required equipment, were turned back on the spot. The road-checks were lifted in 1948, but the driving problems remained. As late as 1960, the Canadian government was still following "a strict Alaska-traveller code: the driver of each car must have $250 and a valid gas and oil credit card, and each passenger must carry $100 when bound for Alaska."[8] There were further complications. The American Automobile Association pointed out in 1958 that only Standard Oil and Chevron credit cards could be used the length of the highway; Texaco's reach extended only to Lower Post, while Gulf and British American cards could get the credit-dependent traveller a bit further but not all the way to Alaska.

While such realities scared off the casual traveller, and angered local business people who had hoped to profit from the opening up of the Far Northwest, the unfinished Alaska Highway still held out great attraction to others. For those seeking a great adventure – something less exotic but more accessible than a paddle down the Amazon or a camel ride across the Australian outback – the Alaska Highway offered wonderful opportunities. Here was every person's adventure, an experience available to

The highway at Mile 191.
J. GARBUS.

anyone with a serviceable automobile, sufficient funds, and enough time to drive the highway and back. It was not an assignment to tackle on a whim; the American Automobile Association recommended in 1954 that people planning to drive to Fairbanks from the United States plan ten days each way — and budget for $800 in total expenses. One of the major legacies of the war was that the Alaska Highway was surrounded by the warm memories of a dramatic, nonviolent, and patriotic task conducted under intense pressure. And now, with the highway still in rough shape, the average North American had an opportunity to experience for him or herself the isolation, wildness, and beauty of this road's exotic route.

From the early years of the post-war era, therefore, the Alaska Highway was engulfed in a curious mix of regional boosterism, adventurism, southern fascination with the North, and frontierism. The people along the highway cared about fixing potholes, eliminating steep hills, and building reliable bridges more than write-ups in American magazines. But they also recognized that the growing mystique of the Alaska Highway, fuelled by the publication of such books as Gertrude Baskine's *Hitch-hiking the Alaska Highway*, Philip Godsell's *The Romance of the Alaska Highway*, Frank Illingworth's *Highway to the North*, and numerous magazine and newspaper articles, offered a foundation for a tourist industry.

Iris Woolcock tackled the Alaska Highway in 1948, driving across North America from Warm Mineral Spring, Florida, in a determined effort to reach Alaska. Her journey was fraught with difficulty and discomfort. Shortly after leaving Fort St. John, she met travellers who had turned back a few miles up the road, claiming that no one with her rig – a jeep and a large trailer – had a hope of making it. Woolcock persisted, helped by bus drivers, university students, and other travellers who gave her a tow over the steepest hills. She pushed on through Whitehorse – the last few miles before the town being among the worst on the entire highway – and on to Alaska. The expedition exceeded her wildest expectations: "Instead of being off in a desolate and lonely place, as most of my friends and relatives thought, I was travelling the friendliest road in the world." She stopped at the highway camps, met dozens of people, and became completely enamoured with the region. She left Alaska that same year, racing to beat the onset of winter as she headed south along the highway.[9]

In the immediate post-war period, little was done to provide travellers' facilities along the Alaska Highway – Woolcock had been wise to take her mobile home with her. Bob and Wilma Knox, recalling a visit to Whitehorse in 1951, remember that "streets were unpaved and dusty and Indians more plentiful than tourists. The few places that had private baths proudly featured the fact in their advertisements, as bathtubs were then rare along the Alaska Highway. Instead of supermarkets two department stores offered groceries and dry goods. Both had wonderful dim interiors and a delightful atmosphere that combined bulk produce with buckskin gloves and moccasins."[10] A few entrepreneurs moved into the area and opened garages or makeshift restaurants and hotels. The American Automobile Association commented in 1954, "The motorist's money will buy only what is available – extremely modest accommodations and very plain fare in cafés that range from the homespun frontier cabin type to modest but clean lunch counters."[11] Iris Woolcock found the Long's establishment at Mile 278 to be an utter delight: "I parked across the road to try to avoid picking up any more nails. When I smelled the odors which came out of

Mrs. Long's kitchen I decided to have my evening meal in their attractive, homelike dining room. My appetite was whetted more while watching her prepare food in the immaculate kitchen open to view from the counter. For a dollar I was served a wonderful roast pork dinner with a big fluffy baked potato, fresh crispy crusty homemade bread."[12]

With traffic at a minimum and restricted to the short summer months, there were not many paying propositions. Several of the first operators on the scene, in a revealing glimpse of the nature of free enterprise, deeply resented the appearance of competitors, arguing that the small amount of traffic could not support more than a few businesses. Along the southern end of the highway, legend has it, two notorious rivals – Tucker and Slyman – competed bitterly for the small seasonal trade; wherever one would open a store, the other would set up another across the road, determined to run his competitor into the ground.

The Americans' withdrawal had left one intriguing and timely opportunity. As the maintenance operations were streamlined and centralized, the government had abandoned a number of construction and maintenance camps. These properties, often complete with dormitories, office space, garages, gasoline-dispensing facilities, and cooking halls, were easily converted into commercial operations. A small group of entrepreneurs seized the opening, secured the salvage rights to the structures, and set up shop. The Canadian government and army welcomed the advent of a small network of highway stations, for it reduced the demand on their crews and camps for assistance. Travellers could now be directed to the small but growing number of commercial operators along the highway. The establishments came slowly, and some disappeared into insolvency shortly after they opened. Others became landmarks for highway travellers: the Rancheria Hotel, opened by Bud and Doris Simpson, the first such establishment along the highway, the distinctive Watson Lake Inn, Clyde Wann's motel at mile 1202 (and the other lodges that he built at other sites along the highway), and Jim Grant's rustic cabins at Highland Glen at Muncho Lake. There was considerable turnover in the hotel business, but a core group stayed. Frank Steele, for one, worked initially for Clyde Wann at Swift River, then leased a place at Watson Lake, and later, in 1957, bought Summit Lodge. As one travel writer wrote

The Donjek River bridge in February 1952. H. DEVITT

in 1960, "If you're looking for deluxe motels with heated swimming pools, barbecue pits and dancing girl revues, we don't have them – yet. Right now, the highway roadhouses tended more to the 'bath is down the hall' variety."[13]

The B.C., Yukon, and Alaskan governments also jumped in and developed rustic camping facilities at appropriate intervals along the highway, providing the more cost-conscious travellers with a welcome alternative to the lodges and motels. There was a certain urgency to the construction of campgrounds; many of the travellers had taken to using abandoned military bases for their stopovers – "they constitute a fire hazard, leave the camps dirty and lift all moveables."[14] It was a trend the Canadian Army strongly discouraged.

Almost imperceptibly a new society emerged along the Alaska Highway. It began in Dawson Creek and Fort St. John and continued in a series of tiny dots on the highway map: Wonowon, Pink Mountain, Trutch, Steamboat, Muncho Lake, Fireside, Rancheria, Swift River, Teslin, Johnson's Crossing, Jake's Corner, Mendenhall Creek, Destruction Bay, Beaver Creek, Northway, Tok, and Delta Junction. Some of the places, unknown to people outside the region, consisted of little more than a highway way-station; others included a commercial operation across the road from an army or Alaskan maintenance yard.

Travellers rattling along the highway seldom stopped long enough to do more than fill up with gasoline, grab a hamburger and a piece of pie, and occasionally pass the night. The travellers' experience of the road was linear, superficial, and rapid; the Alaska Highway was reduced to a series of glimpses, vivid images frozen in photographs or imprinted in a fuzzy blur on one's memory. The sameness of the road stations and the remarkable isolation – usually fifty miles between stops, with virtually no other signs of human habitation around – meant that these tiny outposts attracted only a casual glance, a brief thought of sympathy or envy, and then quick dismissal as the cars and trucks rolled northward.

Many of those who stopped did so unintentionally. The highway took its toll on cars and trucks, particularly those in rough shape before the journey, those driven too quickly or overloaded. Travellers were warned to carry extra equipment – the list of required material in the late 1940s amounted to a veritable garageful of replacement parts, including tires, belts, starters, and the like. The American Automobile Association in 1958 recommended that travellers carry: "two mounted spare tires (preferably six-ply or nylon) and tubes, fuel pump, spark plugs, fan belt, light fuses, cold-patch tube repair kit and pump, car tools, a fire extinguisher, tow rope or cable, and an extra coil and condenser," plus a five-gallon gas can. By the early 1960s, when more service stations had opened along the highway, tourists were advised to carry at least two spare tires but not the plethora of automobile parts recommended earlier – although many continued to strap a jerrycan or two of gasoline onto their vehicles. Travellers coming south from Alaska were still greeted at the customs office with a list of recommended equipment, with particular warnings to carry warm clothes and blankets in winter time.

There were reasons for the caution. With tongue only partially in his cheek, one highway traveller observed that there was a different explanation for the 0 in the Dawson Creek Mile 0 sign: "Riding into Dawson Creek from the Alaska Highway it should be quite plain to everyone, as it is to us, that after sinking into, plowing out of, and straddling across the million-and-a-half deep holes which comprise the entire road surface in that piece of highway immediately entering Dawson Creek, that the 0 referred to in the sign is put there to warn motorists about the holes ahead. After all it matters not which way you choose to go from the sign, there are holes a-plenty awaiting to test your skill as a driver, your auto's durability, your patience, and your physical endurance." Highway travellers, she continued, suffered from a regional illness called "Buttock Bumpingitis."[15]

The winding and twisting, the countervailing curves, the dangerous steep hills and blind corners, which sounded like such an adventure while sitting in a living room in Colorado, California, or Alberta, soon took their toll. The road was interminably long, excruciatingly dusty at times, rough, and ragged. The dust worked its way through the doors and windows, laying a fine film across passengers and upholstery and filling nostrils with a persistent dryness. And when the rains came, as they did regularly each summer, the roads gained a slippery coat that was soon plastered onto vehicles and travellers alike. Through the 1950s and early 1960s, the rains often brought road and bridge wash-outs, adding hours if not days to an already long journey.

The highway munched tires at a ferocious pace. Much of the problem lay with the drivers, who failed to slow for the potholes, drove too fast over rough gravel, or, even more commonly, piled too much equipment and supplies into their vehicles. Hugh Devitt claimed that "grader steel" – slivers of steel shaved off the grader blades during the levelling of the road surface – also contributed to the high mortality rate of car tires.

The tourists were, themselves, a breed apart. The American servicemen posted to Alaska had no choice but to push through. The tourists, on the other hand, had numerous options – and those who wandered north in this era were venturesome souls indeed. Hugh Devitt recalls passing an old Rio truck outside of Fort Nelson, loaded to the top with a family's entire possessions – another pioneer family heading to Alaska, the last settlement frontier in the United States. They did not get very far: "They had just broken a chassis and were just sitting on the highway like an old swayback mule, quite flat on the highway, and on the back of it, so ironically, there was a sign 'Alaska or Bust.' This old truck had clearly busted at Mile 278." Paul Greenan remembers a man who led a modern-day wagon train – more than fifteen vehicles heading for a pioneer life in Alaska: "Well, of course, the convoy could only move as fast as its slowest vehicle. There was always one of them breaking down. I bet they didn't make a hundred miles a day all the way from Dawson Creek to Fairbanks."

Cliff Stringer says that many of the travellers were ill-prepared for their northern adventure. They would, for example, assume that the costs of travel were the same in the North as in the South, only to discover that gas, meals, and accommodation were so much higher than anticipated they lacked the money to get back south again. "People," he says, "didn't know what they were coming to." Frank Steele had a carload of travellers show up at Summit Lodge without a cent to their name. They offered to pay for their gas with a gold watch. Steele refused, offering instead to loan them some money and hold the watch as collateral. They came through again the following fall and picked up the watch, remaining Steele's committed customers thereafter. Steele says, "You had to help them. What are you going to do, keep them on your doorstep? So, you got them on their way somewhere."

One of the most common problems along the highway in this era was the tendency of the drivers to, in the oft-repeated phrase, "take their half of the road right down the middle." Since the road was often narrow, and traffic very limited, drivers could go for miles down the centre of the highway. Lulled into a sense of false security by the absence of oncoming traffic, drivers often went around curves or over blind hills without moving back to the right side of the road. Most of the time, they made it safely, but not always.

The Alaska Highway was pock-marked with warning signs. When Mrs. Light travelled along the Alaska Highway to Whitehorse in 1947, she observed: "The highway is literally covered at the side with signposts: Slow – Steep Hill – Winding Road – Turn – Dumps – Danger – Falling Rocks – Slow – Washout – Detour. Before we had reached the next stop, we twisted and turned down a long incline to a wooden trestle bridge where there was a big sign and a guard at the approach. The sign was at the end of the 1,270 foot narrow bridge over Teslin Lake and gave the speed as five m.p.h., 'Drive Carefully and Steadily,' and the guard clocked each vehicle for speed, no two vehicles being allowed on the bridge at one time."[16] The constant barrage of signs and warnings was hardly designed to encourage confidence – although it did instil caution.

The highway signage was far from complete, however. When Hugh Devitt drove his family to Whitehorse between Christmas and New Year in 1957, he discovered that there were no distance or community markers – just ubiquitous curve and hill signs and mileposts. Immediately upon taking up his position Devitt requested that the proper signs be commissioned, and they were soon posted along the length of the highway. Devitt also had his sign painter, Jack Earl, create a series of more picturesque signs indicating special interest points and tourist attractions, thereby adding "a little diversion to a pretty boring trip to some people on the highway."

For the uninitiated, unprepared, or the foolhardy, the Alaska Highway could easily be a dangerous road. Miles of twists and turns, fog banks of dust, blind curves and hills, and the false security of limited traffic added up to a potentially fatal combination. The army did its best to warn travellers of the dangers; treacherous spots were well and clearly marked. Adding some poignancy to the scene, the army placed small red markers at the site of each fatal accident. The markers were perfunctory, indicating nothing more than the date of the accident and number of people who died, such as, "March 15, 1958, Two Killed."

These simple, powerful messages slowly sprouted, like late-flowering plants, along the Alaska Highway. Most grew alone, but at particularly dangerous spots, a small garden of the markers was planted. It is impossible to know if the fatality markers had any effect, but it is hard to believe that most drivers would not lift their foot slightly off the gas pedal as they approached a short picket fence of the death symbols near a curve or hill. Mickey McGaw confirms this: "There were too many signs along the highway that said two killed here in such and such a year. When you've got your family with you, it scares the daylights out of you."

Still, inevitably, the accidents mounted, though not at a particularly rapid pace, for the highway was not unusually dangerous and the same forces that caused some accidents – bad weather, dust, rough conditions, poor sight-lines – generated extra caution and slower speeds. Marv and Mabel Armitage remember one incident. They were preparing supper when a car pulled into their yard. Mabel answered the door to discover a man standing out front, blood pouring down his face. In his arms he held a small bundle – Mabel assumed it was a baby. "Here," he said

The highway north of Fort St. John in 1943.
PHYLLIS CHURCH.

shortly, "we can't look." His wife and their other child, quiet and fearful, followed him into the house. Mabel, who was shaking at the implication of his words, took the bundle to the couch and slowly pulled back the blankets. To her relief and delight, a small baby smiled back up at her. Once they had cleaned up the man – he had glass in his eyes – they heard the full story. The family's car had run off the road, and they had luckily suffered only superficial cuts. The baby, however, had been bounced around in the back, had fallen in a bunch of diapers, and had made no noise. Her parents had been too afraid to look for themselves.

Chuck Baxter, one of the many northerners whose life is intertwined with the highway, drove up it in the winter late in the 1940s. Travelling in exceptional cold, Baxter came across a car on the side of the road. The car had crashed into a tree that had fallen across the highway, punching out the windshield. The driver and passengers were unhurt, but when they drove back into town they found there was no windshield to be had. Anxious to push on, the travellers had no choice but to bundle back into the car – despite the thirty-below cold – and drive more than nine hundred miles to Dawson Creek. They bundled together in the front seat, wrapped in blankets, heater on full blast, whatever good that might do. Baxter did not see them through the journey, although the thought of them venturing down the highway under such circumstances still sends shivers down his spine.

Travellers in difficulty along the highway, particularly in winter, were often victims of their own mismanagement. Drivers from the American South seemed especially vulnerable to cold weather mishaps. One highway engineer says, "I have a very clear recollection of coming upon an American serviceman nearly frozen to death up at the top end of the highway in the middle of winter. He was driving south and was admiring the scenery, and as he was gazing at the beautiful snow-capped mountains, let his vehicle veer off the road into a snowdrift. The vehicle had gone in on its side and he couldn't move it. He had no shovel, was not properly dressed; he couldn't operate the engine because it was starting to overheat, and he was very close to freezing. I remember being absolutely amazed when I got him into my station wagon, my staff car, that he was dressed in cotton jeans. We were in sub-zero temperatures by then. It never occurred to him that if he lost control of his car he would have no car heater to keep him warm."[17]

This scene – a traveller, almost always an American, driving down the highway in mid-winter, ill-prepared for the Arctic conditions – is a common memory for former highway workers. Paul Greenan remembers a man in a large Cadillac, heater turned up full, wearing only a T-shirt and shorts. Not an unusual scene – except that it was forty below outside. As Greenan comments: "It's fine as long as the heater works, but if the gas line ever froze up on him, and lots of times that happened, he was sure in for serious problems."

Stories soon abounded about long-distance endurance trips, the hazards of Alaska Highway driving, and other travellers' feats on the road. Many of the tales show the effects of time, growing, like a fisherman's recounting of the "one that got away," to unbelievable dimensions. But the individual circumstances were, in themselves, quite remarkable. One of the last military personnel posted to the Alaska Highway maintenance operations, a lieutenant from Quebec, piled his effects into his Corvair and, risking his new car to the vagaries of highway driving, set off from Quebec City on 30 September 1963. According to the story, he completed the trip – some four thousand miles in total – in five days, arriving in Whitehorse on 3 October.

Travellers soon discovered that this was a highway unlike any other. Earle Smith, stationed in Whitehorse with the Royal Canadian

Air Force from 1954 to 1961, offers a wonderful story that occurred during a trip on the highway in 1956: "After waking up one particularly frosty morning, my wife decided she would like to have breakfast at a café or roadhouse. We eventually came to one, pulled up, parked, and went in. There wasn't a soul in sight, but some lights were on. I went snooping around the back, found three drunk, dead-to-the-world, scruffy characters in beds in a shack. I finally got one to open his eyes a bit and told him we wanted breakfast. You can imagine the reply! Well, to make a long story short, he told me to go and make my own breakfast and leave them alone, and he went back to sleep. So, back to the café I went, brought my wife and son in, fired up the grill, cleaned a few months' accumulation of grease off it, found the eggs and wherewithal, and made breakfast for the three of us. Yes, you guessed it! Before I got the bacon, eggs, and toast onto our plates, tourists and other travellers started coming in the door, and before I could explain what I was doing I was getting orders. Once everyone knew what was going on they were happy with the standard bacon, eggs, toast, and coffee I was able to dish out. One of the drunks from out in back finally staggered in, thanked me for the help, told me to keep the money I had collected, and off we went. It could only happen on the Alaska Highway, I'm sure."

The people travelling along the highway varied tremendously – American servicemen heading to Alaska, hunters and fishermen looking for northern adventure, tourists retracing either the Trail of '98 or reliving the adventures of 1942. The range of travellers was remarkable: A worker at a lodge in the Yukon encountered one of the unusual groups travelling the road: "I was all alone and three carloads of gypsies came in one day. All the car doors opened and there were gypsies all over creation. No matter where I went a gypsy was into something. I was warding off the women in the café who wanted to read my palm and tell my fortune. And while they were doing that the kids were in the store filling their pockets with candy and gum and whatever they could get a hold of. The men were at the gas pump filling up their cars and then winding that thing back so I wouldn't know how much gas they got. I tell you, I had two hectic hours till they got on."

Herb Hilscher swears that you can spot an Alaska Highway driver from miles away: "No matter what the make or model, it's a cinch to spot a car that's just driven over this northern road. Like birds of a feather, many of them carry luggage racks on top and/or trailers behind, are well supplied with stickers that say Welcome to Canada, and have mesh bug-catchers shielding the front, and their headlights and bumpers are taped against flying gravel."

Highway workers, who helped those whose vehicles broke down or who picked up the wreckage after an accident, were constantly amazed at the "weird and wonderful pieces of equipment – junk" that drivers brought to the highway. Cars ill-suited for driving on paved southern highways would be pointed north, only to break down from the rattling and shaking far away from replacement parts and repair shops. Not surprisingly, many of the highway workers were less than sympathetic to the plight of the foolhardy and ill-prepared, although they always stepped in to help those in trouble – if only to add a new anecdote to the fund of highway stories that enlivened their winter hours.

Making fun of travellers became something of a highway sport. Knowing that many of those journeying north to Alaska lived in fear of the road and sub-Arctic conditions, workers were known to exploit their lack of knowledge. Bob Brant was sitting in the restaurant at Summit Lake with several of his friends one mid-August when a light snow was falling. Playing to a small audience of travellers – a favourite pastime for those who lived along the highway – one of Brant's friends commented, "Well, I wonder how deep it will get tonight." Playing along, Brant answered, "Oh, it shouldn't get past the centre bar in the window." After Brant had left, an elderly couple slid over to his friend and asked if it was true that the snow would get that deep so early in the year. He told them they were just kidding, but the couple took fright anyway. They cancelled their plans and retreated south, fearful of being caught in a full Arctic blizzard.

The Alaska Highway compensated its travellers for its shortcomings. The scenery never stopped: the grand vistas from Steamboat Mountain, the river scenes along the Liard, the rocky hillsides along Muncho Lake, the stunning beauty of Teslin and Marsh lakes, the breath-taking landscape portrait that filled the windshield on approach to Haines Junction, the chilling blues of Kluane Lake, the marshy tracks south of Northway, the broad views of the Tanana Valley were almost too much to absorb. For travellers accustomed to the crowds and overdevelopment of

much of North America, this was wilderness as seemed to exist only in the pages of *National Geographic* and *Outdoor Life*. It was everyone's opportunity to go where it was truly wild and free.

And there was wildlife, too. Not as much, perhaps, as southerners expected. Wartime stories, exaggerated with the passage of time and distance from the Norhwest, told of enormous moose, caribou herds, and flocks of sheep. Many travellers were disappointed to discover that the ungainly ungulates of the Far Northwest rarely blocked their way – they were fortunate that this was so, for moose were known to attack cars – and that large game animals were a rare sight. There were exceptions – the Muncho Lake area was known for its mountain sheep, as was the well-named Sheep Mountain in the Kluane Game Sanctuary. Early morning travellers often saw moose in the swamps and sloughs along the highway – although the much shorter journeys through Banff and Jasper National Parks usually brought better photo opportunities, as did several of the main roads in Alaska.

The wildlife enhanced the scenery and highlighted the wilderness nature of the Alaska Highway experience but also caused occasional problems. A truck driver by the name of Stevens was working near Mile 1095 when he came upon a bear busily licking the grease off a crane sitting alongside the road:

"Being an enthusiastic if inexperienced hunter, he attacked the bear with his .22 rifle, and after absorbing two rounds, the bear, a trifle annoyed, chased Stevens up the bottom of the crane. In his excitement he dropped the .22 rifle, and the bear remained below licking his chops. It was not until the following morning that some of his fellow employees arrived and dispatched the bear. A more experienced hunter descended to mother earth."[18]

For keen hunters, camp life held wonderful attractions. Bob Brant pointed out that highway hunting differed from most people's definition of the term: "I carried the rifle on the grader and if you saw something, and you liked what you saw, and it looked good, you shot it. So it really wasn't hunting, you know, not in the context of chasing off in the bush and roughing it."

Bears were a regular feature of highway life. Marv Armitage was pressed into emergency service one evening when one of the cooks in the camp ran up to tell him that a bear was staring at her through the kitchen window – the crew's hamburgers were an obvious attraction. Armitage had no choice but to dispatch the beast on the spot, one of several he had to shoot while he worked on the highway.

Of course, those who travelled along the Alaska Highway for adventure and wilderness experiences were not the only people who used the road. There were such folk, to be sure, and many of them wrote about their journey, further exciting southern fascination with the highway. But like all roads, this was a working highway, built and maintained to carry people and supplies across vast distances. Truckers drove up and down the Alaska Highway by the hundreds, carrying supplies to sites across the Yukon and into Alaska. Trailer-loads of fresh food, mail, construction equipment, retail goods, and countless other commodities pressed northward. The truck trade could not capture all the market – both Whitehorse and Fairbanks had regular train service to ocean ports, and regularly scheduled air service provided tough competition for urgently needed freight. But the truckers continued to move up and down the highway, often heading north fully loaded and deadheading south. They became the staple for the highway shops, providing a regular clientele for the gas stations, hotels, and restaurants. Most lodges had special sleeping quarters – driver's hotels – that offered a tiny room for a relative pittance, for the drivers seldom hung around any longer than necessary to catch a bit of sleep and refuel both body and vehicle.

The people who lived and worked along the highway experienced the place, and the road, differently. Whether a Department of National Defence employee in a maintenance yard, a worker for Canadian National Telecommunications in one of the many repeating stations along the Alaska Highway, or a manager with a private company operating a gas station, hotel, or store, the people of the Alaska Highway looked upon the road with special fondness. The highway was, after all, their lifeline to the outside – the world beyond Dawson Creek. It provided contact with their neighbours, who might well be fifty miles away, kept them connected to their community, which stretched like an umbilical cord for hundreds of miles through the wilderness, and provided the steady supply of travellers that kept them in business and at work.

The camps themselves were not impressive places. The Muncho Lake maintenance camp, set in one of the most scenic locations in the Northwest, consisted of a few cabins for families and a couple of apartments for single men. The buildings were not well-constructed for the sub-Arctic climate. Marvin and Mabel Armitage remember that the buildings at the Muncho Lake camp used to have three feet of sawdust piled up on the outside as a form of insulation. Shortly after Cliff Stringer and his wife, Collette, moved into their unit at Coal River, the weather dipped to forty-five below. The oil froze in the lines to the heater, turning their home into a deep-freeze. They had to curtain off the kitchen with blankets and turn the oven on in order to keep the baby warm. Some camps were better than others. Hugh Devitt describes Haines Junction as a "model camp in the Arctic" with its general purpose huts converted into "comfortable living quarters." Each camp had its recreational facilities and events – darts and ping-pong tables in the recreation halls, regular film nights (with the workers taking turns at the projector), and occasional dances, thanks to canned music and the odd employee who could play a musical instrument. The movies, passed from camp to camp along the highway, were not always up to standard. Marion Greenan says, "Sometimes they were so bad we'd run them backwards to enjoy them. That's no fooling. And they were always broken. We'd patch them together."

The people in the camps welcomed visitors, and went out of their way to make them welcome. On her journey up the highway in 1948 Iris Woolcock pulled into the Canadian National Telecommunications station at Coal River and requested permission to park for the night. It was enthusiastically granted, and the next day she had trouble getting away. "[The men] wanted me to meet their wives and they took me around to their various attractive little houses – as usual, the drab old barracks were surprising inside, some of them almost elegant."[19] She left having made new friends and with a new pet – a dog named Peater after the repeating station.

The other recreational outlet – the frontier standard – was alcohol. Social drinking was common, according to former highway residents, but heavy drinkers did not last long in the camps. Fittingly, there were a few special northern concoctions – including moosemilk, a miserable sounding mix, described by Audrey Gaddy as overproof rum with Eagle Brand milk, hot water, and a drop of vanilla. Paul Greenan believes that drinking was a fairly common problem in the highway camps: "It was easier to get a bottle up there. Pretty well every truck driver had an extra one, and some of the help that we used to get in the lodge and restaurant, it was terrible." People trying to escape their drinking problems in the South soon found, Greenan argued, that liquor was readily accessible along the highway – and there were abundant reasons to drink.

Mixing highway work and drink could be dangerous. Hugh Devitt says that he understood some people's desire to drink but wouldn't allow anyone to drive equipment while under the influence. Shortly after he arrived he fired a "float" driver, setting a firm and unmistakable precedent. Harry George, then a camp foreman, used a similarly strong hand. Upon discovering that several men were drinking and gambling to excess and leaving their families short of food, he called them together and laid down the law: "'I'm looking after this personally. The groceries: Your family has got to eat. But if you can't pay the bill next time, you go and you haven't got a job anymore.' You had full control. This stopped the poker game, and if someone wanted to imbibe during work hours, they were long gone." But such measures did not stop drinking in its tracks – life seldom follows such simple patterns. During Devitt's tenure, one of his operators ran a truck trailer into a vehicle driven by an American serviceman, killing the man. Subsequent investigation revealed that the trailer driver had been drinking.

Former highway residents speak glowingly of the sense of community that pervaded the maintenance camps. At Muncho Lake, the Armitages shared a washing machine with the entire camp, and stored their frozen goods in a common walk-in locker. When the Brants arrived at their first posting, they were without furniture; theirs was stuck in Dawson Creek. The other families, however, provided them with the necessities until their supplies arrived. There was, as one long-timer recalled, "a real community spirit because of the isolation of it. Everybody had to join in, and everybody did join in." Hugh Devitt describes it as a "community of 1,200 miles length." (It is telling to note that the American portion of the road did not fit into the Canadians' definition of the "community.") "We had much more active community spirit in the North than one experiences living in so-called outside civilization." Harry George agrees: "The hospitality of the people in the North is out of this world. In the early years you could go to any place, didn't matter, and you were welcome there – you might have to sleep on the floor. We looked after a lot of people – a lot of people coming down the road slept on the floor in our houses, Americans, Canadians, what-have-you, who had run into some trouble and were looked after."

One of the most popular recreations in highway community life was to be found in the curling rinks – unheated, single-sheet Quonset huts. Hugh Devitt and others credit Walt Williscroft with the establishment of the sport along the highway. It was, Devitt says, a masterstroke: "This was one of the finest morale builders that could have been introduced. In my opinion it saved many people from either going around the bend with claustrophobia or cabin fever or becoming alcoholics." As a result, almost every camp had a rink, most of them built in the early 1950s by volunteer labour and with departmental supplies. Cliff Stringer, newly arrived at Coal River, had put everyone to work on building the curling rink: "Love was the brigadier then, and he came through and all my crew, totally everybody, was working on the curling rink. It turned out he was actually a real good curling man. He never said anything about it other than he thought it was a good curling rink." Bob Brant says, "Curling was the big

Milepost 0 in Dawson Creek during the 1950s.
JOHNSON COLLECTION.

thing in the winter time. Always had teams. Everybody curled. Even little kids, before they went to school, they learned to curl." The curling rink became a focus for social and recreational life in the long and often uneventful winter months.

The camps began competing against each other, establishing a curling culture that ran the length of the Canadian highway (but not, in any significant way, extending into Alaska). The Armitages remember making the long journey from where they were at Mile 245 to a bonspiel at Trutch. Almost the entire camp went – kids and all, for there were no babysitters at their camp. They left on a typical winter's day, only to have a Chinook (a burst of warm winter air that can raise the temperature thirty degrees Fahrenheit in a matter of a few hours) hit. The ice on the Trutch rink softened, forcing a cancellation of the games. Not to be deterred, the entire operation picked up and drove back to the camp at Mile 245, where they proceeded with the bonspiel.

The bonspiels quickly became a major focus for winter life — an excuse to travel and an opportunity to spend time with old friends and meet newcomers to the camps, motels, and other operations along the highway. Facilities were pretty basic; most camps had only a single sheet of ice, and in order to accommodate as many as sixteen teams, the competition continued without a break from Friday evening to Sunday afternoon, leaving enough time for the competitors to make it back to their camps that evening. Sleep would be fitted in around games, talking, and partying.

The community spirit emerged in other ways. Liard Hot Springs had first been developed by the American soldiers during World War II. The rustic facilities quickly fell into disrepair after the war. People living along the highway in the 1950s, particularly those at Muncho Lake and Coal River, including highway workers and Canadian National Telecommunications employees, organized a work bee to improve the hot springs and make them usable once again. They rebuilt the boardwalks that crossed several hundred yards of swamp over to the natural springs, cleaned up the campsite, and generally improved the facility. In short order, they had a year-round diversion.

The highway had taken on a life of its own. Native people in the area rarely shared in this community, for only a few worked on the highway and the others rarely joined the commercial world. The non-Natives, however, were bound into the same organizations — the army or CNT on the Canadian side — and were connected by commercial suppliers, common friends, and frequent visits during highway travels. Bob Brant remembers often driving fifty or seventy-five miles to visit a friend and share a cup of coffee, travelling to the next camp for a bingo game, or otherwise finding an excuse for expanding the network of fellowship. The camaraderie spread to the lodge operators as well. Owners up and down the highway shared supplies and equipment as required, knowing that they could call on similar hospitality in their turn. Frank Steele at Summit Lake says the people at Fireside, 150 miles away, would sometimes call up and ask to borrow a case of bread. If he had it to spare, he would throw it on the next bus or truck heading up the highway.

The highway camps were neither large nor particularly impressive places. The outfit at Blueberry (Mile 101) in 1948 included cabins for six to ten families, a large garage, modern amenities (water, sewage, and light), and a small service station and café, run in 1948 by an ex-serviceman. The maintenance staff included a foreman and mechanic; the rest were heavy equipment operators. In many camps the army maintained a school, staffed by a teacher provided by the B.C. or Yukon government. But life in the isolated outposts, with a handful of families and a sprinkling of children, cut off from regular contact with southern society, was far from easy. For young, single men, the maintenance camps offered few opportunities for female companionship. The hunting and fishing attracted their share of enthusiasts, but most young men quickly tired of the tiny settlements and the unending routines. Larger centres – Fort St. John, Fort Nelson, Watson Lake, Whitehorse, and Fairbanks – beckoned. Some people considered their time in the North to be akin to a sentence – something to be endured rather than enjoyed. For them it was only a career stop or an opportunity to make some big money in a subsidized camp. Bob Brant, who has wonderful memories of his time on the highway, says that it was a marvellous place for young people, but that "after we'd been out for fifteen years or so, I wouldn't even think of going back up there to work. It's a young person's country."

The women in the highway camps felt particularly isolated. Ester Peters, who accompanied her husband Frank to his posting at Mile 245, was the only woman in camp; life at home with her seven-month-old daughter was so tedious that she would join her husband in his gravel truck: "I just took the baby's bottle, went out to the highway, and waited until he came along and he'd stop and pick me up. Spent a couple of hours like that."

Such extreme isolation was rare. Lifelong friendships were forged in the camps; at the same time, the proximity that bred such fondness could also generate tension and difficulty. Many families, particularly in the long winter months, when there was little traffic on the road and little to do outside the home, became discouraged, lonely, and anxious to move on. Mabel Armitage recognized that not all women were ready for the highway life: "Actually, the people who liked the area, who could stand being isolated, well, they were fine. People who couldn't, they just didn't stay. It did get to a lot of people; they just couldn't – especially the women – they just couldn't handle it. There were always a few people who would only stay a matter of a few months. They just couldn't handle it. They were gone." Colette Stringer agrees: "I think it was harder on the women than it was on the men. You'd miss your own family. Sometimes we'd stay up there two years to get a month's holiday, because you just got two weeks holiday a year. You were pretty bushed by the time you went to Edmonton after living in Coal River for two years."

Families in the isolated camps faced other problems. Mabel Armitage says that the constant movement of trucks created concern for the children's safety. So they built a fence out of slabs and, whenever the trucks were about, the children were penned in. The army did make every effort to move families with school-age children to one of the larger camps. The schools were tiny — the Brants remember that the school at Wonowon had only nine children in total. Bob Brant says, "They got a good start in education up there because it was almost a one-on-one situation. They had special tutoring." Older children, and those in camps without a school, worked by correspondence. Hugh Devitt says, "It was a good, sound, intelligent camp wife that was the unofficial school marm in some of the maintenance camps."

Women would find themselves recruited for other unusual assignments. Camp foreman Don Bakke and his wife, Trudi, lived at Summit Lake in 1949. One evening, when the rest of the highway personnel were at a wedding at Muncho Lake, some sixty-four miles away, a trucker pulled into camp to report that the road was washed out below Summit Lake. The Bakkes rushed to the scene to discover that a culvert had frozen up, forcing water over the road. The two of them set to with a steam generator, plunging heated metal rods into the culvert to thaw out the ice plug and thus free the backed up water. They worked through the evening and into the early hours of the following morning, no doubt thinking occasionally of their colleagues at the wedding party.

Camp life meant doing without — without the amenities of town or city life, without a variety of recreational activities, and without access to stores. Most people visited the nearest large centre — Dawson Creek or Whitehorse — only once or twice a year. Lil Brant says that ordering groceries — a month's worth at a time, and having to do without if supplies ran low — was her greatest adaptation to life along the highway. Friends in the

Highway wash-out.

South could be recruited for the more unusual requests, and the catalogue – Sears' or Eaton's – became their access to a full department store. The stores outside were a great help. When Colette Stringer needed a wedding gift for two friends she wrote a short note to the Co-op in Dawson Creek. "They sent me up the nicest things for a gift. I think they understood our plight."

Most of the groceries and other supplies were purchased by truck drivers and regular highway travellers. As they passed through a camp, they would collect money and shopping lists from the workers and their families. Once in town – usually Whitehorse or Dawson Creek – they would fill the orders and, on their next trip along the road, deliver the supplies. The truck driver would also do the banking, deliver pay cheques, carry mail and otherwise serve the highway communities. It was a remarkably informal system – called the Pony Express in many of the camps – with few formal IOUs, only the occasional use of receipts, and a healthy dose of trust and goodwill.

Wash-outs and road closures caused occasional shortages in the ill-supplied highway camps. At one point, Paul and Marion

Greenan were down to rice and baloney because of a highway wash-out. Staff were threatening to quit *en masse*. The area superintendent called a meeting and promised that the first trucks – three promised for the next day – would bring food. "First truck came in, everybody was around to unload it. Toilet paper. Second truck, toilet paper. The third truck was paper towels. But they flew in some emergency rations then, and the next day the trucks were there with food."

Freight costs were added to the cost of supplies, of course, although the expense was largely offset by the government's isolated-post allowances. This subsidy covered the difference in the cost of living between major, southern centres and the many smaller, isolated postings in Canada. In the late 1950s, much to the consternation of highway workers, the federal government officials in Ottawa reworked the allowances. Hugh Devitt says, "They beautifully screwed it up, and we had people in the more remote locations getting less than those who were comfortably based in Fort Nelson and Whitehorse and Fort St. John." Faced with a near mutiny among federal civil servants, the government sent a delegation up the highway – where they got more than an earful from the maintenance camp residents and others who suffered because of the reorganization. Devitt succinctly summarizes the tour of the region, "We got results."

The maintenance operations operated with a military, hierarchical structure. The commanders and chief engineers – Walsh, Connelley, Brown, Love, Meuser, Jones, Lilley, Webb, and Spencer, who held these offices at different times between 1946 and 1964 – stood atop the pyramid, operating out of the Whitehorse office and maintaining overall supervision of highway operations. Whitehorse remained the headquarters of the Northwest Highway System – most of the engineering and design staff and the employees in the maintenance operations worked out of Whitehorse and lived in nearby Camp Takhini. Local highway operations were divided into three areas: Southern (miles 0-496), Central (miles 496-917) and Northern (miles 917-1221). The design and maintenance establishment was small – the complete staff numbered only 335 in 1953, of whom 208 were civilians. The scale of operations declined over the next decade. By 1964, the Northwest Highway System had 211 employees – 184 civilians and 27 military personnel.

The system – a military hierarchy imposed on a civilian maintenance system – was complex. Highway workers, however, recall few difficulties. Bob Brant offers an excellent assessment of the arrangement: "We certainly never had any problem with the army personnel coming along and being demanding or anything of that nature at all. We were actually an orphan body in the defence program in the fact that we were highway maintenance, which didn't really fit into any category of the Department of National Defence in those years. It was a bit of spit and polish when you knew someone was coming through, especially if it was top brass – clean up the garage and wash the trucks or something."

Devitt agrees that the arrangement worked well for all concerned. As senior highway superintendent he contacted the three area superintendents routinely, taking advantage of a highway-long party line that allowed conference calls long before the concept entered the corporate boardroom, and, through them, kept in touch with the sixteen separate camps operating during his tenure. Devitt also spent as much time outside Whitehorse as possible, devoting as much as half his time to travel along the road. He, like the others before and after who held his position, would fly out of Whitehorse to Fort St. John and then work his way back up the highway over a week, visiting camps and inspecting the road. The following week, after a short stop in town, he would head north by car, travelling as far as Beaver Creek (mile 1202), the most westerly community in Canada.

As the years passed, and major sections of the highway improved, operations were progressively streamlined. Several highway camps were closed. Kiskatinau (Mile 20) and Fort St. John (Mile 49) were both closed by 1960, and responsibility for this portion of the Alaska Highway passed on to British Columbia authorities. Similarly, the camps at Marsh Lake (Mile 883) and Stoney Creek (Mile 956) were closed, and the large Whitehorse station assumed responsibility for this portion of the road. Koidern (Mile 1156) was closed in 1949, and the maintenance camps at Destruction Bay (Mile 1083) and Beaver Creek (Mile 1202) took over its work.

The Department of National Defence had never been particularly eager to accept, or retain, responsibility for the Alaska Highway. As complaints about the condition of the highway escalated through the late 1950s and early 1960s, the service's desire to rid itself of the road increased. Any arguments about the utility of the highway as a training operation had long since been worn thin, and the department was in no position to plan for the long-term reconstruction of the highway. In the early 1960s the department began plans to pass the northern duty to other hands.

The new custodians would inherit a wealth of knowledge about the highway. A small number of highway employees – the DND referred to them as the Original Group – had joined the army's civilian corps on 1 April 1946 and were still there eighteen years later. These were not the military men of supervisory rank, or the ones who negotiated deals with federal or territorial officials. They were, however, absolutely essential to the operation of the Alaska Highway. Together, they knew what there was to be known about the road, the northern environment, and maintenance and construction procedures. These individuals – particularly Don Bakke, Harry George, James Quong, and Walt Williscroft – had devoted most of their adult, professional lives to the Alaska Highway. They had done more than work, for it was the force of their personalities that gave highway life much of its character and charm. Yet nothing along the highway marks their contribution – unless one counts the bridges that Jim Quong designed and supervised the construction of, or the miles of highway maintained by the crews under Bakke, George, and Williscroft. Nor is there any commemoration of the work of the other long-service personnel who were heart and soul of the professional Alaska Highway community.

Walt Williscroft signed on to work on the Alaska Highway in 1943. He stayed with the Canadian operation in 1946, served as superintendent of the Northern Area from 1946 to 1951, and after that moved to the Southern Area. Harry George arrived on the highway in 1945 and, at the time of the transfer in 1946, accepted a position as superintendent of the Central Area, a job he held for the entire tenure of the Royal Canadian Engineers. Don Bakke, Northern Area superintendent from 1953 to 1964, served with the U.S. Army between 1943 and 1946 and worked his way up the maintenance ladder, with postings at Summit Lake and Trutch Camp. Jim Quong, who also joined during the war, stayed on with the Canadian army's bridge work division, and developed a unique and comprehensive expertise in sub-

Arctic bridge construction and maintenance. The work of these people and dozens of others, from grader operators and mechanics to engineers and shop foremen, is often lost in the description of broader operational activities. From a technical and professional point of view, however, these people were essential to the viability of the Alaska Highway.

The area superintendents worked with a remarkably free hand. Harry George, one of the superintendents, referred to his area of responsibility as a little kingdom, made so by the fact the civilian employees provided the primary continuity in the workforce. The military personnel came and went, usually on two- or three-year rotations. George says, "You'll never see the like of it again. I mean, where you have full control of man and equipment. And to me, the people became associates, not necessarily employees. It was a great team."

The superintendents had another important function – that of intermediary between the military and civilian authorities. Most of the highway workers were civilians who worked under the direction of one of the three area superintendents. Most maintenance camps had relatively little contact with military personnel – the annual army inventory sticks out in many memories. It was the superintendents who took civilian complaints and suggestions up the ladder to the military commanders and who brought orders and suggestions from the headquarters' officials back into the field.

The Alaska Highway made an indelible impression on these men. Hugh Devitt, whose enthusiasm for the highway still sparkles almost thirty years after he left the region, says, "My love of the highway comes from the fact that it was a challenging job for an engineer. You had a real living thing that had to be addressed and managed every day of your life while up there. It was a marvellous opportunity for an engineer to gain first-hand experience in practising his trade."

A few numbers help clarify the military contribution: When the Americans handed over the Alaska Highway in 1946, there were thirty-one permanent and a hundred and four temporary bridges; the RCE built an additional fifty-six permanent bridges and constructed thirty-two steel-pipe or pipe-arch culverts. The Engineers completed fifty-five major highway relocations (not counting minor rebuildings to avoid dangerous curves and blind hills). Most of the relocations involved short distances – less than

Looking down the highway at Mile 183. J. GARBUS.

a mile — but they did eliminate the major danger spots along the highway or replace sections of road particularly vulnerable to wash-outs or landslides. Between 1953 and 1963, 718 major surveys were completed — 98 in 1959 alone. This work, far from dramatic and invisible to all but those highway travellers who found their drive slowed by the surveyors, laid the groundwork for the gradual reconstruction of the highway.

The history of the Northwest Highway Maintenance Establishment provides a departmental reflection on the changes to the Alaska Highway between 1946 and 1964: "Looking back, many changes took place while the Canadian Army was the custodian. The highway opened the hunting grounds, the oil fields, the forests and the mineral wealth of the North to hundreds of thousands, including a great many Alaskans....The amount of traffic on the highway has increased steadily, and with this increase has come a gradual increase and improvement to tourist facilities....The majority of the real old timers, the characters of the Yukon, have passed on. No longer can one leave one's doors unlocked, nor a car on the highway, with the assurance that all will be untouched when one returns. This is a sure sign that some objectionable results of civilization have also left their imprint. Changes there have been, but the charm of the country remains. It is still an exciting, rugged land, rich in scenic beauty — remote from civilization – and a sportsman's paradise."[20] Mabel Armitage had a more succinct summary. Commenting on the many signs warning Windy Road, 3 Miles, Windy Road, 5 Miles, she suggested that a single sign, placed just outside of Dawson Creek, would do: *Windy Road, All the Way!*

The Alaska Highway did not impress many travellers in the years between 1946 and 1964 – except for those who noted its ruggedness, propensity toward dust, and its twisty, seemingly illogical course (several switchbacks on the road toward Haines Junction, in which the road twists sharply on seemingly flat ground, attracted particular comment). But for the people of the North, it was such an improvement on the slow, river-based transportation of the past that even the dust and curves were happily ignored. But the clamour, north and south, was for more – more new bridges, more miles of relocations, and for the paving that advocates claimed would vault the Alaska Highway to the forefront of North American highways. But the dreamers still dreamed, hoping that an improved highway would somehow prove to be the magic needed for the economic boom that had long been forecast for the Far Northwest. It was, even as the Department of National Defence handed over control of the highway in 1964 to the Department of Public Works, a dream as yet unrealized and increasingly, to some, unrealistic.

In September 1963 engineers, politicians, and other speakers from Alberta, British Columbia, the Yukon, and Alaska gathered in Whitehorse for an International Conference on Paving the Alaska Highway. It was not immediately successful, but nor was it the final effort by the advocates of rapid highway reconstruction. Numerous public meetings, from gatherings of mayors and chambers of commerce to high-level ministerial consultations involving Canadian and American officials, were held to consider the prospect of a massive paving project. Hundreds of names were gathered on petitions, beseeching Ottawa and Washington to act. Words proved cheap and easy; getting the governments to come up with the money proved rather more difficult.

7

The Modern Alaska Highway

F
ROM ITS INCEPTION, the Alaska Highway suffered from
one basic and immutable problem. It was an American
highway – in design, conception, and ultimate purpose
– built largely across Canadian territory. The highway
served the growing settlements of the new North – particularly
the oil, gas, and timber-rich region around Fort Nelson, the
new territorial capital of Whitehorse, and a slowly expanding
regional tourist industry – but in the mid-1960s the majority of
its users were destined for the booming new state of Alaska.
Rescued from oblivion by World War II, Alaska had come into
its own during the Cold War. Massive military bases near
Fairbanks and Anchorage, and dozens of smaller installations
across the state, brought a new level of prosperity and security to the region. It was Alaska's boom that drew people onto
the highway.

The challenge for the highway's Canadian promoters lay in
interesting their government in the improvement and maintenance of a highway built by and for American interests. Increased
traffic counts were impressive, but the knowledge that most
travellers pressed through Canadian territories as quickly as possible, to slow only when they reached Alaska, dulled political
interest in the Alaska Highway. However, demands for improvements could not be completely ignored, coming as they did
from Alaskans, the U.S. government, and residents and politicians

along the highway route. With considerable trepidation, the federal government reconsidered its handling of the Alaska Highway. Since the end of the war, sporadic discussions had taken place about the possibility of a Canadian-American agreement to improve or reconstruct portions of the Alaska Highway. Most of the discussions went nowhere, stalled on the inevitable clash of national priorities and concerns over sovereignty.

Most Canadian highway promoters, however, were more concerned about transferring the road from military to civilian control than with issues of sovereignty. The prospect of shifting responsibility for the Canadian portion of the highway from the Department of National Defence to a civilian agency originally surfaced in the 1950s. In 1954, the government agreed to transfer control of the highway to the Department of Public Works (now called Public Works Canada). A departmental investigative team was dispatched to review the need for, and costs of, such a move. The Public Works' engineers recommended in favour of the shift, but nothing was done. The issue faded into the background, to be resuscitated on an annual basis by northern members of Parliament, particularly Progressive Conservative Party backbencher Erik Nielsen, first elected to represent the Yukon Territory in a 1957 by-election.

Pressure from Alaska for the reconstruction of the highway continued, however. Alaskans were eager to capitalize on their new mantle of statehood (granted in 1959) and to promote the many opportunities for investment in the Far Northwest. For many of them, the poor condition of the highway was the state's Achilles heel, providing as it did less than adequate land-based access. To consolidate Alaska's economic vision and assess the practical roadblocks to prosperity, the Alaska International Railway and Highway Commission hired the Batelle Memorial Institution to complete a major study of the region's prospects. The Batelle Report, released in 1961, tossed a tankful of gasoline on the embers of regional discontent concerning the Alaska Highway. The report covered an array of issues, but one quickly caught the attention of highway promoters. Pave the Alaska Highway, the Batelle authors concluded. The estimated cost of improvements, $102.3 million, would, the report confidently concluded, be quickly repaid out of greatly expanded tourist trade and other economic developments.

In this atmosphere, the Canadian government decided to revisit the question of control of the Alaska Highway. The matter arose amid a more general discussion of the reorganization of federal government departments; the anomaly of having the Department of National Defence administer a civilian highway demanded attention. Finally, and to the well-suppressed delight of many within the armed forces, Paul Hellyer, minister of National Defence, announced on 25 October 1963 that responsibility for the Alaska Highway would, on the following 1 April, be passed to the Department of Public Works. Public Works agreed to retain all the civilian employees willing to stay and to assume responsibility for all equipment and maintenance facilities along the highway.

And so, another April Fool's Day ceremony to mark yet another hand-over was organized. Representatives of the Canadian Army and the Department of Public Works gathered on 1 April 1964 atop Two-Mile Hill – at the same location where the celebration was held eighteen years before when the United States Army transferred the Alaska Highway to Canadian authorities. It was an appropriately posh affair, begun with a musical welcome by the band of the Royal Canadian Engineers and marked by the presence of Brigadier G. H. Spencer, commander of the Northwest Highway System, Mr. G. R. Cameron, Commissioner of the Yukon Territory, Lieutenant-General G. Walsh, chief of the General Staff, and Lucien Lalonde, deputy minister of Public Works. The dignitaries turned out in force, as did more than a thousand locals drawn by the ceremony and unseasonably warm weather. But most celebrants reserved judgement about the significance of the event, waiting for more compelling signs that something had actually changed.

What excitement there was surrounding Public Works' new responsibilities arose from one simple fact. Unlike the DND, which had handled its duties with professionalism and dedication but had not made massive modifications to the highway, it was widely assumed that Public Works would quickly apply itself to a substantial reconstruction of the Alaska Highway. Public Works had, after all, an enviable record of highway construction, having assisted the building of the renowned Trans-Canada Highway and with road building within national parks. It was, as well, involved with the much-touted Roads to Resources

Program, which promised major new access routes in northern districts. It seemed safe to assume that the hey-day of the Alaska Highway was about to arrive.

Public Works Canada, as the Royal Canadian Engineers had done in 1946, inherited many key personnel from those in the field. A few military personnel, Major Norm Hendrickson, Captain "Red" Brown, and a few others, transferred over to Public Works on a temporary basis to provide some measure of continuity. Others, like Art Shaw, Hank Collyer, Wally Ward, and Dave McMurray, left the military to stay with the civilian operation. Harry George, Don Bakke, Doreen Truelson, Noreen McLennan, Walt Williscroft, Cliff Lawrence, Jim Quong, Dick Fairey, Norm Felker, and many others who had worked for the army as civilians, now moved over to Public Works. The entire transfer was accomplished with a minimum of difficulty, ensuring that the maintenance operations along the Alaska Highway continued without a hitch.

Bill Koropatnick, senior representative of Public Works, had assembled a talented group under his direction. Some, such as bridge engineer Jim Quong, had been around since the war years. Others, including Koropatnick's second-in-command, Ed Kellett, and Jim Fulton, Al Wright, Pat Kennedy, Jimmy Fullerton, Howard Truman, Cec McLennan, Herman Furst, and Adolf Gaubinger, already stationed in Whitehorse to carry out the engineering on the Roads to Resources program, became the nucleus for management and engineering. The Department of Public Works reorganized in 1967, decentralizing operational authority, regional offices and subordinate districts. Bill Koropatnick became regional director, Pacific Region, and moved to Vancouver. R. K. (Dick) Coates, who had transferred to Whitehorse as highway construction engineer in 1964, became district director of the Yukon and Northern B.C. District, with responsibility for the Alaska Highway in Canada.

Traffic on the Alaska Highway was already substantial by the summer of 1964. At Mile 1202, total two-way traffic for 1964 topped forty-one thousand vehicles; a significant increase over the roughly twenty-five thousand cars and trucks which had passed that point ten years earlier. American use of the highway remained very high. More than three-quarters of vehicles crossing the Canada-U.S. border were American. Near Whitehorse,

in contrast, most people using the highway were Canadians. Yet at Mile 101, close to 40 per cent of the summer traffic was from the United States. Not surprisingly, traffic fluctuated according to the seasons: the monthly average at Mile 1202 was 3,475 vehicles in 1964, ranging from a low of 1,221 in February to 7,660 in July.

Despite the shift to Public Works, the federal government remained unconvinced of the need for immediate and costly reconstruction. Faced with the politically daunting and overly optimistic conclusions of the Batelle Report, the government chose to commission its own study of the need for highway improvements. In 1964 it turned to the Stanford Research Institute, which submitted a much more cautious report two years later. The Stanford Report offered some bitter news for highway promoters: there was no economic justification for paving the entire Alaska Highway; most of the main economic activities in the area, including mining, oil exploration, and timber operations, could continue just as easily on an unpaved road. Erik Nielsen was incensed. The report's conclusions ran counter to his sense of the situation. The intention of the Liberal government, he asserted, was to "justify a further delay in the government coming to some kind of decision with respect to the paving of the highway."[1]

Reaction to the report was heated throughout the Northwest. Alaskan Senator Ted Stevens contributed, "Paving the Alaska Highway is the road to the future and anybody who doesn't understand that doesn't belong in either the government of Canada or the United States today."[2] Erik Nielsen, speaking to the Alaska Travel Promotion Association, echoed Stevens' sentiments: "It simply boils down to the fact that it is false economy to continue to refuse to pave – not just from a capital and operational point of view of revenue to be realized from increased uses that paving would bring, to say nothing of the savings which would result from decreased wear and tear and maintenance."[3]

While political attention focussed on the repaving debate, the Department of Public Works began work in the mid-1960s on a major bridge replacement and upgrading program. The primary thrust in this initiative came from Jim Quong, who by this time had over twenty years' experience along the road and unparalleled knowledge of Alaska Highway bridge construction, and from the Department of Public Works' bridge design section in Ottawa. The project proceeded at a steady, if unspectacular pace, seldom appreciated by the legion of travellers who agitated for further attention to highway reconstruction.

While the Stanford recommendations offered a bitter pill to highway residents and business people, the report included a bit of sugar coating. While the larger project – repaving and improving the entire highway – should be relegated to the back-burner, the report concluded, work should begin immediately on the improvement of several key sections of the highway. The Stanford Report specifically singled out the first segment of the Alaska Highway, from Fort St. John to Fort Nelson, a heavily travelled but poorly located portion of the highway. In addition, it recommended that a short section of highway be paved around each community to solve the problem of dust and mud caused by highway traffic passing through the towns. Residents of Fort Nelson and Watson Lake, in particular, had perennially complained about the problem of choking dust.

Armed with the report and a raft of departmental studies and assessments, and aware of the limited support within the government for a major reconstruction project, Honourable

Arthur Laing, minister of the Department of Indian Affairs and Northern Development, approached the federal cabinet for approval of a less ambitious but politically palatable proposal dubbed the Limited Improvement Program. DIAND and Public Works jointly recommended that substantial sums be provided for the southern third of the highway, one of the worst portions of the entire highway, heavily travelled and of particular importance to Canadians. This proposal offered just what the politicians wanted – a solution that addressed the major northern concerns without requiring the massive infusion of funds required for a full-scale reconstruction. It was a superb political arrangement, for it allowed for an expansion or contraction of highway work as financial and political needs dictated. It did not completely satisfy the people of the Far Northwest, but the Limited Improvement Program did put construction crews on the highway and began the long, difficult, and costly process of reconstructing the road.

Money began flowing northward in 1964, not enough to satisfy the regional boosters, but in sufficient quantity to get the road work started. Bridge work began in earnest, leading to the improvement or replacement of all temporary or substandard river and stream crossings. The program provided additional funding for the areas in greatest need of repair; the initial allocation was directed toward the ten miles immediately north of the end of the pavement at Mile 83. The federal government grafted an additional program onto the process – the 1960s and 1970s were, after all, the age of program announcements in Canada. The Paving Through Settled Areas program provided funds for the improvement of the highway through communities, finally solving the mud and dust problems that had so angered the residents of the highway settlements.

The actual work of rebuilding the Alaska Highway fell to civilian contractors, hired after public tender by Public Works. The contracts were hotly contested, with a small number of local firms competing with big construction companies from Edmonton, Vancouver, and other cities. Although there was strong pressure for local preference, Public Works resisted. The local firms did not have the high freight costs faced by outside companies and had greater access to local labour, so their involvement, especially that of General Enterprises in

Whitehorse, ensured competitive bidding. Contrary to popular assumptions about the lucrative construction contracts, many of the successful bidders found that the work was not always remunerative. Construction delays, faulty costing, or unexpected design problems could wreak havoc with a well-planned construction schedule and shoot gaping holes in a tight budget. More than one firm went broke because of the difficulty of completing a contract along the Alaska Highway.

Public Works, the front-line agency that bore the brunt of public criticism about the Canadian section of the road after 1964, repeatedly petitioned the federal government for additional funds and a more expansive reconstruction agenda. It discovered that, more often than not, the Northwest's limited power on the national political stage thwarted its proposals. Budget submissions enjoyed inconsistent success, reflecting the priorities of national politics more than the needs of the highway. The election of the Progressive Conservative Party to national office in 1979 and again in 1984, brought Erik Nielsen to a position of considerable prominence. In the Joe Clark administration (1979-1980), Nielsen was the minister of Public Works – well-positioned to accelerate highway construction.

The Alaskan side was another matter. The road had been completely paved by the early 1960s, although the results have been somewhat mixed. When Bob and Wilma Knox crossed the border, they discovered that the "relatively smooth, dust-free surface provides a sensation even the diehard Alaska Highway purist can momentarily relish." But as they drove north, they discovered that the sub-Arctic climate had extracted its toll on the asphalt as well: "Frequently, we found this 'paved' stretch so wrenched by frost-heaves, so full of sharp chuckholes that, despite its lack of dust, it offered no more comfortable or rapid travel than the gravel."[4] The highway was, however, on the Alaska government's short list of major roads, and was therefore slated for steady improvement. The Alaskan section was repaved a second time after 1964 and a third time in the 1970s. By the early 1980s, the Alaskan portion of the highway was in first-rate condition, matching southern highways of similar size and importance. Even the difficult sections through muskeg and permafrost immediately north of the border were brought up to standard.

This shovel was almost destroyed in a rock slide west of Fort Nelson.
HOWARD BURRELL.

Over the years, the highway developed as an unusual patchwork. Sections of paved road of the highest civilian standard gave way, with little warning, to stretches of gravel highway little changed from World War II. Increased traffic pounded unceasingly on the road surface. The construction of the Alyeska Pipeline across Alaska in the early 1970s sent hundreds of heavily loaded semi-trailer rigs up the highway, to return, lightly loaded and travelling fast, a few days later. The invasion of heavy equipment, unparalleled since the war years, took its toll on the highway, particularly when the trucks moved along the road in the muddy spring season, banging pot-holes into the soggy road surface.

The federal government never moved fast enough to satisfy local and tourist opinion. Journalist Iris Warner wrote in 1970, "American travellers, used to paved highways, invariably drive too fast and many come to grief. Irate at broken axles, flat tires, dust-filled cars and trailers, snapped propane lines and loosened hinges they are petitioning their Congressmen to 'get this highway paved.'"[5] On an almost annual basis, reports filtered along the highway of tourists turning back after only a short drive along the southern portion of the road. The news infuriated tourist operators farther north, who saw their bread and butter being repelled by an incomplete, dusty, and bumpy road. Protests took many forms – letters, petitions, legislative appeals, and a variety of organized statements, including Pave the Highway walks in Whitehorse and Fort Nelson in 1970.

But the government, try as it might, could not generate the economic data to justify a full-scale and rapid reconstruction of the Alaska Highway. Public Works was, instead, charged with the slow and steady reconstruction of the worst sections of the road, a plan that would eventually lead to a completely paved highway from Dawson Creek to Fairbanks but which, until then, left many travellers and highway residents angry and impatient.

In the early 1970s, Public Works had targeted the southern portion of the highway – as far north as Fort Nelson – for immediate reconstruction. The plan was simple. The federal government would pay for, and supervise, the rebuilding and paving of this, the most heavily travelled section of the road. Upon completion, responsibility for maintenance would be transferred to the British Columbia government. There was one hitch. British Columbia would have nothing to do with it. Even though maintenance of roads is a provincial responsibility, the B.C. government refused repeated federal requests that it take over the B.C. section of the highway. The public rationale for this odd position was the international character of the road; the practical reason was that it was costly to maintain and, compared to other provincial roads, lightly travelled. What's more, the existing arrangement whereby the federal government paid for the costs of maintenance and reconstruction was eminently suitable to the provincial government.

The federal government's interest in a rapid reconstruction of the southern portions of the Alaska Highway dimmed considerably in the face of British Columbia's intransigence. Why, Public Works officials wondered, should the federal government fast-track a construction project of major benefit to B.C. when provincial authorities refused to negotiate a permanent transfer of maintenance responsibilities? Work on the Fort St. John to Fort Nelson section did not stop completely – it was, after all, greatly in need of repair and improvement – but it proceeded at a much slower pace than initially planned. The highway was caught in the Canadian vice of federal-provincial politics.

Administrative changes followed the political debates and struggles over the Alaska Highway. Public Works had never intended to retain responsibility for maintenance indefinitely. Shortly after their arrival in 1964, its officials began negotiations with the Yukon territorial government, a process slowed by concern among some Ottawa-based civil servants that the Yukon government was not up to the task of taking on the highway. But in 1972, the Yukon government entered into an agreement with the Department of Public Works to maintain the Yukon section of the Alaska Highway, and retained responsibility for highway design and reconstruction. Most of Public Works' highway and equipment-maintenance employees transferred to the territorial government; a few, such as long-time employee Don Bakke, retired and took the option to move "outside" at the government's expense. A small number of other employees also took advantage of the government's once-in-a-lifetime offer to pay for moving expenses and left for the South. The Yukon government's Department of Highways doubled in size overnight. Within a short period, the two sets of crews and equipment were intermingled, and a unified Alaska Highway maintenance system was soon in place.

The federal government wished to make a similar deal with the B.C. government, but continued provincial intransigence foiled any logical devolution. From the provincial government's perspective, the arrangement was (and is) ideal – the federal government pays for the reconstruction and maintenance while the province picks up the gasoline taxes, permits, and licence revenues related to highway travel. There have been provincial promises to take over the highway – once reconstruction is complete – and various federal threats to force the province to accept its constitutional responsibility for the highway. It has all been to little avail, although Public Works has managed to extract itself from day-to-day administration of the highway. Instead of passing responsibility on to the province, Public Works contracts out maintenance for the B.C. portions of the highway. Cantlon & Parker of Fort Nelson got the initial term contract for miles 83 to 300 in 1966; B.G. Linton Construction bid successfully for miles 300 to 456 in 1967, and Nanaimo Bulldozing secured the contract for miles 456 to 626 in 1968. These private contractors, working under Public Works' supervision, look after routine maintenance; Public Works, as in the Yukon, retains responsibility for highway redesign and reconstruction.

This, too, brought sweeping changes to the highway communities. As the maintenance contracts were let – one per year for three years – DPW camps and equipment were sold off; the auctions organized by the Crown Assets Corporation were impressive regional spectacles, drawing buyers from far afield to capitalize on the dispersal of equipment, paints, furnishings and other DPW supplies. As in the Yukon, employees had to choose between staying with the organization or finding a new job.

By the mid-1970s, the Alaska Highway was an engineering oddity of the first order. Setting out from Dawson Creek, travellers moved along a well designed, paved highway until they passed Fort St. John, where they dropped off the pavement and onto the familiar dust and gravel of the old Alaska Highway. On the gravel sections, travellers were slowed repeatedly by construction activity and highway detours around relocation work. Interspersed with sections of new, but unpaved, road and old gravel surface were paved segments of high standard. The contrast was startling, as cars, rattling and dust-covered after miles of gravel surface, shot onto a paved section. The immediate quiet upon hitting the pavement only emphasized the constant noise of driving on an unpaved road. When the gravel surface again approached, after a peaceful hiatus of ten or twenty miles, drivers could feel themselves tensing for the return to noise, bumps, and rattles of the old Alaska Highway.

And so it continued along the road. Large sections remained unchanged from the 1950s. The approaches to Fort Nelson, Watson Lake, and Whitehorse had been paved, providing a small respite of driving comfort in the middle of a ribbon of dust. It was not that the road was in bad shape; by gravel standards, the Alaska Highway was, with the unavoidable seasonal variations, in superb condition. In fact, it was the construction zones – the paved sections of subsequent years – that caused the most problems, particularly for those drivers loath to slow down even when repeatedly warned to do so. The rest of the highway was not as straight and smooth as a paved route, and many of the sharp corners, blind hills, and other driving challenges remained in place, but it was easily managed and safe. North of the Alaska-Yukon border, however, the highway reverted to full southern standard. For those who had ventured from the far South, it was like a reward for perseverance and determination, particularly after the tortuous twists and turns of the last two hundred miles of the Canadian section.

But the Alaska Highway of the 1970s and early 1980s was a far cry from the road of myth and legend, the one that, according to travellers' tales, had wrecked mufflers, dashed rocks by the dozens into windshields, smashed gasoline tanks, destroyed tires, and demoralized even the toughest driver. The application of bituminous surface treatment (nick-named Chinese pavement) on unpaved sections proved to be an effective interim solution to the paving dilemma. The BST bound the gravel surface together, effectively controlling highway dust and providing a road surface that most travellers had difficulty differentiating from pavement. At several points, highway crews painted a centre line on the BST-treated surface, adding to the confusion between paved and gravel road. Asphalt and BST pavement markedly improved the quality of the road. The clouds of dust, storms of surface gravel, and pools slick with mud after rain had largely been eliminated.

But the best preparations can do little to protect a long, vulnerable ribbon such as the Alaska Highway from the omnipotent hand of nature. Flooding remains commonplace along the highway. Certain stretches, near Muncho Lake, Racing River, and along the shores of Kluane Lake, are vulnerable to seasonal storms. The mountains surrounding Muncho Lake, one of the most picturesque spots on the entire highway, have few trees and little soil; the rock-covered hillsides scarcely slow the flow of water at all, and during heavy storms torrents pour off the mountains, through rock-filled gullies, and over the ill-protected highway. Wash-outs occur with some regularity. The situation is strikingly different near Kluane. Here, when the earthen mountainsides are subjected to occasional heavy rainstorms, the water mixes with the soil, creating a potent and all-but-unstoppable mass of oozing mud, which is washed down onto the highway. The muck is exceptionally difficult to move, particularly while the rains continue, for as part of the pile is removed from the lower edge, more is being washed down from above.

During the summer rains, blockages of the highway happen from time to time; most are cleared in a day or two. R. C. Buckstar recounted his near brush with disaster: "Returning from Big Delta, Alaska, I was driving at night on the Alcan near Muncho Lake when I noticed my lights appeared to be striking a void in the road ahead. I stopped the car, took my flashlight, and walked the road ahead. The thaw in the mountains had swelled streams beyond capacity causing an overspill. Ahead in the former

Springtime run-off pours over the Alaska Highway at Mile 480. JIM QUONG.

roadbed was a gully some twenty feet across, six feet deep, extending the entire width of the road."[6] On occasion, entire stretches of the highway have washed out, cutting off the north's most important land-line to the south.

In 1974, the highway experienced some of the worst flooding in its history. There had been exceptionally heavy snowfalls the previous winter. The following summer was cool, and mountain-melt slow. Warm weather arrived in early July, to be followed, in a murderous combination, by exceptionally heavy rainfall. The rains began on 15 July. Water gushed off the mountainsides and down the rivers and streams. As the creeks leapt their bounds, tons of debris swept off the hills. The rubble plunged into culverts, filling them as firmly as a plug in a bathtub drain. Water, driving down the hills at a furious rate, built up behind the culverts and began to eat away at the road surface. Within a matter of hours, dozens of miles of the highway had been rendered impassable. The storm continued, interrupting telecommunications and stopping hundreds of travellers in their tracks.

The Muncho Lake area was turned into an island, as the raging waters cut off the highway at both ends and brought the level of the lake to unheard of levels. Miles of the highway simply disappeared – at Muncho Lake, Trout River, and elsewhere in the district. In total, 130 miles of the highway were rendered impassable. The Racing River bridge, its foundations eaten away by the raging waters, lost one of its approach spans. To complicate matters further, the Stewart-Cassiar Road, an alternate road access to the outside, washed out in the same storm, stranding the entire northwest and adding to the urgent need to reopen the Alaska Highway.

Travellers were caught all along the highway. Department of Public Works personnel, particularly Denny Anderson, project manager from Fort Nelson, Wally Wondga, contract inspector, and Jim Quong, checked out those people stranded in the wash-out sections – the 50 at Summit Lake, 50 at Toad River Lodge, others at isolated sites, and the largest group, 175, trapped at Muncho Lake. The Provincial Emergency Planning group, assisted by the RCMP, flew food and other supplies (as well as a social worker and public health nurse to the group at Muncho Lake) to the stranded travellers. Concern for the people's immediate safety dissipated with the end of the rains. The task of keeping an eye on the stranded travellers fell to the RCMP, who maintained regular patrols along the highway and ensured against privations and undue hardships.

At Fort Nelson and Watson Lake, the ends of the washed-out sections, large communities of stranded highway travellers congregated. Dozens of would-be travellers turned back at the southern end; those who had to continue north crowded into Fort Nelson's hotels and campgrounds and soon flooded the small town's facilities. The community pitched in to make the best of the situation, turning the ball field into a makeshift campground, providing entertainment for the unexpected visitors, and throwing community facilities open to all users.

To the north the road was not closed until Trout River, more than a hundred and fifty miles to the south of Watson Lake, was filled to capacity. For a day or two, travellers continued south, filling up the campgrounds and other highway accommodations. On 17 July, a roadblock was set up south of Watson Lake to prevent additional travellers from continuing down the highway. The crowd was more uneasy than the group at Fort Nelson; the vast majority of the travellers were anxious to press on immediately. They were families eager to get home after a lengthy holiday, military personnel transferring to new postings, and commercial travellers losing money each day they were stranded.

I have my own memories of this catastrophe as I was in Whitehorse at the time, having driven through the same rainstorm to return to town after a week in Watson Lake. I was in charge of a three-person crew of car-counters; we sat beside the highway, in three eight-hour shifts, keeping track of the cars passing by us. When the road went out, the highway crews were desperate for workers. We were tracked down in Whitehorse and ordered to return to Watson Lake as quickly as possible. We rushed back, convinced we were about to be assigned some crucial task in the reopening of the highway – visions of emergency lessons on driving a bulldozer and the prospect of many hours of overtime flashed through our fanciful teenage minds. We reported to the maintenance yard in Watson Lake and were told to get down to the roadblock at the south end of town and keep all but essential traffic off the road. Hiding our disappointment, we went first to our hotel – only to find out that it had rented the rooms we had only recently vacated, and that, like many workers along the highway in the 1940s, we had access to a bed for only eight hours a day.

Our work consisted of, on those rare occasions when someone drove to our spot, jumping out of the truck, waving a stop sign, and informing the driver that he or she could go no farther. Some, who wished to press on, were persistent. We listened to stories about how factory operations would stop if the driver could not get through, of corporate or government planning activities we were personally fouling, and other such tales of woe. We informed them, as directed, that they would be reported to the RCMP if they tried to proceed. The Stewart-Cassiar Road reopened on July 20, thus siphoning off some of the huge mob then gathered in Watson Lake.

We remained at the roadblock, the principal source of information for dozens of travellers anxious to continue down the highway. It was a thoroughly engaging experience. The seniors were the most patient, for their holidays knew few firm schedules and they found the whole thing rather exciting. Families were quickly exasperated. There is not a lot to do in Watson Lake at the best of times, and with supplies of milk, fresh food, and beer running low, tempers flared. Each morning, however, a good-natured group of travellers, anywhere between fifteen and fifty of them, would gather at the roadblock for the latest update. They swapped stories with us and among themselves and talked about their various Alaska Highway adventures. Many were anxious to learn more about the North, and we were happy to tell them. I remember trying very hard to explain the nuances of curling to a group from the American South. They got the concept – the similarity to shuffleboard makes it fairly obvious – but they had difficulty understanding the attractions of pursuing this bizarre ritual on ice, in the middle of a sub-Arctic winter.

For a minority of travellers, the Canadian government was moving much too slowly to open the road. They wanted immediate action and were prepared to petition the U.S. government to step in. One petition – I doubt it went anywhere except into an evening camp-fire – called for the U.S. Air Force to fly in Hercules planes to evacuate the stranded passengers. In the middle of the muddle, officers from the U.S. Army did travel to the area, meeting with military personnel and arranging their financial and personal matters. Rumours of this intervention reached far and wide, leading anguished Canadian officials to wonder if Canadian sovereignty had, in some way, been violated.

We stayed in Watson Lake until the roadblock was lifted. The stranded travellers from Muncho Lake passed through on July 22. The crowd stranded in Watson Lake waited for them at our roadblock, cheering the first arrivals, who responded with an enthusiastic honking of horns. Two days after the first caravan arrived, the first vehicles from Watson Lake were allowed to leave. They lined up early in the morning, and we gathered, for the final time, at the roadblock. We waved them on as they passed by the dozens, temporary friends now fleeing south, with a great northern adventure story to tell. We returned to our old task, counting cars passing by Jake's Corner. The rest of the summer was, to say the least, an anticlimax.

The task of restoring the Alaska Highway to its normal standard was enormous. Equipment and crews from the maintenance contractors on the southern highway, and from the Yukon Territorial Government's highway operations, were diverted *en masse* to the wash-outs. Working feverishly, night and day, the crews patched together temporary bridges, filled in washed-out sections, buttressed the existing road bed, replaced culverts, and otherwise put the Alaska Highway back together again. In sections, such as the one around Peterson Canyon, the old military tote road was pressed back into service. Remarkably, given the extent and nature of the damage to the road, the Alaska Highway was open to two-way traffic by July 26, only eleven days after the rains started. Reconstruction work, however, had just begun. Several bridges, including the one across Racing River, had to be rebuilt. Most of the work was completed by freeze-up in 1974, leaving only a limited amount of resurfacing and bridge work for the following year. The entire operation cost the Canadian government more than $1.3 million.

Destruction visited the Rocky Mountain section of the highway again the following year, when wash-outs forced its closure on June 26 and 27. It was, climatically, a replay of the previous year, another summer of exceptionally heavy rain. The rapidity and severity of the run-off, this year, caused greatest damage to bridges and proportionately less to the road surface. Bridges at MacDonald Creek, Racing River, and Toad River were severely damaged, ensuring travel delays and considerable cost in bringing the highway back into service.

The floods of 1974 had provided Public Works with a battle-tested plan of attack. Maintenance crews and equipment in the area were dispatched immediately and reconstruction work began promptly. The bridge repairs took the longest. Work started on the Racing River bridge on July 5 but was not finished until July 14. Still the wash-outs did not have the same crippling effect as the previous year's. Most travellers were able to return to Watson Lake or Fort Nelson, where they waited for work to be completed. As well, the Stewart-Cassiar Road remained open, providing travellers with a viable route in and out of the territory.

Once again, highway residents helped the travellers make the most of the situation. The citizens of Fort Nelson made a particular effort to welcome the stranded tourists. Bingo, parties, baseball games (including one that pitted the visiting Americans against the home team – won by the Canadians), and pot-luck suppers provided much-needed diversion. There was a much smaller crowd in Watson Lake this time; the Stewart-Cassiar Road turn-off lies only a few miles west of the town, and most travellers simply continued along that muddy but scenic route to the south. When the highway reopened – initially to cars and small trucks – on July 8, the convoy south from Watson Lake comprised only forty vehicles. The expedition from Fort Nelson, escorted by RCMP cruisers, included 310 cars and vans, 303 campers, 120 towed trailers, 93 motor homes, and a few other vehicles.

As it had done the year before, Public Works Canada quickly turned its attention to restoring the Alaska Highway to its proper standard. Work was not completed by winter freeze-up, and some of the bridge work continued through the winter. But by May of 1976, the highway was back to its pre-flood condition. The flooding had proved very expensive – more than $1.3 million in 1974 and more than $2 million the following year. Public Works' effort was not, however, devoted entirely to restoring the road to its original condition. The highway engineers learned valuable lessons from the experience of unusually high water levels, and applied these lessons to the reconstruction. Special efforts were made to buttress the road shoulders, depositing rip rap (large boulders) along exposed edges, reinforcing bridge foundations, building protection around culverts (which, as in 1974, had plugged with forest debris), and otherwise protecting the Alaska Highway from flood waters that the engineers hoped they would not see again for many years.

The forces of nature cannot be kept at bay by the wishes and best efforts of engineers. The rains returned, and will again. In the summer of 1988, for example, a major portion of the Alaska Highway along the west shore of Kluane Lake was buried under a mountain slide. It took many days to dig the muck off the road surface and, equally important, to stabilize the hillside sufficiently to protect against further slides. Traffic again piled up at both ends of the blockage, although many escaped the problem by driving around by way of Dawson City, the Top of the World Highway, and Richardson Highway in Alaska to Tetlin Junction on the Alaska Highway. The serious floods of 1974 and 1975 have not been repeated, although the possibility remains.

The 1970s' wash-outs, particularly the 1974 disaster, reminded northerners of their dependence upon the Alaska Highway.

Another wash-out on the
Alaska Highway.
PUBLIC WORKS CANADA.

People didn't starve as a consequence; there was road access to the ocean at Haines, and, via the White Pass and Yukon Route railroad, which was still running at that time, regular deliveries of supplies from Skagway. News got through, as did deliveries of fresh food and other necessaries, and people could get out, by air or by ferry, if fortunate enough to get a reservation or desperate enough to convince one of the carriers to take them. For tourists and residents alike, however, the floods reminded the people in the Northwest that there really was only one road to the region, an access route that depended on the ability of the maintenance and construction crews to keep it open. If northerners needed any reminder of the importance of the Alaska Highway they were given it during those few summer days in 1974 and 1975 when they did not have the road.

The floods escalated demands that the Canadian government tackle the reconstruction of the Alaska Highway. The next major project came, however, from unexpected quarters. The U.S.A. had maintained a strong interest in the Alaska Highway. It was, after all, the only road access to Alaska and hence of primary importance to regional plans. Since a substantial portion of the highway traffic was destined for Alaska, the poor quality of the road was seen by Americans as a serious liability. Iris Warner foreshadowed subsequent developments when she observed in

1970, "Yukoners, with their whole mining and tourist economy at stake, are aware that their American neighbours wait for no man. If the highway is not paved for their pleasure, they will simply step up the efficiency of the Alaska Ferry System and leave Canada, and her highway, to dust and mud."[7]

The United States government had proposed a variety of cost-sharing and joint ventures to improve and pave the Alaska Highway. Several American legislators – mostly from Alaska or the border states – authored bills calling for Canadian-American cooperation on the reconstruction of the road. The Canadian government was not, according to Erik Nielsen, much interested: "The fact is that the United States is eager to do more to help pay for the cost of paving the highway than we have a right to expect but even so, the Canadian government is dragging its feet, and more, it is adopting stratagems and policies to avoid paving and confrontations with respect to paving."[8] The Federal-Aid Highway Act of 1970 authorized the president of the United States to negotiate with the Canadian government for the paving of the Alaska Highway, a project that stalled before detailed discussions ensued.[9]

In the early 1970s, the U.S. government approached Canadian authorities with a new plan – to improve and pave the Haines Highway from Haines, Alaska, to Haines Junction in the Yukon and the 205-mile-long portion of the Alaska Highway from the Yukon settlement to the Alaska-Yukon boundary. The motive was simple. The Alaska State Ferry System (now called the Alaska Marine Highway) provided regular service between the various ports of the Alaskan Panhandle, ending at Skagway at the head of Lynn Canal. People wishing to continue on to the rest of Alaska were dependent upon the twisting, rocky, and rather terrifying Haines Highway, a road that, after the war, had initially not been kept open through the winter months. They then had to drive along some of the worst portions of the Alaska Highway, particularly the stretch from Burwash to the border. The Haines Road and this portion of the Alaska Highway were, conversely, of minimal importance to the Canadians, given the tiny amount of Canadian traffic.

The Americans' solution, surprising and a little audacious, was that they would pay for the entire project. Negotiating a proper arrangement took some time – since the Americans were paying, they expected to be able to call the tune; the Canadian authorities, however, were determined that the design and as much of the construction as possible would be done by Canadian personnel. By January 1975, Public Works Canada and other federal negotiators had reached a deal with the American authorities: the Americans' would pay for the project, and, in return, Canada would allow U.S. companies to bid on construction projects. The Canadians also agreed, after rejecting an American request that the highway be maintained "forever," that the Canadian right of way would be guaranteed for twenty-five years, with indefinite extensions as long as both parties agreed. The Shakwak Project – named after the ancient valley through which much of the reconstructed route lies – was started on 11 January 1977.

The cooperative project was a fitting return to the spirit of the original construction of the Alaska Highway. But work did not proceed as smoothly or as quickly as it had thirty-five years earlier. Environmental impact assessments were required, a tip of the governmental hat to the new social and ecological realities of the 1970s. As well, the U.S. Congress had authorized only $58.6 million of the $200 million estimated for the completion of the project – the sum, based on an estimate over a decade old, was used by the sponsor of the bill and had not been determined in consultation with engineers familiar with the road. Work began, focussing initially on the Haines Road – particularly one remarkable stretch of switchbacks that took the road from the Three Guardsmen Pass to the Chilkat River valley – and the Alaska Highway immediately north of Haines Junction. Construction crews headed into the field to tackle the biggest joint Canadian-American project in the region since 1946.

But the Shakwak Project was fuelled by different forces than the wartime Alaska Highway had been. As a political initiative, it was acutely dependent upon its congressional backers. When Senator Mike Gravel lost his Alaskan seat in the 1980 primary election, concern about the project spread. The budget-conscious Republican administration of Ronald Reagan elected that year quickly lost interest and balked at requests for additional funds. Instead of the one, coordinated, bold stroke to reconstruct and pave the entire route from Haines to the Alaska-Yukon border, the undertaking slowed to a crawl. Nevertheless the major contracts commissioned after 1977 – except for work in the northern section, toward Beaver Creek – were completed as planned, resulting in a substantial improvement of the Haines Road and the Alaska Highway from Haines Junction to Kluane Lake. Work did not halt completely, and negotiations leading to a potential restart of the entire Shakwak Project still continue. The state of the road north of Haines Junction reflects the difficulty of reconciling the conflicting interests of highway travellers, national budgets, politicians, engineers, and, most importantly, Canadians and Americans.

The debate over the Shakwak Project, and the erosion of the ambitious plans of the 1970s, drew the contrasting visions of the Alaska Highway into sharp focus. For some, the road is simply a conduit between the South and Alaska, with the intervening region – from Dawson Creek to Fairbanks – being little more than a barrier to speedy access. People in the region see the highway quite differently. It remains the primary, but no longer the only, access route to the South; an increasing number of travellers are being enticed to use the Stewart-Cassiar Highway, a mining and lumbering road that has been episodically upgraded since the early 1970s, or to opt, as Iris Warner had warned, for the Alaska Marine Highway. Most northerners no longer see the Alaska Highway as a long-range access route; its primary purpose is to carry people from Teslin to Whitehorse, Tok to Fairbanks, and Fort Nelson to Fort St. John. Only a small number of northerners regularly travel longer distances along the highway, for the time required to drive its length and back again can rapidly consume short holidays or work time. *Milepost* magazine, the Alaska Highway traveller's bible, recommends five to seven days for the journey between Dawson Creek and Fairbanks, although the ambitious can get through more quickly. Many opt, instead, for the convenience of air travel.

Highway residents are, consequently, primarily concerned with the state of the road from their community to the nearest large centre and secondarily with their connection to the southern highway grid of British Columbia and Alberta. (Tourist promoters are something of an exception, for they see the quality of the entire route as integral to their efforts to draw travellers north.) Complaints to highway maintenance offices are usually about local conditions, and can be extremely spirited. Seasonal

Former headquarters of the Northwest Highway System, Camp Takhini, Whitehorse, Yukon.

PUBLIC WORKS CANADA.

battles over pot-holes (one wag described the best way to judge the depth of a highway pot-hole: "Knowing the height of your car or van, you measure how much is sticking out of the hole. The difference is the depth of the hole.") and the routine construction delays are a constant topic of northern conversation.

As the highway has changed, so has life along the road. Improvements in automobile technology have undercut the viability of many of the smaller road stations. Larger gasoline tanks, combined with improved gas-mileage, eroded the demand for services at the stops between the main centres, and many service stations and restaurants open in the 1960s have now closed. A number of other facilities, including such important stops as the main hotel and restaurant at Muncho Lake, close for the winter months, when highway traffic drops to a mere trickle. Improved communications, including cheaper telephone service, better radio and satellite television service, and the availability of video cassettes, has mitigated the isolation of former times. Today even the smallest centre has access to the latest news and information and no longer relies on community events for recreation.

The culture of highway maintenance remains basically the same. As the smaller highway camps closed, and larger towns built up around others, however, the dominance of the maintenance establishment declined. But still the highway bosses retain the old sense of connectedness to their workers. Marge Coates, whose husband served as district director, recalls her horror at discovering one winter day that he was about to head off to a camp 150 miles beyond Whitehorse. It was fifty below with a blizzard blowing. She remembers his explanation: "Well, the men have to work in all kinds of weather, so it's the least I can do to keep my date." Not all the administrators saw things his way – as the highway workers soon recognized – but the ones that did were held in high esteem by their employees.

Other aspects of Alaska Highway culture remain much in evidence. The curling bonspiels, fishing derbies, and other social events that traditionally drew people together from along the road continue. Political boundaries, however, exert considerable influence, much more so now that private contractors and the territorial government, rather than the Department of National Defence and Public Works Canada, maintain the entire Canadian section. The Alaska-Yukon boundary has been an impressive barrier for many years, and only recently has that started to break down. Attention, and community loyalties, focus on local and regional activities. Dawson Creek, Fort St. John, and Fort Nelson have comparatively little to do with Yukon highway communities, which look to the government town of Whitehorse. The small highway settlements in Alaska, similarly, have only sporadic contact with people to the south; Fairbanks and Anchorage are their primary points of reference. Most of the highway towns, particularly Dawson Creek, Fort St. John, and Fort Nelson in the south, and Whitehorse and Fairbanks farther north, have diverse and complex economies that do not depend as much on the Alaska Highway as in the past. Even the smaller centres – Watson Lake, Teslin, Haines Junction, and Tok – are not as firmly tied to the road as they were only two decades ago; increased government programming, different tourist attractions, and other activities have made them more than highway towns.

The Alaska Highway
through Watson Lake.
YUKON GOVERNMENT PHOTO.

As well, the introduction of satellite television in the early 1970s broke the dependence on regular camp films and undermined the sense of community so lauded by earlier residents along the Alaska Highway. When people from across the area are drawn together, as they are for the popular Arctic Winter Games, it is on a regional basis and not because of their connection to the Alaska Highway.

Transiency was a hallmark of highway life in the 1960s and after, particularly for the workers in the small camps. When Dick and Marge Coates arrived in Whitehorse in 1964, somebody approached Dick and asked, "How long are you up here for?" He replied, incredulously, "My goodness, it sounds like I've gone to jail. What do you mean?" He was told that many people came up for a fixed term, usually three years. The Coates were unusual in that they had come to the Yukon with no predetermined date of "escape."

The summer work crews were and are notoriously transient. Since there are generally not enough skilled workers available in the Northwest for the intense summer work season, recruitment extends far outside the region, particularly for engineering crews. In order to secure a suitable complement of workers, hiring is done in early May, often among university students just released from their studies. Construction work does not begin immediately, but the workers are put on salary and given small, preparatory jobs to keep them on staff until the real work begins. By mid-August, with university beckoning and with healthy bank balances after a couple months of overtime wages and, often, free room and board, the summer employees begin to quit, giving themselves an unpaid vacation before school starts. The construction and maintenance crews, however, are left short, and have to scramble to find replacements on short notice for the remainder of the construction season.

While elements of the highway community remain intact, much has also changed. Life in Fairbanks differs significantly from life in Fort Nelson, and Fort St. John is a very different community than Whitehorse; what similarities exist are primarily those related to climate, northern location, unstable economies, and the presence of a large First Nations' population. But in the smaller towns, such as Watson Lake, Teslin, and Tok, and the road stations – Fireside, Coal River, Liard River, Swift River, Johnson's Crossing, Destruction Bay, Northway – one still feels the full impact of the Alaska Highway.

Life in these places is tied to the rhythms and realities of the road. When it washes out, as it does from time to time, activities grind to a halt and supplies dry up. The arrival of tourists, previously in late June but now as much as a month earlier, signals the beginning of a brief but intense working season. Gloriously long hours of sunlight and the promise of a somnolent winter energize the people to operate the hotels, staff the gas pumps, and keep the grills hot. For four or five months, work is a busy round of fixing the tire on a Winnebago, giving directions to a German couple on a year-long expedition across North America, offering small-talk and postcards to a bus full of tourists, and pumping gas into one of the dozens of small vans, station wagons, and cars crammed with travelling gear.

Frank Steele, who operated the lodge at Summit from 1957 to 1976, remembers intensely busy summers, with as many as twenty cars lined up for gas, a crowd in his restaurant, and lots of money flowing into the lodge. The long hours of work – from 7:00 a.m. to 11:00 p.m. through the summer – gradually got to him. He rarely had time to explore the surrounding countryside and never once climbed the mountain in front of his lodge. Finally, he had had enough: "I'd had so many years of dealing with the public that I was getting bad tempered and ratty, and I found that I was snapping at my customers – just being mean. I couldn't help it. So I knew I had to sell and get out."

For the tourists, most with a well-thumbed current edition of *Milepost* magazine jammed into the folds of the front seat, the sense of mystery and adventure remains much as before – even with the road substantially paved, the Alaska Highway is a remarkable departure from the normal North American driving experience. The veterans – those on the way back down the highway – are eager to offer travel secrets to the vehicular version of the *cheechako* of 1898; the newcomers, still trying to distinguish between the stories they have heard about the highway and the reality of the modern road they are travelling, lap up words of wisdom and advice. In campgrounds, at gas stations, and in information booths, the tourists gather to recount adventures, tender advice about facilities and attractions, and compare damage to their windshields. One lodge operator had a great line for any highway traveller he saw without a nick in the windshield. As he went to serve gas, he would holler out, "Just stand back. I'm going to throw a rock at you, because you can't drive out there without a broken windshield. You have to have one." It is hard to know if anyone took him seriously.

Even before they depart for the North, most travellers dip into the vast literature about the Alaska Highway. Information abounds on how to ready a vehicle for the northward expedition and how to avoid the many pitfalls of sub-Arctic driving. The detail is commonsensical – cover the headlights with wire or plastic protectors, carry an extra spare tire, drive slowly and cautiously on the gravel, and, most emphatically, protect oneself from dust: "Keep all the windows tightly closed and turn on your fan full bore – the pressure buildup inside the car keeps a lot of dust out if you can stand the warmth in hot weather.... And for clothes and various other articles, those zippered plastic bags – the heavy ones – help a lot."[10] The articles, in fact, persist

Rubble blocks the highway after a flash flood at Mile 474.
JIM QUONG.

long after there is any particular need for warnings or advice; it has become part of the culture to consider the entire undertaking as some special expedition to the far outback.

The Alaska Highway has earned a reputation as a tough and challenging drive – not one for the ill-prepared or incautious. The reality is less dramatic, as those who live in the Northwest know, but stories still abound of the dangers and discomforts of driving the road. The account of Tom and Marnie Brennan's 1967 excursion is not unusual. The two set out from Massachusetts, heading for adventure and a new life in Alaska, towing a houseboat behind their International TravelAll: "Because of the houseboat, they were able to drive only fifteen miles an hour on the Alaska Highway. They were on the highway for twelve days. One thousand five hundred miles of two-lane road, of which the houseboat occupied a lane and one-third. More than a thousand miles were unpaved. Full of potholes and bumps, and shrouded in dust. Traffic was backed up behind them for miles. The houseboat bucked and plunged as if it had been set adrift in heavy seas. Dust covered everything; the inside of the houseboat, their belongings, themselves. With every bump, another dish would break, another lamp would fall over, another piece of furniture would slide across the houseboat floor. The dust obscured mountains, obscured the sky, obscured the road. For more than one thousand miles, in midsummer, they drove with their windows shut tight, because of the dust."[11]

There is, of course, a great deal to remind one that the Alaska Highway traverses a great, majestic, open land. On one of my trips up the highway, in early September 1981, taking my wife, Cathy, on her first trip to the Yukon, we stopped at the Liard Hot Springs. A sign at the entrance to the boardwalk informed travellers that the hot springs were closed. I confidently convinced my less-than-courageous partner that the sign was there for tourists, not "real" northerners. We set off, past a few smaller signs suggesting that to continue was inadvisable. At the first of the hot springs' pools, there was an even larger sign – EXTREME DANGER! I turned to my wife, only to discover that she was already hot-footing it back to the van. I caught up with her and, as we drove on to Whitehorse, teased her mercilessly about her lack of fortitude. Always the gentleman, I told this story two nights later around the dinner table while visiting friends in Whitehorse – my account elicited no great laughs. My friends informed me, rather solemnly, that a trained biologist had been mauled by a bear at the hot springs the day before we were there; the animal had not yet been caught. Cathy said nothing, but her sharp kick under the table left a vivid bruise. It was a solid reminder that signs, especially those along the Alaska Highway, are to be obeyed.

Some of the old signs are gone. In the 1960s Public Works removed the accident markers – long a standard along the highway. Erwin Johnson, manager of engineering after 1967, decided to take them down. His rationale was fairly complex: the signs had not been kept up to date (they stopped erecting signs in 1964), the signs apparently had little effect on the drivers, they were a "knife-twisting" reminder to the families of highway victims, and they were rather poor advertising for a road that was not, by North American standards, unusually dangerous. Perhaps more ironic was the fact that the little forests of signs had not necessarily marked the worst sections of the highway; many of the tragedies had actually occurred on some of the better stretches of the road. The signs came down.

The Alaska Highway's foremost magazine, *Milepost*, takes its name from one of the road's unique features. During the war, distances along the road were measured in miles from main centres; camps, for example, were often given such inspiring titles as 50N, meaning fifty miles north of the nearest community. Once the highway was completed, mileposts were erected along the entire route. Most communities were known as much by their milepost designation as their formal name – Whitehorse was 918, Haines Junction 1016, Beaver Creek 1202, and so on. The mileposts were not particularly accurate. In 1961, for example, Whitehorse was actually 911 miles from Dawson Creek (Mile 0), not 918 as its milepost stated. The difference was due to road straightening and relocation. It was a matter of some assurance to be able to keep track of distances as one ventured along the road.

The mileposts, small wooden posts, which bore the mile number on a painted metal flap, were an integral part of highway lore. So much so, in fact, that tourists loved to take a milepost or two home with them. The more creative found the milepost that matched their home address; others simply grabbed the more standard ones – mileposts 500 and 1000 were constantly being stolen. Replacing missing posts became a regular part of summer maintenance. (There were similar problems with route markers, particularly when, in 1976, the Yukon government introduced attractive ones bearing the territorial crest.) Efforts were made to make the main targets less attractive; milepost 1000, for example, became a metal post set in concrete. The familiar metal flaps of the wooden posts became too expensive and difficult to replace; plastic numbers tacked directly onto the wooden posts took their place.

An even greater change occurred in the mid-1970s, when the Canadian government launched its metrification program. Across the country out went the old imperial measurements to be replaced, in this instance, with kilometres. In 1975, the Yukon government replaced the old mileposts with kilometre posts. Two summer students, of whom I was one, received the august task of tearing out a segment of northern history and replacing it with signs of the new Canadian modernity. It was a perplexing task; we had to wait for a divisional engineer, whose car had a very accurate odometer, to drive along the route, starting in Watson Lake. The problems started just outside of Watson Lake. What was the kilometrage (metrification does not resonate with highway travel) at the B.C.-Yukon boundary? A number was designated, although reconstruction and straightening the highway almost immediately rendered the figure inaccurate – a sign at the border now reminds travellers that there is considerable discrepancy between B.C. and Yukon distances, requiring a "one time only" leap forward to compensate.

Our task involved ripping out the old mileposts (creating a wonderful pile of scrap lumber in the process) and, following the engineer's markings, planting the new kilometre posts. Travellers were less than pleased with our efforts. Those coming from the North resented the unexplained shift (proper explanatory signs went up after we were done); those from the South were only too willing to vent their displeasure at this latest government initiative. Pierre Elliot Trudeau and the Liberal Party were not particularly popular in that neck of the woods, and we suffered an undue share of abuse for their decisions.

The aged posts could not be reused and were destined for the scrap-heap; as historical mementos, however, they were much sought after. This, of course, placed us and our superiors in a difficult situation. It would have been inappropriate to sell the mileposts – although many such offers were made – and none were sold. It was, nonetheless, extremely hard to decide between the various requests from friends, colleagues, and local people for specific posts. One option, made much easier by the decision to go from metal flaps to plastic numbers, was to create a limited number of clones (several 918s, or 1016s), which were given to those requesting them on the strict condition that they keep them absolutely private and never display them in public.

Over time, tourists came to greet the transition from the mileposts to kilometre posts with good humour. The fact that the *Milepost* magazine soon took to listing distances in both miles and kilometres satisfied most travellers; to some Americans, it was rather quaint, a hint that they were, despite much evidence to the contrary, actually in a foreign country. Soon thereafter, distance signs experienced the same fate as the mileposts. In this instance, however, we were rushed into the field to replace the signs before formal authorization to proceed had been granted. Metal replacement tags, indicating the distances between centres in miles rather than kilometres, were hastily

Johnson's Crossing.

painted and dispatched to the different highway maintenance yards to be placed over the kilometres until formalities had been completed.

The travellers themselves are a rather interesting breed. The locals observe the rituals of tourist travel with a combination of resignation, fascination and, mostly, good humour. The repeated questions ("Where can I see a moose?" "Are there any *real* Indians around?" "How far to Fairbanks?" "Is the road this bad all the way?" "Can I get unleaded gas in Beaver Creek?" "Are we in Alaska yet?" "What do those numbers on the mileposts mean?") get a bit tiresome, as does the arrogance of a tiny but vocal number of travellers. But since the tourists are the highway community's bread and butter, the queries, well-intentioned, repetitious, or offensive, are generally handled with equanimity, the better ones filed for future reference and wintertime discussion.

One of my favourite stories about arrogant tourists occurred when I was helping out a friend at a gas station in Haines Junction in the early 1970s. An American from the Deep South – judging by his accent and licence plate – pulled in and began ordering us around. He expected us to clean his entire car, which seemed to have been slimed by a mud-monster. "Boy," he snorted, "my window isn't clean yet." We cleaned his windows, headlights, tail-lights, checked his oil, filled his gas tank, and managed to hold our tempers. When we were done, he pulled out a wad of American dollars: "Boy, 'y'all have change for a hundred?" He was on his way soon enough – though we had to plunder the cash register and then explain the niceties of Canadian-American exchange rates and our reasons for not having a till full of American bills – no doubt completely unimpressed with the service. He left behind him enough anger in that little gas station to fan the flames of anti-tourist sentiment for an hour or two until a travelling grandma and grandpa arrived. Deeply interested in how two teenagers actually lived along the Alaska Highway, they barraged us with excited questions about our experiences in the area, unwittingly giving us free rein for our memories, imagination, and bravado. In so doing, they put tourists, American ones at that, back in our good books.

While it is perhaps Canadian sanctimoniousness that ascribes tourist arrogance exclusively to Americans, highway workers know that aggressive and rude American tourists were not unusual – although they were in a decided minority among American travellers. Highway crews working at roadblocks often had difficulty stopping certain drivers – they remembered them, perhaps inaccurately, as being Americans – who insisted on being allowed to proceed, even if the road was completely washed out. One engineer says, "They feel that the road is theirs because their country built it. They keep saying, 'Canada has had it for twenty-five years and they haven't changed a thing on it.'"[11]

Such tourists are, of course, in a decided minority. The vast majority, entranced by the Far Northwest and intrigued with living conditions in such an isolated and unique region, are polite to a fault, anxious to learn anything they can about the place and people. An endless barrage of questions – when we were counting cars along the Alaska Highway people used to stop partly to find out what we were doing and partly to pump us for information and insights – from those truly interested in the region more than compensates for the occasional "ugly" tourist.

The locals' principal complaint about the thousands of travellers who pass through each summer is that very few stop to look around. Alaska remains the destination for the vast majority of tourists; the highway is as much a conduit as an attraction for this annual mass migration. For this reason, most travellers pause only for gas, an occasional restaurant meal, to sleep overnight in a highway hotel (although the proliferation of recreational vehicles has cut into even this trade), or to stock up on souvenirs – proof that they have, indeed, travelled the Alaska Highway. Most stop at the standard highway attractions – Mile 0 in Dawson Creek, the signposts in Watson Lake, downtown Whitehorse, Soldier's Summit, Sheep Mountain on the shores of Kluane Lake, the Santa Claus House in North Pole – but otherwise they rush through northern British Columbia, the southern Yukon, and eastern Alaska, scarcely slowing until they reach Fairbanks or turn off for Anchorage. Most rarely stray off the highway proper, and leave the North with only a high-speed sense of a narrow corridor.

Perhaps the epitome of this rush through the Northwest was the annual caravans, usually of Airstream Trailers when they were popular in the 1960s. These well-organized, carefully planned expeditions brought dozens of cars and trailers onto the highway. Other travellers cursed the mammoth caravans, which sometimes amounted to more than a hundred units and slowed traffic for miles on end, particularly on the winding sections of the road. The vehicles were usually spaced apart to provide an opportunity for faster cars to pass, but on twisting stretches, not much could be done. One could spend several hours working one's way slowly past the seemingly never-ending line of cars and trailers, sucking up their dust, catching a few well-aimed rocks in the grill or windshield, and feeling one's blood pressure rise by the minute.

The caravans were lauded by local chambers of commerce. On the surface they were a retailer's dream, as several hundred flush tourists arrived *en masse*. The towns went all out for them, providing them with space to park their vehicles and otherwise welcoming them. Frank Peters' home town would put on a big show for the caravans: "At Watson Lake they used to park in our compound, and they'd have church services and movies when they were there. Watson Lakers themselves used to have a bake sale for them." The caravaners left a good impression, not the least because "there was never a piece of paper on the ground

Campground at Kluane Lake, Yukon.

after they left." The caravans were virtually self-contained; they did, however, bring a handsome infusion of tourist cash into the local economy.

Not all the expeditions worked so well. Frank Steele recalls a group of caravaners who pulled into Summit Lodge. "They were bickering, fighting, arguing," Steele recalled, "and nobody was speaking to the other one. And the ones that were speaking were yelling at each other. I asked them, what is this group and what are you doing. 'Oh', one says. 'We're on a goodwill tour to Alaska.'"

But all too soon for those whose commercial fortunes are tied to the annual lemming-like rush up (and even faster retreat down) the Alaska Highway, the migration ends. By late August, the flow is almost entirely southward, as travellers flee before cold nights and the possibility of snow. By mid-September, tour companies shut down their operations and the university students who make up a large portion of the summertime work force return to school. The crews on the reconstruction projects remain in the field a few weeks longer until onset of the fall snows and the beginning of the bitterly cold northern winters.

Winter along the Alaska Highway bears little resemblance to the frenetic pace of the summer season. Tourist travel disappears, leaving the road open for local traffic, school buses near the main towns, military migrants from bases in Alaska, and the ubiquitous long-haul truckers. Highway crews, recovering from the frantic pace of summer work, shift to the work of snow-removal and keeping culverts ice-free. Several roadside hotels, restaurants, and gas stations close down; those that stay open still reduce staff and activities, sustained by the promise of another boom the following summer.

Most southerners see the Far Northwest as a snowy and wind-ravaged landscape, impassable to all but the most intrepid and foolhardy. In reality, winter travel along the Alaska Highway is generally as safe and reliable as during the summer months; the occasional winter storms are not appreciably worse than the hard rains of summer. But with little traffic along the highway, mechanical breakdowns or minor accidents can turn into major tragedies in the sub-zero temperatures of mid-winter. However, common decency and the code of northern travel also ensure that other travellers, infrequent as they might be, rarely pass by a motorist in trouble.

For people who live along the highway, winter driving presents few difficulties. The low temperatures of the region – readings of minus forty (the Fahrenheit and Celsius scales meet at this point) are fairly common, and it is not unusual for the mercury to fall to minus fifty Fahrenheit – limit the amount of slush and ice along the highway. At extremely low temperatures, the snow on the road takes on the qualities of dry sand, crunching under foot and tire, and providing sure traction for pedestrian and automobile alike. Heavy snowfalls are rare along much of the highway, although there are a few trouble spots (but nothing remotely close to the exceptional snows experienced along the Haines Road between Haines Junction and Haines, Alaska). The snow carries additional benefits; more than a few drivers, having lost control of their vehicles, have been the beneficiaries of a relatively soft and safe landing in a snow-filled ditch.

Few experiences can match the beauty of winter driving along the Alaska Highway, particularly in such picturesque areas as Muncho Lake, approaching the St. Elias Mountains, and along Kluane Lake. Snow-covered mountains, shimmering pink and orange in the muted light of the winter sun, provide a superb backdrop to the darkened carpet of sub-Arctic evergreens. Through such scenes of stunning power, the Alaska Highway lies like a gentle bridal ribbon. The biting wind of a winter breeze, chilling enough to make the skin crawl while still inside a vehicle, often brushes the road with light strokes of blown snow. You drive on with a sense of isolation, vulnerability, and awe, unless, of course, you are a local who simply accepts this stunning setting as the basic canvas of your life. It is a scene all too seldom seen by tourists or southerners, for they are kept away by accounts of winter dangers and the North American fear of extreme cold.

Winter driving along the highway at night-time – a common state given the shortness of daylight in mid-winter – gives one a profound sense of isolation and darkness. Headlights throw a narrow beam through the seemingly lightless world, reaching only a few feet beyond the shoulders of the road. Other travellers can be seen at great distances, welcome beacons of human contact in a seemingly lifeless land. Homes near the highway, gas stations or small settlements, sit bathed in unnatural illumination, islands of light in the midst of a black wasteland. It is utterly dark unless one has the wit to turn off the headlights. (Drivers are warned that, as a car approaches from the other direction, they should put their headlights back on right away. Few things can be more disconcerting than having a vehicle's lights erupt in front of you unexpectedly as you are driving along an isolated stretch of northern highway.) It takes a few seconds for the eyes to adjust, but slowly, as the iris expands, searching for bits of light in the deep evening, a new world unfolds. The night that was so forbidding and unfriendly recedes.

Sparks from the winter moon bounce off the snow-covered landscape, their brilliance magnified many times by the virginal carpet. Mountain tops glow in the winter light, ice-covered lakes shine with unexpected brilliance. On those special nights when the northern lights sparkle colourfully across the sky, the beauty of the scene can defy description, crossing the thin barrier from majestic sight to spiritual experience. In the winter you see a completely different side to the Alaska Highway, stripped of its summer migrants, seasonal workers, temporary facilities, and uncharacteristic weather and driving conditions. During the cold season, another face emerges: that of Native communities, the few permanent non-Native residents, the insularity of the major communities, which burrow in on themselves for much of the winter season. In winter trucks are the most common vehicle on the road, reminders of the fundamental role of the highway as a provision route for the Far Northwest.

The Alaska Highway remains one of North America's great driving adventures. While many of the leisured classes now travel to the North by airplane or cruise ship, a steady stream clamber into their cars, camper vans, and recreational vehicles and head north. The trip to Alaska still takes weeks of planning, anticipation, and preparation. For most tourists, the experience more than matches the expectations. Hundreds of miles of virtually uninhabited territory, the majestic landscape revealing few scars of modern industrial civilization, provide a superb backdrop to a unique vehicular adventure.

The road, of course, is far from the rough, rustic pathway left by the United States at the end of World War II. Most of the highway meets southern road standards and expectations. The millions of dollars spent on reconstruction and relocation through northern British Columbia, the Yukon, and Alaska have eliminated almost all signs of the highway of wartime legend. There are glimpses here and there of the old road – a winding piece of gravel track, largely obscured by underbrush, curving off from the modern highway – but they are ephemeral and go unnoticed by the vast majority of travellers.

The area between Kluane Lake and the Alaska Boundary, slated for reconstruction under the incomplete Shakwak Project, provides the best introduction to the highway that was. Built low to the ground (unlike the miles of elevated road that precede and follow this section), the road winds and twists through miles of muskeg and slough, desperately searching for high and dry ground. Here, frost heaves and ground water continue to eat away at the highway surface, keeping the road crews on their toes through the summer months. Traffic often slows to a near crawl, as cars and trucks back up behind the ubiquitous recreational vehicles that, seemingly unaware of the convoy forming behind them, lumber slowly along the highway. Only the occasional straight stretch provides faster drivers with the opportunity to race pass the mobile obstacles.

But this section of the highway is an exception, the winds and twists more a symbol of differing Canadian and American priorities than an indication of the engineers' ability to deal with the problems of muskeg and permafrost. Most of the other sections that long bedevilled highway crews and infuriated travellers – the rough ground south of Fort Nelson, the slippery surfaces north of Coal River, the twisting miles west of Whitehorse – have succumbed to the engineers and road contractors. These gains came slowly, and only after much research and experimentation. The muskeg areas around Fort Nelson, for example, presented tremendous difficulties, but eventually Public Works engineers discovered that ditches dug some distance away from the sides of the road dried out the muskeg under the road surface, thus providing a more stable, permanent base for the highway. For the vast majority of its distance, the Alaska Highway is a fine road, made more remarkable by its isolated location, comparatively limited traffic, and the region's harsh climate.

A tiny number of travellers, the ones whose image of the Alaska Highway rests in the legends of the 1940s and who persist in seeing the Far Northwest as a nineteenth-century frontier beyond the pale of southern civilization, are disappointed with the experience. Where, they ask, are the rivers to ford? The muddy miles to plough through? In the 1970s, when tourists had more reason to misunderstand the nature of the Alaska Highway, such tourists came north with jerrycans of gas and extra tires strapped to their vehicles, and with a fully operational winch at the ready to pull them over the expected obstacles. The discovery of a serviceable road, easily and safely travelled, collided with their expectation of adventure and excitement in the northern hinterland.

For the principal users of the Alaska Highway, the slow but inexorable improvements have been less than adequate. Newspaper editors from Fort St. John to Fairbanks, and particularly in Whitehorse, repeatedly decry the poor condition of stretches of the highway and wonder if the oft-touted government commitments to the reconstruction of the road can survive yet another round of budget cuts and retrenchment. British Columbia's adamant refusal to negotiate the transfer of the southern portions of the highway to the provincial Department of Highways continues to cast a pall over long-term planning.

Lurking further away – the hidden knife secretly poised to strike a blow to the heart – is the possibility of portions of the highway route being flooded for a hydro-electric dam. B.C. Hydro actively investigated the construction of a major dam on the Liard River in the early 1980s, only to back off when the cost and environmental estimates were done. Although B.C. Hydro has publicly stated that the Liard project is off, the untapped hydroelectric potential of the Liard River system remains, leaving the prospect of a massive flooding of the Alaska Highway route on the books.

But the major threat to the highway is one that officials and highway managers seldom discuss in public – too little traffic. Since the 1930s, promoters of the Far Northwest have promised that the construction of a road to the region, or the improvement of the wartime highway, would touch off a travellers' boom from British Columbia to Alaska. The tourists have come, and in sizeable numbers, but not as many as regional promoters anticipated. As highway planners have repeatedly discussed during their preparation of budget submissions, there are not enough people using the road to justify the millions of dollars required to rebuild it. There are plenty of reasons for the shortage – the exceptionally long distances to be travelled, the length of time required for a return trip, the relatively high costs of gasoline, meals, and accommodation along the road – but the fact remains that the highway has not attracted the thousands upon thousands of visitors promised by highway promoters.

There are actually several highways contained within the ribbon that stretches from Dawson Creek to Fairbanks. The extreme south end, from Dawson Creek to Wonowon, is part of the local

Teslin, Yukon, with the Nisultin River bridge in the foreground.

YUKON GOVERNMENT PHOTO.

highway network, scarcely distinguishable from the other main roads that criss-cross the Peace River country. Oil and gas, logging, and mining activities in the Fort Nelson region generate much of the traffic on the next portion of the road, one of the busiest on the entire route. Only a small number of travellers drive farther up the highway; the section from Fort Nelson to Watson Lake is among the least used of the entire system and so is assigned one of the lowest priorities in reconstruction plans.

The highway from Watson Lake through Whitehorse to Haines Junction is a central part of the Yukon Territory's highway system and much of the traffic between these communities is tied to territorial activities. The stretch from Haines Junction to Tok, Alaska, has perhaps the most unusual travel patterns. Few Canadians venture along this portion of the highway – and the small settlements of Destruction Bay, Burwash, and Beaver Creek generate little traffic. Most of the travellers are Americans, coming from or through Haines and heading north on the highway. This portion of the road serves primarily as a connector between the Alaska Marine Highway ferry system and the rest of the state. The highway from Tok to Big Delta and Fairbanks is, like the southernmost segment of the road, an integral part of the regional system, serving Alaskan needs and drawing only a relatively small percentage of its total traffic from the southern reaches of the Alaska Highway.

The Alaska Highway remains a single entity on the maps – a lengthy twisting ribbon of road snaking from the Peace River country to the central Yukon River valley. The absence of a consistent standard from south to north, the fact that the highway comes under four political jurisdictions (British Columbia, Public Works Canada, Yukon, and Alaska), and varying traffic patterns raise questions about the future of this famous road. The development of alternative road access to the South, particularly the gradual improvement of the Stewart-Cassiar Highway through northern British Columbia, and the improved ferry service along the coast, has diminished the Alaska Highway's significance. These slow developments have also eroded the sense of community and common cause that once bound the entire highway corridor together – or at least the Canadian sections of the road.

Significantly, the fiftieth anniversary of the construction of the Alaska Highway put it back on centre stage throughout the region. Years of preparation and planning, countless meetings, and great expectations surrounding the event have reminded the citizens of the highway corridor of the historical and cultural importance of this road to their lives and communities. The Alaska Highway may yet again be at the forefront of attention both in the Northwest and in North America generally.

Five years ago, when work on this book started, few people were interested in the Alaska Highway. There was a steady stream of "I travelled the highway" or "I worked on the Alaska Highway" books, sure sellers in northern bookstores to tourists anxious for proof of their own adventure. But this was scarcely evidence that the region was taking the highway story to heart. The fortieth anniversary celebrations in 1982, particularly in

No longer a rough road north.

YUKON GOVERNMENT PHOTO.

Fort St. John and Whitehorse, created a short-term local ripple, but little of the enthusiasm spread throughout or outside the region. As the fiftieth anniversary year – 1992 – approaches, however, local boosters, historical enthusiasts, and public figures have turned their attention to the Alaska Highway. The idea of celebrating a half-century on the world's most remarkable highway found favour with regional governments, which have funded a variety of anniversary projects. The year 1992 is likely to be something of a coming-out party for the Far Northwest.

Government promotions usually follow, not create, public interest, and this is certainly the case with the planned Alaska Highway anniversary celebrations. Greater awareness of the Alaska Highway owes something to the simple passage of time. As the veterans of the construction era pass on, and as nostalgia for the life and times (but not the horror and uncertainty) of

World War II increases, interest in the highway grows. There are signs along the road – from oral history projects and museum displays in Fort St. John and Fort Nelson to Watson Lake's wonderful wartime USO re-enactment staged in the summer months – of increasing interest in the Alaska Highway. It is to be seen, as well, in Big Delta's determination to hold on to its pride of place in Alaska Highway lore, and its friendly battles with Fairbanks for designation as the real end of the highway.

Twenty years ago, the highway was a way for northerners to get outside and a conduit for tourists anxious to buy tin cans of Alaska Highway dust and stickers declaring I Drove the Alaska Highway – and Survived. (Flo Whyard, Bob Erlam, and John Scott of Whitehorse started canning Alaska Highway dust in 1964. The label invited the owner to "Relive that exhilarating thrill of driving the Alaska Highway. Stand in front of your electric fan on a hot day and pour the contents of this can slowly into the whirling blades. This mixture is recommended for obscuring licence plates and dimming headlights." The Alaska Highway dust came with an unequivocal guarantee: "If after eating a tin of this genuine Alaska Highway Dust you are not satisfied it is similar to the dust you ate on the Alaska Highway, we will supply you with another tin at cost."[12]) Today, if I might risk a bold generalization, the Alaska Highway is an integral part of the region's history, culture, and life. The passage of time has seen the road straightened, widened, and (mostly) paved; it has also seen the maturation of regional society, and a greater awareness of the significance of the past in the creation of the modern North.

Now, perhaps, the Alaska Highway's time has come. On the eve of the fiftieth anniversary of the Alaska Highway, it is time to recall the history of a unique, remarkable, and delightful road, which ranks among the world's greatest driving adventures.

The final word properly belongs to two of the people who helped build the Alaska Highway. Robert Black went north to work for Campbell Construction Company in October 1942; his wife, Dell, and their eighteen-month-old son, John, joined him in April 1943. They worked at several camps along the southern highway, piled up a tidy nest egg, and left for the south in March 1944, having never driven the entire highway. Twenty-six years later, they returned, driving as far north as

Whitehorse; "From Fort St. John north, the roads were gravel, with large potholes, dust flying that made vision almost impossible, and mud like gumbo when it rained. We turned back, disappointed, although we had enjoyed walking and reminiscing at our deserted camp site." Not readily deterred but more cautious, they returned again in 1987, flying to Edmonton and boarding a tour bus for the journey north: "But what a difference! Road's all hard topped. But our camp site had been bypassed – and that was a disappointment." But they, like thousands before and countless thousands to follow, had finally achieved their lifelong ambition: "WE HAD TRAVELLED THE ENTIRE ALASKA HIGHWAY."

Acknowledgements

WHILE WRITING IS GENERALLY a solitary enterprise, in my case conducted on a word processor in the hot and stuffy attic of my Oak Bay home, the successful publication of a book invariably owes a great deal to the assistance of others. I am especially blessed in this case, for I have been aided immeasurably by a number of people.

This project began in earnest five years ago, when I was approached by John McTaggart of Public Works Canada, which has been involved with the Alaska Highway since 1964. Public Works Canada wished to commission a history of the highway as part of its contribution to the 1992 Alaska Highway celebrations. It kindly provided me with the research funds and logistical assistance that made this book possible. I wish to thank John McTaggart, Joe Marston, John Hudson, and N. M. Hoy, Regional Director General, for their early work on the project, and Toni Timmermans for her assistance and encouragement with the later stages. Ms. Timmermans arranged to have a number of highway veterans read this book in draft form; their helpful and enthusiastic response was a major boost for me. Special thanks to Basil Dowd for his useful comments.

The good people at McClelland & Stewart have been of tremendous help. Doug Gibson responded enthusiastically to my initial proposal and provided much encouragement at an early stage. Dinah Forbes has worked carefully and conscientiously on the various drafts of this book; her good humour, sharp editorial eye, and infectious enthusiasm have been truly delightful.

While I happily absolve her of responsibility for any errors and infelicities of style that remain in the book, I also know that its good qualities owe a great deal to her efforts.

There are others who have helped me at various stages in my writing. My research assistants – Judith Powell, Brenda Clark, Barbara Kelcey, and Jacob Marshall – helped tremendously with the archival and newspaper research and conducted many of the interviews. The secretaries in the Department of History, University of Victoria, particularly Dinah Dickie, June Bull, and Karen McIvor, were of great assistance. Denise Bukowski of the Bukowski Agency in Toronto is an extremely able agent. Her enthusiasm for this project and her helpful advice in the early stages kept this book on course. Bill Morrison, my writing partner on many other projects, kindly read through the manuscript – while on the White Pass and Yukon Route train from Skagway and while on a bus to Dawson City, no less – his counsel and careful editorial eye are both greatly appreciated. I have been helped tremendously by archivists and librarians across Canada and the United States. John Greenwood, chief of the Historical Division, U.S. Army Corps of Engineers, and his assistant, Martin Gordon, gave me access to the files of his organization and much cheerful encouragement. Staff at the U.S. National Archives (particularly in Suitland, MD), the National Archives of Canada, the Alaska State Archives, the British Columbia Provincial Archives, the Edmonton Municipal Archives, and especially the Yukon Territorial Archives provided a great deal of professional advice and much good service.

I have drawn heavily, once again, on my family in the preparation of this book. My father R. K. Coates, spent many hours with me talking about the Alaska Highway (particularly its engineering aspects); my mother, Marge Coates, filled in a lot of the details about social life along the highway corridor. My children, Bradley, Mark, and Laura, have now all spent time in the Far Northwest and know a bit more about the land and history that preoccupies their father. I know that they do not (yet) share my passion for the region, but I think they understand me a little better for having been along parts of the Alaska Highway. Cathy Coates, my wife, remains a pillar of strength in my chaotic life. Her support makes my research trips and hours of writing possible; her enthusiasm and love makes it all enjoyable.

I have saved the final word for the dozens of Alaska Highway folk who participated in the research for this book. The willingness of Alaska Highway veterans to contribute made this project both feasible and exciting. While I could only include a small portion of what they told me, I hope that the story as told here properly respects the memories of those who so kindly shared their information with me. The following people, in particular, provided much useful material in the form of answers to questionnaires, photographs, copies of diaries, or other Alaska Highway memorabilia. (I may have missed some of those who so kindly contributed to my research; if so please accept my apologies):

Norman Allison, Donald Amos, C. E. "Red" Anderson, Marvin and Mabel Armitage, Thelma Ashby, A. G. Askew, Kaare Aspol, Coreen Bafford, Duncan Bath, Chuck Baxter, J. E. Bedford, Bill Bennett, Charles Biller, Robert and Dell Black, H. M. Blackwood, Bob and Lil Brant, Agnes Brewster, Barbara Brocklehurst, Vera Brown, A. Brutto, Howard Burrel, D. K. Campbell, Phyllis Church, Ruth Clemo, Aleatha and Marshall Close, Dick and Marge Coates, Muriel Coates, Gileen Colcleugh, Muriel Gwen Collip, J. D. Cooper, C. T. Cotton, Crawford Cowieson, Sylvia Cranston, G. B. Criteser, W. H. Croft, Bob and Barb Dempster, Hugh Devitt, Evelyn Dobbin, G. C. Drake, Tom Dunbar, George Ford, Alex Forgie, R. Fowler, Lorne Frizzell, Merle and Audrey Gaddy, Stacia Gallop, Raymond Ganser, J. Garbus, Harry George, Gordon and Lorna Gibbs, M. E. Golata, W. A. Gorham, Willis Grafe, Rex Graham, P. and M. Greenan, Nancy Greenwood, Harold Griffin, Cyril Griffith, L. G. Grimble, Clarence Haakenstad, Selmer Hafso, Fred Hammond, Harvey Hayduck, J. D. Hazen, Chuck Hemphill, Ed Herzog, Richard Hislop, M. Hope, John Hudson, Gunnar Johnson, Mary Johnson, Vernon Kennedy, Charles Knott, Con and Dot Lattin, Phyllis Lee, Brig. Gen. H. W. Love, Laura MacKinnon, Mickey and Effie McCaw, A. C. McEachern, R. C. McFarland, Helen McLean, Donald Miller, Adam Milne, Bruce Milne, Roy Minter, J. Mitchell, T. E. Molyneux, John Mueller, Claus-M. Naske, Walter Nelson, E. O'Neill, Bob Oliphant, R. A. Panter, Ben and Addie Parker, Ena Parsons, Joan Patterson, Gerry Pelletier, Frank and Esther Peters, Walter Polvi, Hampton Primeaux, A. J. S. Protherow, William T.

Pryor, Jim Quong, Peggy Read, Cale Roberts, K. L. Rudhardt, Donald Saunders, Ray Savela, L. H. Schnurstein, Carl Schubert, Rudy Schubert, June Scully, Bernice Sillemo, Bud and Doris Simpson, Earl and Barbara Smith, Lake Southwick, Frank and Agatha Speer, Mildred Spencer, Frank Steele, Cliff and Colette Stringer, John and Ruth Stringer, Jolyne Sulz, Jim and Iris Sutton, Norman Swabb, Duane Swenson, Ray Talbot, Jim Tedlie, Joan Thomas, Jean Waldon, E. R. Walker, Jean Walker, H. Walker, Paul E. Warren, Harvey Weber, Bud and Barb Webster, Olga Whitley, E. J. Wiggans, J. Williams, Wendell Williamson, L. E. Willis, L. Williscroft, Bruce F. Willson, Vern and Alice Wilson, Henry Wright, Peggy Wudel.

Notes

Chapter 1

1. Harold Griffin, *Alaska and the Canadian Northwest* (New York: W.W. Norton, 1944), p. 102.

2. F. S. Wright to City Clerk, Edmonton, 30 May 1938; F. S. Wright to Herbert Putnam, Library of Congress, 30 May 1938, Edmonton Municipal Archives (EMA), RG11, Class 90, file 23.

3. Aitken to Hodgson, 2 May 1941, EMA, RG11, Class 90, file 29.

4. T. A. Crerar to Mayor John W. Fry, 23 June 1941, EMA, RG11, Class 90, file 29.

5. Morris Zaslow, *The Northward Expansion of Canada, 1914-1967* (Toronto: McClelland & Stewart, 1988), p. 216.

6. M. V. Bezeau, "The Realities of Strategic Planning: The Decision to Build the Alaska Highway," in Ken Coates, ed., *The Alaska Highway* (Vancouver: University of British Columbia Press, 1985), pp. 25-38. *See also:* Shelagh Grant, *Sovereignty or Security? Government Policy in the Canadian North 1936-1950* (Vancouver: University of British Columbia Press, 1988), p. 75.

7. J. D. Hickerson to Mr. Berle, 31 January 1942, United States National Archives (NA), RG59, Decimal file 842,154, Seattle-Fairbanks Highway/354.

8. Zaslow, *The Northward Expansion of Canada*, p. 216.

9. Basis for Estimates – Alaska Highway Project, 18 March 1942, NA, RC30, Box 188.

10. John Greenwood, "General Bill Hoge and the Alaska Highway," in Coates, ed., *The Alaska Highway*, pp. 39-53.

11. C. L. Sturdevant to Colonel W. Hoge, 3 March 1942, Army Corps of Engineers (ACE), 72-A-3173, Box 15, file 52-1.

Chapter 3

1. Julie Cruikshank, et al., *Life Lived Like a Story* (Vancouver: University of British Columbia Press, 1990), p. 249.

2. Gertrude Baskine, *Hitch-hiking the Alaska Highway* (Toronto: Macmillan, 1944), p. 88.

Chapter 4

1. Riggs to Sturdevant, 21 March 1942, ACE, 72-A-3173, file 50-39.

2. Heath Twichell, 4 March 1942, Yukon Territorial Archives (YTA), 82/546.

3. Heath Twichell, 3 March 1943, YTA, 82/546.

4. Griffith Williams, "Alaska's Connection," *Pacific Northwest Quarterly*, vol. 76, no. 2 (April 1985), p. 62.

5. Greenwood, "General Bill Hoge and the Alaska Highway," p. 46.

6. Fred Rust, "History of the Eighteenth Engineers Regiment (Combat) in Yukon Territory" (mimeograph), p. 5.

7. *Ibid.*, p. 49.

8. *Ibid.*

9. Recollections of Archie McEachern.

10. This description is taken from "History, Organization and Progress of the Military Road to Alaska," prepared by Brigadier General Sturdevant, ACE, 72-A-3173, 16/20.

11. "The Long Trail: 341st Engineers on the Alaska Military Highway, 1942-1943" (mimeograph report).

12. Harold Richardson, "Alcan – America's Glory Road, Part III – Construction Tactics," *Engineering News-Record*, 14 January 1943.

13. ACE, Organizational History, 886th Ordnance HAM C., August 1942-April 1945.

14. "The Long Trail."

15. Rust, "Eighteenth Engineers Regiment," pp. 9-10.

16. *Ibid.*

17. Recollections by Leslie Schnurstein.

18. H.W. Richardson, "From a War Correspondent's Notebook – 1," Whitehorse, 25 June 1943, ACE, X-2-10.

19. Griffin, *Alaska and the Canadian Northwest,* p. 119.

20. Harold Richardson, "Alcan – America's Glory Road, Part II – Supply, Equipment and Camps," *Engineering News-Record,* 31 December 1942, p. 35.

21. Rust, "Eighteenth Engineers Regiment," p. 11.

22. Recollections by Leslie Schnurstein.

23. Heath Twichell letter, 3 April 1942, YTA, 82/546.

24. Richardson, "Alcan – America's Glory Road, Part II," p. 42.

25. Annex No. 3 to G-2 Periodic Report No. 108, NA, RG407, Box 32, file 91-DPI-2.1.

26. Paul Thompson to Commanding General, 18 August 1942, ACE, 72A3173, Box 16, file 50-26.

27. Gudrun Sparling file, YTA, 82/48, pt. 2.

28. *North Star Magazine,* November 1944.

29. *Washington Post,* 16 March 1943.

30. Recollections of Walter Nelson.

31. Recollections of Harold Griffin.

32. Notes provided by Harold Griffin.

33. *North Star Magazine,* November 1944, p. 19.

34. Unit History 19th QM Salvage Repair Platoon, NA, RG407, Box 22956, file OMPL-19-0.1.

35. Heath Twichell letter, 26 July 1942, YTA, 82/546.

36. History of the Alaskan Operations 93rd Engineer Regiment (GS), NA, RG407, Box 19550, file Engr. 93-3.0.

37. Ruth Gruber to Secretary, U.S. Department of the Interior, 11 June 1943, NA, RG165, OPD 291.21 (Section II), Cases 21-52 (Negroes and the Negro Race).

38. Recollections of Lake Southwick.

39. Recollections of Cyril Griffith.

40. Annex to G-2 Periodic Report No. 94, NA, RG407, Box 32, file 910-DPI-2.1.

41. Recollections of Harold Griffin.

42. "The Long Trail."

43. Log Book, 18th Engineers, Alaska Highway, April 1942-January 1943, p. 11-14, Glenbow-Alberta Institute, Seaton Papers, A. S. 441.

44. Notes provided by Harold Griffin.

45. Annex No. 3 to G-2 Periodic Report No. 51, NA, RG407-7-91-DPI-2.1.

46. F. Rainey, "Alaska Highway: An Engineering Epic." *National Geographic Magazine*, vol. LXXXIII, no. 2 (Feb.-Mar. 1943), p. 155.

47. *Edmonton Journal*, 15 December 1942.

48. Recollections of Laurent Cyr.

49. C. A. Penner to K. B. Hannan, 18 September 1943, YTA, YRG1, Series 1, vol. 61, file 35402.

50. Knox McCusker, "The Alaska Highway," *Canadian Surveyor*, vol. 8 (July 1943), p. 9.

51. Testimony of Joe Jacquot, 21 April 1976, National Archives of Canada (NAC), RG126, Exhibit 618.

52. A. Weber, "The Dawson Creek Explosion," (typescript).

53. Metheson to O.C., RCMP "G" Division, 14 April 1943, YTA, YRG1, Series 3, vol. 10, file 12-20B.

54. Entertaining Orientation of USO Show Overseas Unit #100, c. 1943, NA, RG338, NWSC, Box 7, file 353.8.

55. Phillips to Director, Special Service Division, 21 December 1943, NA, RG338, NWSC, Box 7, file 353.8.

56. Richardson, "Alcan – America's Glory Road, Part III," p. 133.

57. Recollections of Charles Knott.

58. Recollections of Cale Roberts.

59. Gibson to Commissioner, RCMP, 11 December 1942, YTA, TRG1, Series 3, vol. 10, file 12-20B.

60. Alleged Killing of Game Animals by U.S. Soldiers, 1 July 1943, NAC, RG85, vol. 944, file 12743, part 1.

61. *Ibid.*

62. Recollections of Willis Grafe.

63. Annex No. 3 to G-2 Periodic Report No. 104, p, 10, NA, RG407, Box 32, file 91-DPI-2.1.

64. *Ibid.,* Periodic Report No. 89.

65. Malcolm MacDonald, *Down North* (Oxford: Oxford University Press, 1945), p. 237.

66. Captain Richard Neuberger, "Opening of the Alaska Highway," quoted in Grant, *Sovereignty or Security?*, p. 255.

67. *Ibid.,* p. 9

68. Details taken from the "Alaska-Canada Highway" dedication program.

69. Grant, *Sovereignty or Security?*, p. 256.

70. Hickerson to Mr. Secretary, 20 May 1943, NA, RG59, file 711.42/255.

71. Heath Twichell, "Cut, Fill and Straighten: The Role of the Public Roads Administration in the Building of the Alaska Highway," in Coates, ed., *The Alaska Highway.*

72. Grant, *Sovereignty or Security?* p. 119.

73. "The Long Trail."

74. Office memoranda, 1944, Army Day Message, NA, RG338, Box 10, NWSC.

75. Rust, "Eighteenth Engineers Regiment," p. 65.

Chapter 5

1. Twichell, "Cut, Fill and Straighten," p. 57.

2. J. S. O'Connor to Commanding General, Army Services Forces, 14 July 1943, ACE, 72-A-3173, Box 15, file 50-15.

3. Recollections of Duncan Bath.

4. Baskine, *Hitch-hiking the Alaska Highway,* p. 251.

5. Twichell, "Cut, Fill and Straighten," p. 62.

6. Recollections of Alex Forgie.

7. Recollections of John Mueller.

8. Recollections of Duncan Bath.

9. Johnson to General Reybold, 13 November 1943, ACE, 29-52A434.

10. Rust, "Eighteenth Engineers Regiment," p. 43.

11. Richard Finnie to Ken Watts, 10 July 1943, ACE, 72-A-3173, Box 14.

12. Recollections of Kaare Aspol.

13. Rogers to George Black, 20 May 1942, ACE, 72-A-3173, Box 15, file 52-1.

14. Report by Constable Francis, 17 May 1944, NAC, RG27, vol. 1488, file R-171, pt. 1.

15. Statement by Major Thurston, 9 January 1945, NAC, RG27, vol. 1488, file R-171, pt. 2.

16. Baskine, *Hitch-hiking the Alaska Highway*, p. 18.

17. *Toronto Evening Telegraph*, 25 February 1943.

18. Parkinson to Henwood, 7 July 1944, NAC, RG36/4, vol. 112, April '44-Sept '44.

19. Belanger to Western Wage Labour Board, 19 June 1944, NAC, RG36/4, vol. 112, Agenda Book, April '44-Sept '44.

20. Dawson Creek Diary, 19 December 1942, NAC, NWSC, Reel 14.

21. *The Alaska Highway: The Interim Report of the Committee on Roads*, 79th Congress, 2nd Session, House Report No. 1705 (Washington: Government Printing Office, 1946), p. 179.

22. Okes Construction Bulletin, 6-2, Termination of Employment, 3 August 1942, NA, RG59, Decimal file 842.154, Seattle-Fairbanks Highway/450.

23. Recollections of Homer Blackwood.

24. *Edmonton Journal*, 21 June 1943.

25. Recollections of Ray Savela.

26. Recollections of Thelma Ashby.

27. Recollections of Cyril Griffith.

28. Recollections of Kaare Aspol.

29. Recollections of John Mueller.

30. "Henepin Avenue to the Bering Sea," *North Star Magazine* (November 1944), pp. 24-25.

31. Recollections of Gordon and Lorna Gibbs.

32. Recollections of Alex Forgie.

33. Recollections of Kaare Aspol.

34. *Northwest Newscast*, 19 August 1945.

35. Cruikshank, *Life Lived Like a Story*, p. 250.

36. McCusker, "The Alaska Highway."

37. Cruikshank, *Life Lived Like a Story*, p. 250.

38. Black to Strong, 27 January 1945, NAC, RG36/7, vol. 40, file 28-23, pt. 1.

39. Recollections of Hampton Primeaux.

40. LeCapelain to Colonel K.B. Bush, Chief of Staff, 18 August 1943, NAC, RG85, vol. 958, file 13439.

41. Callahan to Heeney, 17 November 1943, NAC, RG36/7, vol. 40, file 28-23, pt. 2.

42. *Financial Times*, 2 October 1943.

43. Jeckell to Gibson, 30 May 1945, YTA, YRG1, Series 1, vol. 59, file 34362.

44. A. W. Klieforth to Hickerson, 16 September 1943, NA, RG165, ODP 336, Canada, Section I, case 1-21.

45. Thompson to O'Connor, 5 September 1942, ACE, 72-A-3173, Box 16, file 50-26.

46. Gibson to Jeckell, 20 September 1944, NAC, RG85, vol. 957, file 13417, part 1.

47. F. S. Strong, Jr., *What's It All About: Thoughts from the Nineties* (privately published), p. 152.

48. *Edmonton Journal*, 11 July 1944.

49. *Edmonton Bulletin*, 25 July 1944.

50. Recollections of R.C. McFarland.

51. Eugene Wilkenson, "My First Trip on the Alcan Highway" (typescript), courtesy of Joe Garbus.

52. Recollections of Cyril Griffith.

53. Earl Gingrich, *Eastern Passage to the Alaska Highway* (Winterburn: Gingrich, 1986), p. 142.

54. Black to Gibson, 1 February 1945, NAC, RG85, vol 967, file 14-876, pt. 1.

55. Cited in R. Diubaldo, "The Alaska Highway in Canada-United States Relations," in Coates, ed., *The Alaska Highway*, p. 109.

56. *Ibid.*

57. *Star Weekly*, 28 June 1952.

58. Riggs to Delano, 14 May 1943, University of Alaska Fairbanks Archives, Gruening Papers, Box 6.

59. Gruening memorandum, 4 December 1943, Franklin D. Roosevelt Library, N1-N3Y, General, map room container # 171.

60. Short Report on the Northwest Highway System, 1 April 1946-31 March 1947, NAC, RG22, vol. 252, file 40-7-4, pt. 9.

61. Griffith Taylor, "Arctic Survey, IV: A Yukon Doomsday: 1944," *Canadian Journal of Economics and Political Science*, vol. 14, no. 3 (August 1945), p. 438.

62. P. Seddicum to Foster, 9 April 1947, NA, RG59, Decimal file 842.154, Seattle-Fairbanks Highway/4-947.

63. *Maclean's*, 15 November 1943.

64. Glen to Cameron, 30 April 1946, YTA, YRG1, Series 1, vol. 70, pt. 4, file 1.

65. Zaslow, *The Northward Expansion of Canada*, p. 217.

66. Curtis Nordmann, "The Army of Occupation: Malcolm MacDonald and U.S. Military Involvement in the Canadian Northwest," in Coates, ed., *The Alaska Highway*, p. 92.

67. *Ibid.*, p. 113.

68. Zaslow, *The Northward Expansion of Canada*, p. 226.

69. Baskine, *Hitch-hiking the Alaska Highway*, p. 310.

Chapter 6

1. Royal Canadian Engineers (RCE), *Highway Maintenance, 1946-1964* (Northwest Highway System, 1964), p. 9.

2. Pierre Berton, *The Mysterious North* (Toronto: McClelland & Stewart, reprinted 1989), p. 119.

3. Seattle-Fairbanks Highway, 7 November 1949, NA, RG59, file 842.154.

4. Iris Woolcock, *The Road North: One Woman's Adventure Driving the Alaska Highway, 1947-1948* (Anchorage: Greatland Graphics, 1990), p. 137.

5. *The Seattle Times*, 24 February 1963.

6. RCE, *Highway Maintenance, 1946-1964*, p. 23.

7. Claus-M. Naske, "The Alcan: Its Impact on Alaska," *The Northern Engineer*, vol 8., no. 1., pp. 112-18.

8. Herb Hilscher, "Highway to Alaska," *The Lion* (April, 1960), p. 16.

9. Woolcock, *The Road North*, 87.

10. Bob and Wilma Knox, "The Alaska Highway," *BC Outdoors* (February 1971), p. 13.

11. American Automobile Association, *Alaska and the Alaska Highway* (Washington: AAA, 1954), p. 10.

12. Woolcock, *The Road North*, p. 68.

13. Hilscher, "Highway to Alaska," p. 28.

14. Walsh to Phinney, 27 July 1946, NAC, RG36/7, vol. 50, file AH5-4-7.

15. Woolcock, *The Road North*, p. 125.

16. *Whitehorse Star*, 4 September 1969.

17. Recollections of Hugh Devitt.

18. RCE, *Highway Maintenance, 1946-1964*, p. 12.

19. Woolcock, *The Road North*, p. 73.

20. RCE, *Highway Maintenance, 1946-1964*, p. 40.

Chapter 7

1. House of Commons, *Debates*, Session 1966, vol. 7, 18 November 1966, p. 10087.

2. *Whitehorse Star*, 29 September 1969.

3. *Ibid.*

4. Knox, "The Alaska Highway," p. 18.

5. *Whitehorse Star*, Tourist Edition, Summer 1970, p. 14.

6. R.G. Buckstar, "Some Northern Roads Advice," *Alaska Sportsman* (February 1968), p. 44.

7. *Whitehorse Star*, Tourist Edition, Summer 1970, p. 14.

8. *Whitehorse Star*, 29 September 1969.

9. *Whitehorse Star*, 1 February 1971.

10. Buckstar, "Some Northern Roads Advice," p. 44.

11. Joe McGinniss, *Going to Extremes* (New York: New American Library, 1980), p. 31.

12. *Whitehorse Star*, 10 February 1964.

13. Knox, "The Alaska Highway," p. 20.

Index

Brown, Dorothy, 159
Brown, Russ, 118
Brown, Vera, 59
Brown, William, 171
Buckstar, R. C., 251
Bulat, Mike, 59
Bureau of Public Roads (U.S.), 208, 209
Burke, George, 47-48
Burwash Landing, Yukon, 47, 60, 64, 68, 70, 71, 72, 78, 147, 175, 259, 281

Calgary, Alberta, 27
Callahan, T. H., 178
Callison, E., 69
Cameron, G. R., 241
Camp Clayburn, Louisiana, 47
Camp Takhini, Yukon, 16, 205, 233
Campbell Construction Company, 168
Campbell, Lt. Col., 127
Campbell, Robert, 42
Camsell, Charles, 132, 190
Canadian National Railroad, 49
Canadian National Tele-
communications, 225, 226, 229
Canadian Northern Railway, 20
CANOL Project, 31, 37, 46, 86, 190, 203
Cantlon & Parker, 249
Capes, C. F., 36
Capital Dome, 81
Carcross, Yukon, 37, 61, 84, 103
Carey, J., 24
Cariboo Road, 10
Carmacks, Yukon, 40
CBC, 132, 134
C.F. Lytle and Green
Construction. *See*, Lytle and Green Construction
Charlie Chaplin, 11
Charlie Lake, B.C., 48, 107, 209

Chevron Oil, 210
Chilkat River valley, 260
Civilian Conservation Corps, 54, 143
Coal River, 15, 202, 225, 226, 227, 229, 231, 265, 278
Coates, Cathy, 268
Coates, Dick, 13, 16, 242, 264
Coates, Marge, 263, 264
Coates, Muriel, 186
Collip, Muriel, 129, 158
Collyer, Hank, 242
Committee on Public Roads, 32
Compton, Major, 102
Conrad, Yukon, 40
Contact Creek, B.C., 130
Cook, Les, 36
Corps of Engineers, 31, 34, 36, 37, 63, 66, 68, 81, 82, 85, 88, 138, 141-142, 148, 170, 185, 197
Craft, Dick, 175
Cranston, Sylvia, 117, 118, 120
Crerar, T., 28
Crosson, Joe, 132
Crown Assets Corporation, 249
Cyr, Laurent, 110

Davidson, Laddie, 159
Dawson City, Yukon, 9, 19, 21, 33, 40, 178, 257
Dawson Creek, B.C., 9, 10, 15, 16, 38, 39, 40, 47, 48, 49, 51, 52, 53, 54, 55, 56, 58, 60, 63, 78, 82, 84, 85, 90, 93, 95, 102, 109, 111, 113, 114, 115, 117, 118, 120, 121, 124, 125-127, 129, 134, 143, 149, 155, 156, 162, 170, 171, 178, 180, 181, 188, 198, 209, 214, 215, 216, 217, 225, 231, 232, 250, 261, 263, 269, 273, 279
Delta Junction, Alaska, 12, 214
Denali National Park, Alaska, 9
Denver, Colorado, 48
Department of Highways (Alaska), 208

Department of Indian Affairs and Northern Development (Canada), 245
Department of Mines and Resources (Canada), 138
Department of National Defence (Canada), 13, 195-238 *passim*, 240, 241, 263
Department of Public Works. *See*, Public Works Canada
Department of the Interior (U.S.), 105
Department of Transport (Canada), 63, 66
Destruction Bay, Yukon, 12, 214, 234, 265, 281
Devil's Lake, North Dakota, 27
Devitt's Folly, 203
Devitt, Hugh, 202-203, 205, 216, 218, 225, 226, 227, 231, 233, 234, 236
Dew Drop Inn, 48
Dimond, Anthony, 32
Donjek River, Yukon, 72, 206, 207
Dowell Construction, 45, 143-144, 145
Drake, North Dakota, 27
Dyea, Alaska, 19

Earl, Jack, 218
Easto, Dora, 173
Edmonton, Alberta, 26, 27, 28, 33, 34, 37, 45, 46, 48, 51, 53, 55, 59, 60, 63, 82, 108, 109, 143, 155, 162, 184, 193, 197, 198, 203, 245
Edmonton, Dunegan, British Columbia Railway, 149
Edwards, Jack, 73
18th Engineers, 84, 92, 107, 120, 130, 140, 153
843rd Signal Corps, 120
Elliott, E. W., 172
Erlam, Bob, 283
Estevan, Saskatchewan, 27
E.W. Elliott, 45, 143-144, 147